AF737980

Towards a Vegan Jurisprudence

Towards a Vegan Jurisprudence

The Need for a Reorientation of Human Rights

Jeanette Rowley

LEXINGTON BOOKS
Lanham • Boulder • New York • London

Published by Lexington Books
An imprint of The Rowman & Littlefield Publishing Group, Inc.
4501 Forbes Boulevard, Suite 200, Lanham, Maryland 20706
www.rowman.com

6 Tinworth Street, London SE11 5AL, United Kingdom

Copyright © 2020 The Rowman & Littlefield Publishing Group, Inc.

All rights reserved. No part of this book may be reproduced in any form or by any electronic or mechanical means, including information storage and retrieval systems, without written permission from the publisher, except by a reviewer who may quote passages in a review.

British Library Cataloguing in Publication Information Available

Library of Congress Cataloging-in-Publication Data Available

Library of Congress Control Number: 2020942798

Dedicated to the struggle for emancipation
and to those defending their right to live with respect for others

"Veganism in law disrupts the idea of exclusive protective rights. It is the institutional recognition of our natural, compassionate, ethical response to the suffering of nonhuman animals. It is a contributing factor in a social justice movement for a paradigm swift in our concept of social and legal justice."

(Jeanette Rowley, The IVRA Conference, Milan, 2019)

Contents

Acknowledgments

This book has been has been on the back burner for some time due to the competing demands of actively promoting veganism in law, developing an international network of likeminded legal and academic professionals committed to securing vegans' rights to live with respect for other animals, and advocating for vegans involved in cases of discrimination.

Over the last ten years or so, I have met and worked with so many people around the world, many of whom have contributed to my thinking, either through discussions, presenting at our conferences, or explaining personal accounts of discrimination. I owe an enormous debt of gratitude to you all.

The origins of this book are in my PhD of the same title, and I am grateful to Lancaster University for giving me the opportunity to conduct research into what veganism means for human rights. My supervisors, Professor Stephen Wheatly and Dr Bella Bonita Chatterjee, provided the challenging and supportive academic environment in which to think through the issues, and I thank them both for their professionalism, commitment, enduring patience, and support. I also wish to thank Professor Upendra Baxi for his support and encouragement to publish, anonymous peer reviewers for their valuable comments, and Becca at Lexington for her patience and for making the publication process simple enough for me to fit it into a hectic schedule.

Most importantly, I acknowledge the nonhuman animal others and their subjugation and suffering as the primary motivational force for this book. This book would not need to have been written were they adequately acknowledged and accommodated in human justice. I hope my response to their call has some value in their struggle for emancipation.

Introduction

This book is about the relationship of veganism[1] to human rights, the related issue of our duties to nonhuman animals, and why we need to examine and change our concept of human rights. It is motivated by the abhorrent subjugation of other animals and the need to think through social domination and prejudice to bring about a paradigm shift in the way other animals feature in human justice.

At the root of my thinking about veganism and human rights is the uncontested, collective social regard that animals matter morally, and the fact that in some jurisdictions vegans have been granted the protection of law. Subsequent to the legal accommodation of vegans, policies and practices that give effect to animal protection have been implemented. For example, the legal accommodation of vegans has resulted in plant-based food in schools, personal protective equipment for employees, such as shoes, boots, gloves, and other workwear such as uniforms, and many more adaptations of practices and policies in both the public and private sector.

The legal accommodation of vegans is not, however, straightforward or consistent in a rule of law that has entrenched prejudice against other animals. Ten years ago, popular press reported a 'prison source' as holding the view that provisions for vegans in prison makes a mockery of punishment. In the same report, an ambiguous statement appears to suggest that some prison officers consider provisions for vegans as privileges that can be withdrawn.[2] Ten years later, I still receive personal correspondence from vegan prisoners, some of whom are forced to escalate their cases of discrimination to the Prisons and Probation Ombudsman.[3]

The discussion in this book is critical of exclusive human rights. It recognises the material and corporal existence of other animals, their sentiency, and the urgency of reforms to end their suffering, but it opens up a new mode of thought, one that points to human responsibility to ground an argument for inclusive protective rights. It centres on the observation that the life-directing convictions of vegans come within the principles of the human right to freedom of conscience,[4] and that in some parts of the world, including the United Kingdom (UK), vegans alleging unlawful interference with their vegan practice or discrimination can be protected in law.

My approach to dealing with exclusive human rights and animal rights presents the idea that veganism is a logical extension of a widespread moral regard for other animals and that the human rights claims of vegans re-present the precarious, vulnerable, mortal animal other and their suffering under the individual human right to freedom of conscience.[5] I frame the legal recognition of vegans in human rights not as matters of the personal and private conscience but acknowledging and evidencing the catalyst for our protective rights enterprise: that rights recognise responsibility and duty to vulnerability and suffering in community, and that the human 'free conscience' is first and foremost dutiful in the face of vulnerability and suffering.

My view is that the protection of vegans under the human right to freedom of conscience brings human rights to a threshold where the moral standing of nonhuman animals is visible in the exclusive rights project that was formulated to deal with the suffering of others. I believe that since vegans are recognised in law, we have a moral duty to reorient human rights away from the principles of the primacy of human autonomy and reason that have taken precedence in current human rights, and ensure that legal cases about compassion for other animals are not assessed as matters of personal and private conscience.

My discussion about veganism and human rights promotes an alternative philosophical basis for the idea and practice of human rights. This philosophy replaces the primacy of human autonomy and reason with duty to suffering and, thus, grounds a protective rights enterprise that includes nonhuman animals and necessarily promotes vegan values. In this system, vegan values and the convictions of vegans are facilitated and normatively manifested, but it is also acknowledged that it may not be a perfect system that is able to permit a vegan desire for uncompromising practice. Justice is necessarily remorseful and the development of an inclusive justice for nonhuman animals (one that represents and justifies the normalisation and legal protection of vegan values) remains fraught with complexities and unfortunate realisations.

My discussion, nevertheless, offers a new dimension on the issues of human and animal rights, the protection of vegan ethical responsibility, the foundation for, and the limits of, legal protection for vegans, and the possibility of an alternative system of inclusive, but remorseful, justice that recognises the rights of nonhuman animals and our duties to them.

My motivation for writing this book stems from a longstanding interest in the relationship between human society and the status of nonhuman animals, and many decades as a vegan, animal rights activist. My specific interest in the human rights claims of vegans was fuelled in 2010 by the observation of a tension in the UK concerning the status of veganism as a qualifying belief under Article 9 of the European Convention on Human Rights (the Convention[6]), and the role of the UK Equality and Human Rights Commission (the Commission) which has a statutory duty to oversee human rights and monitor equality initiatives.[7] In a Draft Code of Practice for Employers, published to accompany new equality legislation, the Commission explained that veganism comes within the scope of the protected characteristic 'religion or belief.'[8] The publication gave example scenarios featuring vegan employees that sought to explain to employers the steps that could be taken to accommodate the needs of vegans in the workplace. The guide explained that employers should do whatever they reasonably could to show regard for the needs of vegans, suggesting, for example, separate food storage and preparation areas, and the possibility of other measures depending on available company resources.

These useful examples raised eyebrows in the UK Parliament, were removed from the Commission's final published *Code of Practice*, and were replaced with alternatives to 'reflect the principles in relevant case law.'[9] At the time, I felt that the removal of these helpful examples was contrary to the principle of inclusion because it meant that the legal status of veganism was relegated in the dissemination of important information, and that vegans were denied a point of reference to support their requests for accommodation of needs. I therefore set about thinking and researching the relationship of veganism to law in the hope of being able to contribute to the normalisation and protection of veganism and vegans, in support of animal liberation.

I suggest that the legal claims of vegans are unique in that whilst other disadvantaged groups—for example, women, religious minorities or disabled people—make human rights claims for themselves, the claims of vegans represent, first and foremost, the moral standing of nonhuman animals.[10] In the dominance of a culture that is based on the consumption of other animals, vegans sometimes experience unfair treatment and discrimination in personal, social, and employment contexts. Some of these experiences motivate equality and human rights claims under the right to freedom of conscience: for example, by vegans who are required to wear uniform or personal protective equipment that are made from the skin or hair of nonhuman animals, or by vegan parents who have tried to obtain vegan food for their children in school. In such circumstances, vegans have reported experiencing coercion and a feeling of being required to assimilate into a way of life that is contrary to their moral convictions.

Veganism has no official definition for the purposes of law. The definition promoted by The Vegan Society states that it is:

> [a] philosophy and way of living which seeks to exclude—as far as is possible and practicable—all forms of exploitation of, and cruelty to, animals for food, clothing or any other purpose; and by extension, promotes the development and use of animal-free alternatives for the benefit of humans, animals and the environment. In dietary terms it denotes the practice of dispensing with all products derived wholly or partly from animals.[11]

Veganism can, thus, be regarded as the acknowledgment of and a comprehensive response to suffering, and a manifestation of ethical responsibility to the moral standing of nonhuman others. On this view, the human rights claims of vegans emerge in an extension of justice that includes other animals in the moral community. The claims of vegans are grounded by a notion of responsibility and, first and foremost, present the suffering of other animals as a matter of justice. As such, the rights claims of vegans are uniquely claims for the protection of others: although by making rights claims, vegans may obtain a small tangible benefit, they are raised to promote the rights of others that they wish to respect and protect. In short, the rights claims of vegans honour the rights of others not to be harmed.

There are various comments and responses to veganism in case law. The convictions of vegans have been held to be within the scope of the Article 9 right to freedom of conscience[12] under the Convention. Veganism has now also been confirmed as coming within the scope of the equality law in Great Britain: in *Mr J Casamitjana Costa v The League Against Cruel Sports*, Judge Postle referred to the 'overwhelming evidence,' submitted by the applicant, in support of his ruling that vegans meet the legal test for the protection of equality law.[13] A prior high-profile case in the UK, in 2011, was the case of Joe Hashman, whose employment was unlawfully terminated on the basis of his commitment, as a vegan, to actively oppose foxhunting. Southampton Employment Tribunal Centre heard that his belief in anti-foxhunting was grounded in the sanctity of life and was within the scope of legal protection.[14] In *R (Williamson),* Lord Walker commented that vegetarianism is an uncontroversial example of what could constitute a belief within the legal meaning,[15] and a belief in vegetarianism, as a manifestation of a perceived relationship with nonhuman animals was indeed accepted as coming within the scope of law.[16] A more recent employment tribunal held, however, that vegetarianism did not qualify for protection under UK equality law, whereas veganism might because it was cogent and cohesive.[17] This was subsequently confirmed in the case of *Casamitjana* (above).

Vegan values have been referred to, in a UK court, as a component of a broader positive philosophy within which to raise children.[18] In the UK, vegan children have nevertheless been required by law to receive vaccinations made using substances derived from nonhumans.[19] In *Rukavina v Croatia,*[20] the court heard that a multidisciplinary team of experts had been brought in to respond to the applicant's allegations that his ex-wife was putting the heath of his daughter at risk by 'keeping her on a vegan diet.'[21] The specialist team was composed of a psychologist, a psychiatrist, a paediatrician, and a social worker who reported to the court that the child was healthy but that her mother's insistence on a vegan diet put her at risk regarding her 'normal psychophysical development.'[22] Similarly, in *Genna & Dennis,* the Family Court of Australia was required to assist disputing parents and employed the services of a dietician as the final arbiter of what the child should eat when in the father's care.

The word 'vegan' has been conflated with child abuse.[23] Media in France report that the judiciary authorised the removal of a child from vegan parents on the grounds that the child was in danger.[24] In health care, veganism has been problematised as an extreme diet or a manifestation of psychological disorder.[25] In Switzerland, media report that a soldier was not allowed to join the army on the grounds that his veganism was an unsuitable ethical orientation.[26] A vegan in the United States of America (US) felt obliged to define her ethical orientation as Hindu in order to receive an alternative medical test in place of a standard type that used derivatives of cows' blood.[27]

These examples of cases regarding vegans concern various legal concepts and principles, but all of them highlight that the judicial approach to veganism is not grounded by an entrenched duty to give open and honest due regard to other animals. Rather, they challenge vegan individuals who live according to the ethical conviction that it is wrong to exploit nonhuman animals to justify why law should protect what are deemed to be their interests. They highlight the centrality of the human individual in law and further entrench social and political confusion about the meaning of other animals in human society.

The application of legal principles to balance the rights of human individuals sometimes produce case outcomes that rest on 'good' grounds for limiting the rights of vegans to manifest their practice. For example, cases involving health care and the best interests of the patients, or the wider duty to protect public health. Some, however, show ignorance or disregard for the convictions of vegans and the importance of their practice, while others show that nonhuman animals have sufficient moral standing (paradoxically, in a human rights system of justice that denies nonhumans have any basic rights at all) to validate the human rights claims of vegans, apparently without extensive discussion or debate. In this illogical and confused approach to other animals, vegans are required to justify, and sometimes compromise, convictions that are, ultimately, a manifestation of a widespread social and moral regard for the well-being of other animals.

This book frames the discussion about accommodating vegans in law in terms of a tension in human rights between human supremacy and the prioritisation of human reason and the acknowledgment, observed in the very mission of a protective rights enterprise rights, that human society feels compelled or, put another way, is obliged to acknowledge and deal with suffering. Critically, it foregrounds an important and necessary discussion in human and animal rights concerning the convictions of vegans and the exclusion of nonhuman animals from the protective rights enterprise, the human obligation to deal with suffering, and the current ethical orientation of human rights: the primacy of autonomous human reason and the subsequent norm of adjudicating cases concerning the right to freedom of (vegan) conscience in terms of human individuality and the individual personal and private domain of consciousness.

Given the widespread acknowledgment that animals matter, the convictions and commitments of vegans and the fact that vegans have, in some cases, been granted the protection of law, the discussion in this book offers another way to think about the idea of protective rights. This idea looks to the 'suffering narrative' of human rights to ground rights for nonhuman animals, and validate the claims of vegans; not as individual claim rights in an exclusive system of protective rights but in recognition that freedom of conscience, and therefore the right to manifest free conscience, is essentially bound up with responsibility to other animals and their suffering.

Currently, the human rights claims of vegans are raised under an individual right to freedom of conscience but are claims that represent a collective value or, arguably, a moral imperative to care about the suffering of other animals. In this book, I combine the suffering narrative of human rights with what I refer to as the suffering narrative of veganism to explain how the rights claims of vegans represent the essence of the protective rights enterprise: the dutiful response to suffering.

Firstly, I propose that veganism is an ethical commitment to the moral standing of animals and that it represents a recognised moral imperative to attend to their suffering. My thinking relies on the observation that other animals suffer, a general social value for not wishing them harm and the established value that intentionally harming other animals is morally wrong. Clear, existing social concern for the suffering of animals is evidenced by the significance of certain animal welfare measures, such as legal recognition that animals are sentient, and regulations, including provisions under criminal law that target and prohibit (some) cruel treatment. I take the view, that veganism as a response to animal suffering and the proactive efforts of vegans to avoid harming other animals are entirely logical in a global society that acknowledges that animals matter morally. According to The Vegan Society definition, vegans do not consume products derived from the living or dead bodies of other animals, do not buy or wear fur or 'leather,' and generally aim to avoid all forms of animal exploitation in recognition of animal suffering. Vegans, therefore, aim to manifest dutifully coexistence, according to convictions of conscience, by trying to avoid causing or participating in imposed suffering and harm. In this first stage of my thinking, I refer to the suffering narrative of veganism as a manifestation of a wider ethical regard for other animals.

Secondly, I examine human rights and the normative legal values and principles that determine the relationship between current human rights and veganism. I present the idea that the rights claims made by vegans in their appeal to law (to be free to practice duty to other animals) are raised in response to acknowledged animal suffering, that their claims of conscience are logical because they are supported by an unequivocal, existing social concern for other animals, but that the grounds on which they raise their (and our collective) moral regard for nonhuman animals is the individual human right to freedom of conscience that is based on the primacy of human reason. This leads me to consider a problem: the logical claims of vegans are assessed as mere individual claims of conscience, rather than as claims about our collective and already acknowledged concern for other animals. The collective social norm that animals matter morally and the logical vegan appeals to law regarding their commitment to protecting other animals by refraining from participating in exploitative practices are, I propose, relegated by the primacy of individual human reason that underpins human rights and the right to freedom of conscience.

Noting a widespread social, political, and legal concern for nonhuman animals that supports veganism as the representation of an already existing profound moral regard for other animals, I propose that the existing human rights approach to the claims of vegans is illogical and suggest that their claims should be assessed differently than as matters concerning disadvantage in relation to personal and private conscience. To give effect to a widespread concern for the suffering of animals, ground the legal rights of vegans, and contribute to the development of compassionate policies, I propose that a protective rights enterprise (i.e., human rights) should be based on an inclusive philosophy that explains and grounds fundamental rights in terms of ethical duty in a community of individual beings that suffer. This leads me to consider the utility of the suffering narrative of human rights which, being grounded by an ethics of alterity, promotes duty to suffering over the primacy of individual autonomy.

The third stage of my thinking is, thus, inspired by the philosophy of Emmanuel Levinas. It explains that Emmanuel Levinas's ethics of alterity constitute a theory of asymmetrical ethical responsibility that supports rights for other animals and the rights claims of vegans. It observes that asymmetrical compassion is intrinsic to a humanity that is bound, in community, through an innate regard for suffering others. By developing existing discourse on the utility of Levinas's philosophy for human rights, this third stage of my argument applies the principles of Levinas's philosophy to nonhuman animals on the basis that they are legitimate, suffering others who demand an ethical response, and to whom the human subject responds. This stage of my argument identifies that Levinas's ethics of alterity is grounded in a strong level of protection for nonhuman animals as a matter of justice and, on my argument, gives expression to vegan values and the validity of their claims in law.

The fourth stage of my thinking builds on the idea that Levinas's ethics of alterity, when applied to the groundwork of an alternative protective rights enterprise, have utility for the protection of nonhuman animals in a system of inclusive ethical justice. I suggest that we are duty bound to recognise that other animals have (at least) five basic rights that can be viewed in three groups: the right to life and liberty, the right to self-defined identity and the right to support and assistance. I suggest that we are duty bound to respect these basic rights of nonhuman animals as a matter of justice, that they ground the naturalness of the rights claims of vegans and oblige us to reorient away from assessing the claims of those who bring animals' suffering to the forefront as matters concerning individual human conscience. This is a non-negotiable requirement invoked by a responsibility that is critical to a humanity that is, first and foremost, ethically responsive to the suffering of others.

In 2003, Sarah Soifer identified that veganism created an 'emerging and difficult dilemma' for law.[28] Since the outset, ten years ago, of research for this book (which started life as a PhD topic), I have sought global support for the idea that veganism presents to law an intersection of human and nonhuman moral standing, and interest has grown within the academy. In 2012, I founded the International Vegan Rights Alliance to bring together, inspire, and motivate academics and legal professionals interested in the development of vegan law. I presented on vegan inclusion at the Toulouse Equality, Diversity and Inclusion conference, and gave a groundbreaking lecture on the utility of using human rights law to advance veganism in Luxembourg, at the International Animal Rights Gathering. By 2014, the idea that vegans could make use of law to advance veganism was growing and I published the results of the first small-scale survey conducted in the UK about how vegans felt in relation to new equality law,[29] and the first supportive short guide for vegans: *Vegan Rights: questions and answers*. In 2015, I received a request to write a chapter on the relationship of veganism to human rights—for a proposed edited collection of critical perspectives on veganism. This was published in 2016.[30] Also in 2016, one of my new colleagues and a friend I acquired through my work, Ralph Müller-Amenitsch, published *Vegan im Recht* (Vegan Rights) in Germany.[31] This publication was developed by Müller-Amenitsch and another of our newfound friends, Petr Kudelka, and published by PETA Austria. I later learned of the independent work being done in the area of vegan litigation by Adam Karp in the United States of America, who included a chapter on vegetarian and vegan litigation in his 2016 book on 'Understanding Animal Law.'[32] In 2017, another of my new associates and now publishing collaborator, Dr Carlo Prisco, published *The Right to Vegetarianism*, in which he makes a connection between the ways law is developing in response to a historical ethical regard for nonhumans and a growing demand to eat a vegan diet.[33] Though Dr Prisco's approach is entirely different from the one taken in this book in that he emphasises more comprehensively the historical human interest in animals' well-being and the development of a moral imperative not to eat them, he also independently observes the way in which positive law for vegans gives expression to the moral standing of other animals, their exclusion from basic moral rights and how these circumstances challenge the orthodoxy of human rights.

These scholarly contributions to the discussion illustrate the development of new ways of articulating the moral and legal standing of other animals. Importantly, they bring new insights to debates about the legitimacy and validity of exclusive human rights in the context of a moral imperative to consider the suffering and exclusion of nonhuman animals.

There is also, of course, a huge recognised body of human rights and animal rights literature in the background to this new branch of discourse on the intersection of human and animal rights, which also has a place in this introduction.

Some human rights scholars—for example, Costas Douzinas, Connor Gearty, and Michael Hass—have recognised the importance of dealing with animals within the context of human rights.[34] Gearty argues that an ethically minded public requires the idea of human rights to be revisited because it identifies naturally with nonhuman animal suffering. For Gearty, '[t]he raw fact of an animal suffering should be enough in itself to engender strong feeling of solidarity and underpin joint campaigns. . . .'[35]

The argument for an integrated debate concerning nonhuman and human rights issues resonates with some animal rights scholars, such as Kelly Oliver, Alasdair Cochrane, and Anne Peters.[36] Though there are a number of positions and approaches in this combined scholarship, it is fair to say that it predominantly relies on nonhuman sentience as the ground for inclusion. None of the existing literature deals with the human rights claims of vegans, their specific presentation of the suffering of nonhuman animals, and, therefore, none of it considers potential implications of vegan claims in law. This book contributes to these discussions by taking a different approach which considers the human rights claims of vegans for the moral standing of nonhuman animals in the context of the theory that human beings are inescapably duty bound to respond to suffering.

Upendra Baxi has no doubt that the target of human rights is to deal with suffering. In assessing the ethics of human rights, Baxi, Costas Douzinas, William Paul Simmons, and Joseph Indaimo express the utility of the philosophy of Emmanuel Levinas's ethics of alterity.[37] Though these scholars believe that Levinas's philosophy pertains to inclusion on the basis that human rights are first and foremost a recognition of others, none develop a full discussion as to whether Levinas's theory can be applied to nonhuman animals as legitimate others and what implications this may have for the human rights claims of vegans.

The idea in this book goes beyond two current thresholds in existing literature: it challenges the anthropocentric assumptions of current human rights, and it offers a new way of speaking of nonhuman animal and vegan rights. By examining the inclusive potential of Levinas's philosophy, it first develops the existing theory that human rights recognise duty to the other and must permit duty to otherness to be realised in practice. It then argues that nonhuman animals can be included as legitimate others, and that the claims of vegans are, therefore, characteristically natural in their re-presentation of the inescapable ethical duty expressed in the protective rights enterprise for a community of others.

Given that this book identifies ethical responsibility to nonhuman animals as the grounds for the human rights claims of vegans, it is worth also introducing the various strands of existing admirable and principled animal rights theory, and explaining why it does not ground the argument for a reorientation of human rights solely on sentience, interests or animal consciousness.

An attempt to bridge the gap between human rights and animal rights was recently undertaken by Alasdair Cochrane.[38] He argues for a reorientation from human rights to sentient rights on the basis that suffering is the universal principle to ground protective rights. This reliance on the primacy of the sentiency of animals is historically relevant and typical of other literature that advocates for the moral and legal standing of nonhuman animals.

This book does not ground its argument in the well-established idea that sentiency alone should ground protective rights. One reason for this is that the concept of sentiency can be disadvantaged by the parameters of anthropocentric human reason. For example, the supremacy of human reason in Peter Singer's utilitarian approach and Tom Regan's groundbreaking 'inherent value' approach to animal rights, ultimately, unfortunately fail other animals.[39] Singer on utilitarian grounds and Regan on the grounds that it is not possible to give an explanation of the inherent value of nonhuman animals. For Singer, human interests will always outweigh those of other animals, and for Regan, inherent value is related to being a 'subject of a life', defined as any normally developing mammal aged one year or more.[40] Though both of these thinkers recognise the significance of animal suffering and the sociopolitical conditions that sully the moral standing of nonhuman animals, both ultimately reluctantly retain the view that other animals can generally be considered less important than humans.

The recognition of animal sentience often leads to anthropocentric discussions about the extent to which other animals will or may suffer in certain contexts. This can lead to permissible harms, such as animal experiments and lawful mutilations, for unnecessary human gain. In these discussions, discrimination between human and other animals revolve around the existence or not of observable complex characteristics of cognitive abilities. For example, language ability, memory, a perception of desires, goals, or the future—that apparently justify human superiority.

Mark Rowlands and Alasdair Cochrane admirably argue that animals have interests and consciousness,[41] but discourse that focuses on animal interests can also be problematic for establishing duty to other animals. Robert Garner, for example, has commented on the frustrating conclusion that it may be permissible to experiment on animals.[42] He notes the possibility in this discourse that as long as an animal's interests are met and no pain or suffering is endured, it may be acceptable to conduct experiments or perform amputations on animals in the interests of human advantage and progress. Arguments put forward for animal rights on the basis that sentient animals are in possession of consciousness or interests are persuasive but have not, thus far, resulted in widespread emancipation.

A number of other theorists have contributed to the discussion on how to extend justice to other animals and explained what that justice would or should look like. Martha Fineman grounds rights for animals in vulnerability and dependence,[43] and Martha Nussbaum develops a capabilities approach.[44] The more recent 'political turn' in animal rights turns away from moral theorising and explains a model for practical justice based on a notion of animal citizenship in which nonhuman animals are co-opted into organised human society.[45] Domestic animals become equal (to human) citizens, wild animals have their own territories over which they are sovereign, and liminal animals (those who chose to live at the margins of human society without interaction) also have basic rights. A concept of citizenship offers nonhuman animals an immediate and practical (rather than theoretical) solution to their oppression.

These historical and contemporary accounts of animal rights seek to accommodate the moral standing of nonhuman animals in an inclusive system of justice. What these theories have in common is that they implicitly and explicitly observe the human preoccupation with other animals and their significance in the shared community. It is this responsiveness that is paramount in this book. It centres on why, in the first-place, humans care, and are compassionate about nonhuman others, how this human characteristic is represented in the project that is human rights and, I suggest, how it can be argued to feature in the rights claims of vegans.

With reference to animal rights, the book's originality is that it centres duty to other animals in human mode of thought; not to remove animals from the centre, but to make responsibility for measures of justice central to the discussion. It explains a philosophical theory that supports the moral standing of other animals, explains their basic rights and the absolute pre-conditions for their inclusion into a human system of justice. It then relates this to a reconceptualisation of human rights that supports the rights claims of vegans and their accommodation in law. My hope is that the explanation of a theory of ethical pre-conditions for including nonhuman animals and vegans in the justice of protective rights will positively support the existing well-respected body of knowledge on justice for other animals.

This book also makes an original contribution to human rights discourse by applying the ethics of alterity to nonhuman animals and considers the implications for animals, humans, and human rights. Existing postmodern, realist, deconstructionist, and posthuman human rights literature identifies the elimination of suffering as the mission of human rights. In this regard, it promotes the utility of Levinas's ethics of alterity, but it does not consider the exclusion of nonhuman animals or the possibility of the positive impact of veganism in human rights. This book applies the established principal insights of Levinas's ethics of alterity to nonhuman animals to explain that their precarious mortality, understood through a concept of ethical responsibility to suffering, grounds their moral and legal standing. The moral standing of nonhuman others is then used, for the first time, to reconceptualise the claims of vegans as re-presenting the original ethical responsibility intrinsic to the free conscience.

In summary, the book builds on the idea that ethical responsibility in the face of suffering is inherent and intrinsic to the community of humanity and that it grounds modern human rights. I argue that the philosophy grounding the suffering narrative of human rights validates the rights claims of vegans because it includes other animals in its reach. I maintain that the success of the rights claims of vegans are limited in a framework of protective rights that excludes nonhuman animals and prioritises and entrenches an orthodoxy of human reason. I argue that duty to suffering animals is inherent in a protective rights enterprise formulated in a community of others, and that the right to vegan freedom of conscience can be reconceptualised as the re-presentation of an inescapable ethical response to the precarious existence of animals and their basic rights.

THE STRUCTURE OF THE BOOK

To reiterate, this book addresses the question of whether there is an alternative ethical orientation for human rights that would better accommodate the claims of vegans. It explores the nature of veganism, the human rights claims of vegans, the normative principles and values intrinsic to the relationship of current human rights to veganism, whether there is an alternative philosophical model for human rights that can deal more favourably with the claims of vegans, what this philosophy entails, and what broad implications such a model may have. The book addresses these questions in a logical progression of chapters using a step-by-step approach.

Chapter 1 develops what I refer to as a suffering narrative of veganism. It examines the nature of veganism, literature on oppression and intersecting oppression, and the social conditions in which the human rights claims of vegans emerge. It concludes that the claims of vegans re-present the vulnerability and suffering of other animals but are assessed as matters of personal and private individual conscience. This leads to a discussion in chapter 2 about the centrality of the human individual in human rights.

Chapter 2 examines the extent to which individual conscience, community justice, and suffering feature in human rights. It finds that though there is evidence that modern human rights are grounded by a concern with suffering, they have been built upon the idea of individual, autonomous, rational agency. The chapter observes that on these grounds, nonhuman animals are denied basic rights and that the vegan presentation of ethical responsibility is subject to an orthodoxy of individual human autonomy[46] that does not recognise or promote the need to deal with suffering 'in community' or the widely accepted moral standing of other animals.

Based on the argument that the orthodoxy of autonomy is problematic for the claims of vegans, the chapter recommends consideration of an alternative philosophy to reorient human rights. This philosophy is Levinas's ethics of alterity. It defines human nature as essentially and universally compassionate and innately responsible to others in recognition of a universally shared perception of the negative forces of mortality.

Chapter 3 explores the principles of Levinas's ethics of alterity and its currency in contemporary human rights discourse. It explains that human rights scholars identify Levinas's philosophy as an opposing emancipatory thesis. In his thesis, Levinas argues that a dominant, entrenched Western philosophy of human reason has created a constraining and unethical totality. Levinas argues that rather than the ability to reason, responsibility to the other is the primary characteristic of humanity. The recognition of responsibility rather than autonomy is observed in the human desire to welcome and live in community with others. For Levinas, the pre-social connection between others is evidence of ethics. Humanity is ethical through non-abstract face-to-face encounters that facilitate responsibility. The chapter explains that ethical responsibility is the acknowledgment of the unique other combined with a desire to extend compassion. It involves respecting individual experience of life in the world and obligates a subject to support another.

Chapter 3 goes on to explain that the fundamental ideas in the ethics of alterity are critical because the Levinasian other has moral standing as the other to whom the subject is obliged to respond. The other presents themselves in a 'saying' without a 'said': 'It is me in my world. Here I am, how will you respond?' It is in this context that the human rights claims of vegans can be reconceptualised as ethical claims of conscience that cannot be subject to speciesist notions of human supremacy that permit and validate anthropocentric legal concepts that moderate duty. These concepts—such as the primacy of individual conscience human personal disadvantage, and legitimate aim and proportionality—when applied in adjudication of cases that concern duty to other animals and considered through the lens of the ethics of alterity only serve an oppressive totality that subjugates nonhuman others.

Levinas's ethics of alterity do not include a robust discussion of nonhuman otherness. Accordingly, the next chapter, chapter 4, asks whether nonhuman animals are legitimate others to whom the subject is ethically responsible and examines the views of authors commenting on the place of animals in Levinas's work. It concludes that other animals invoke responsibility and should be considered in matters of justice. As such, nonhuman animals are brought to the moral community as those who are owed asymmetrical, direct duties of ethical responsibility. Such a responsibility requires the acknowledgment and recognition of nonhuman uniqueness, a prohibition on killing and intentional harm, the recognition of a duty to permit individual experience of life, and the acknowledgement that responsibility espouses a duty to assist nonhuman others in face-to-face relationships. The chapter concludes that the extension of moral community to nonhuman animals has specific advantages for the claims of vegans.

Chapter 5 discusses the implications emerging from the argument that the ethics of alterity concern asymmetrical ethical duties to nonhuman animals. It firstly outlines, in abstract, how a reoriented framework for human rights might be conceptualised. It then explains the basic moral and legal entitlements of other animals.

This chapter explains that the basic rights of nonhuman animals constitute ethical pre-conditions on which the claims of vegans are normalised and can be accommodated through a reconceptualisation of the right to freedom of conscience. It considers the implications of such a conclusion by explaining the complexities and challenges of a subsequent inclusive justice that would give expression to the moral standing of nonhuman animals and vegan values. Ultimately, the discussion concludes by acknowledging that the idea that justice always and necessarily requires sacrifice, and points to the problematic reality that in a normalised vegan world normative justice will, necessarily, be remorseful. This conclusion raises the plausibility of 'uncompromising' vegan practice and acknowledges the complexities in thinking about the required paradigm shift to inclusive compassionate justice.

Notwithstanding the existing difficulties and challenges, and those yet to be uncovered, the conclusion of this book is that human rights can be grounded by duty to suffering in an extended community of vulnerable others, and that the rights claims of those who advocate for other animals can be litigated differently by re-presenting the original ethical demand formative to a (human) protective rights enterprise.

The discussion in this timely book is likely to be of interest to vegans and animal rights activists because it opens up new ways to discuss the relationship between humans and other animals, to articulate rights and equality claims and to develop political campaigns. It will also be of interest to scholars dealing with animal rights or human rights and the intersection of the two, those who are interested in the ontology or ethical orientation of human rights, those interested in exploring the philosophy of Emmanuel Levinas, and, of course, those interested in the developing field of academic literature on the subject of veganism, and the now established academic area of vegan law.

NOTES

1. For the purposes of this book I refer to the definition of The Vegan Society in my use of 'veganism' and 'vegan.' I interpret this definition as explaining the philosophy of those who wish to avoid exploiting other animals in recognition that other animals are sentient, and it is morally wrong to subjugate them. I acknowledge the various strands of emphasis in contemporary veganism, but for the avoidance of

doubt, my use of these terms encompasses much more than the adoption of the dietary element of vegan practice.

2. Daily Mail Reporter, 'Animal rights extremists given 'vegan' work boots and 'ethical' make up in jail (and guess who's footing the bill)' Mailonline (12 January 2010) <https://www.dailymail.co.uk/news/article-1242535/Animal-rights-extremist-given-vegan-boots-ethical-make-jail---whos-footing-bill.html> accessed 24 May 2020.

3. Personal correspondence.

4. Throughout this book 'the right to freedom of conscience' refers to the human right to freedom of 'thought, conscience and religion.' The original wording of this right is provided in the Universal Declaration of Human Rights at Article 18, "Everyone has the right to freedom of thought, conscience and religion; this right includes freedom to change his religion or belief, and freedom, either alone or in community with others and in public or private, to manifest his religion or belief in teaching, practice, worship and observance." When commenting on lawful interference with this right, unless the provision in a specific treaty is explained, the book uses the general principle that any restrictions imposed on the manifestation of this right must be grounded by a law that is necessary in a democracy to ensure respect for the rights and freedoms of others, to protect moral values, public order and general welfare in a democratic society.

5. I use the word 'suffering' in the widest context to include the inevitable impact of biological existence and socially imposed oppression.

6. Convention for the Protection of Human Rights and Fundamental Freedoms (European Convention on Human Rights, as amended) (ECHR) Article 9.

7. Jamieson Alastair, 'Vegans should be protected from discrimination, says equality watchdog: Vegans and atheists should have the same protection against discrimination as religious groups according to guidance on new equality laws proposed by Harriet Harman' *The Telegraph* (2010) <http://www.telegraph.co.uk/news/religion/7392222/Vegans-should-be-protected-from-discrimination-says-equality-watchdog.html> accessed 18 October 2019.

8. Equality and Human Rights Commission, 'Employment Statutory Code of Practice (Draft for Consultation)' (Equality and Human Rights Commission 2009) 32, 252, accessed June 2010. The website of the Equality and Human Rights Commission (https://www.equalityhumanrights.com/en) no longer carries a copy of this document. An online copy can be viewed at <https://www.elaweb.org.uk/sites/default/files/docs/Draft%20Employment%20Code%20of%20Practice%201109798532.pdf> accessed 12 October 2019.

9. Equality and Human Rights Commission, 'Employment: Statutory Code of Practice' <https://www.equalityhumanrights.com/en/publication-download/employment-statutory-code-practice> accessed 22 October 2019. A request under the UK Freedom of Information Act 2000 was used to find out why the examples had been removed. The author has retained these documents on file. The inclusion of vegans raised eyebrows in Parliament, see the Parliamentary debate during the Equality Bill's third reading: HL Deb 23 March 2010, vol 718, cc 851-858.

10. In recognition of a well-established observation that prejudice against nonhuman animals is reinforced by language, this book will support expressions such as 'nonhuman animal(s),' 'nonhuman(s),' and 'other-than-human animal(s)' but may sometimes use 'animal(s)' interchangeably with these terms.

11. The Vegan Society, 'Definition of veganism' <www.vegansociety.com/go-vegan/definition-veganism> accessed 6 October 2019.

12. *H v UK* (1993) 16 EHRR.

13. Protected as 'ethical veganism' *Mr J Casamitjana Costa v The League Against Cruel Sports*: [2020] 3331129/2018 (ET)- Preliminary. It should be pointed out that protection for non-religious beliefs under the Equality Act 2010 is to be guided by the human right to freedom of conscience as stated in the European Convention on Human Rights.

14. *Hashman v Milton Park Dorset Limited* [2011] EqLR 426 (ET) See also Wardrop Murray, 'Foxhunting Views Placed On Par With Religion After Landmark Legal Ruling' (*The Telegraph*, 9 March 2011) <http://www.telegraph.co.uk/news/uknews/law-and-order/8368934/Foxhunting-views-placed-on-par-with-religion-after-landmark-legal-ruling.html> accessed 18 October 2019.

15. *R (Williamson) v Secretary of State for Education and Employment* [2005] 2 AC 246.

16. *Alexander v Farmtastic Valley Ltd and Others* [2011] 2513832/10 (ET).

17. *Conisbee v Crossley Farms Limited* [2019] 3335357/2018 (ET). In this case, Judge Postle (the same judge as in Casamitjana) contrasted vegetarianism and veganism and alluded to the possibility that veganism could meet the legal test for protection.

18. See comments in S (CHILDREN) [2012] EWCA Civ 210. This case concerned vegan children taken into foster care due to the volatile relationship of the parents. The alternative lifestyle and loving environment in which the children were raised was acknowledged as very positive for them.

19. *F v F* (Welfare of Children: Immunisation) [2013] EWHC 2683 (Fam). The court declares the MMR vaccination should be given to vegan children of divorcing parents and warns that an order will be issued if they cannot agree. See also a similar case: *BC v EF* (Parental Responsibility: Immunisation) [2016] EWFC 69 (05 December 2016). In this case the extensive research undertaken by the mother and presented to the court was remarkable, but the court declared that the vaccine was in the best interests of the child and that the mother's view was not balanced.

20. *Rukavina v Croatia* App no 770/12 (ECtHR, 6 January 2015). The father cited the mother's preference of a vegan diet for their young daughter as emotional abuse.

21. *Rukavina v Croatia* App no 770/12 (ECtHR, 6 January 2015), point 56.

22. *Rukavina v Croatia* App no 770/12 (ECtHR, 6 January 2015), point 28.

23. *Melville v Muller* 2006 BCSC 895 (CanLII): No evidence that eating a vegan diet is detrimental.

24. The Connexion, 'Vegan mother has baby taken away' (*The Connexion*, 8 January 2014) <https://www.connexionfrance.com/Archive/Vegan-mother-has-baby-taken-away> accessed 24 October 2019.

25. *WCAT-2012-02217 (Re)*, 2012 CanLII 54414 (BC WCAT) (Canadian Workers Compensation Appeal Tribunal). The case was brought to determine compensation for food supplements following injury sustained in the workplace. See also *H (Re)* 2011 CanLII 63119 (ON CCB). This case concerned the legal capacity of a fifteen-year-old girl and medical intervention.

26. Christopher Harres, 'Vegan Soldier Rejected by Swiss Army for Failing to Wear Leather Boots' (*International Business Times*, 26 January 2016) <http://www.ibtimes.com/vegan-soldier-rejected-swiss-army-refusing-wear-leather-boots-2280206> accessed 18 October 2019.

27. Sarah Soifer, 'Vegan Discrimination: An Emerging and Difficult Dilemma' (2003) Loyola of Los Angeles Law Review 1709. See also *Friedman v Southern California Permanente Medical Group* 102 Cal, App 4th 39, 125 Cal Rptr 2d 663 (2002), in which an offer of employment was withdrawn when the applicant refused to be vaccinated against mumps. The Californian Supreme Court confirmed the decision of the lower court that veganism was not within the scope of protective regulations.

28. Sarah Soifer, 'Vegan Discrimination: An Emerging and Difficult Dilemma' (2003) Loyola of Los Angeles Law Review 1709.

29. Jeanette Rowley, 'Vegan Equality Survey' <https://eprints.lancs.ac.uk/id/eprint/74384/1/Vegan_Equality_Survey.pdf> accessed 24 May 2020.

30. Jeanette Rowley, 'Human Rights are Animal Rights' in Jodey Castricano and Rasmus R Simonsen (eds), *Critical Perspectives on Veganism* (Palgrave Macmillan 2016).

31. Ralf Müller-Amenitsch, *Vegan im Recht* (Ventil 2016).

32. Adam P. Karp, *Understanding Animal Law* (Carolina Academic Press 2016).

33. Carlo Prisco, *The Right to Vegetarianism* (Hamilton Books 2017). In this work, Prisco reclaims the use of the word vegetarianism as meaning a plant-based diet that excludes all animal products.

34. Costas Douzinas, *The End of Human Rights: Critical Legal Thought at the Turn of the Century* (Hart Publishing 2000); Conor Gearty, *The Hamlyn Lectures: Can Human Rights Survive?* (Cambridge University Press 2006); Michael Hass, *International Human Rights: A Comprehensive Introduction* (2nd edn, Routledge 2014).

35. Gearty (2006) 154.

36. Kelly Oliver, 'What Is Wrong with (Animal) Rights?' (2008) 22(3) Journal of Speculative Philosophy 214; Alasdair Cochrane, 'From Human Rights to Sentient Rights' (2013) 16(5) Critical Review of International Social and Political Philosophy 655 doi:10.1080/13698230.2012.691235; Anne Peters, 'Global Animal Law: What It Is and Why We Need It' (2016) 5(1) Transnational Environmental Law 9.

37. Upendra Baxi, *The Future of Human Rights* (3rd ed, 2nd impression, Oxford University Press 2009b); Costas Douzinas, *The End of Human Rights* (2000); William Paul Simmons, *Human Rights Law and the Marginalised Other* (Cambridge University Press 2014); J A Indaimo, *The Self, Ethics and Human Rights: Lacan, Levinas & Alterity* (Routledge 2015).

38. Cochrane, 'From Human Rights to Sentient Rights' (2013) 16(5) Critical Review of International Social and Political Philosophy 655 doi:10.1080/13698230.2012.691235.

39. Peter Singer, *Animal Liberation* (1st paperback edn, Thorsons 1983); Tom Regan, *The Case for Animal Rights* (2nd edn, Routledge 1988).

40. Tom Regan, *The Case For Animal Rights* (2nd edn, Routledge 1988) 247.

41. Mark Rowlands, *Animal Like Us* (Verso 2002); Mark Rowlands, 'Making Light of the Ethical? The Ethics and Politics of Animal Rights' (Penultimate Version. To appear in Andrew Woodhall and Gabriel Garmendia da Trindade (eds), *Ethical and Political Approaches to Nonhuman Animal Issues: Towards an Undivided Future* (Palgrave Macmillan)). This version available at <https://www.academia.edu/24880242/Making_Light_of_the_Ethical_The_Ethics_and_Politics_of_Animal_Rights> accessed 4 October 2019; Alasdair Cochrane, 'Do Animals Have an Interest in Liberty?' (2009) 57(3) Political Studies 660.

42. Robert Garner, 'Abolitionism: Anatomy of an Ideology' Conference Presentation (International Animal Rights Conference, Luxembourg, 13-16 September 2012).

43. M A Fineman, Emory University, 'Vulnerability and the Human Condition' <http://web.gs.emory.edu/vulnerability/> accessed 23 October 2019.

44. Martha Nussbaum, *Frontiers of Justice: Disability, Nationality, Species Membership* (Harvard University Press 2007).

45. Sue Donaldson and Will Kymlicka, *Zoopolis: A Political Theory of Animal Rights* (Oxford University Press 2011).

46. This useful succinct expression can be found in the work of Simon Critchley. It is used to describe the way human reason has dominated modern Western philosophy. In human rights, it conveniently refers to the way this dominance has influenced the idea of human rights. It is the primacy of reason and its dominance that is contested and reviled in the philosophy of Emmanuel Levinas. See Simon Critchley, *Infinitely Demanding: Ethics of Commitment, Politics of Resistance* (Verso 2012) and Emmanuel Levinas, *Totality and Infinity: An Essay on Exteriority* (Alphonso Lingis tr, The Hague 1969/2000).

Chapter One

The Suffering Narrative of Veganism

INTRODUCTION

This chapter draws on a limited range of the now burgeoning body of literature to explore veganism. Developing a suffering narrative of veganism, I examine the vegan rejection of animal exploitation in the context of literature on animal suffering and oppression, and the idea that veganism has value for the development of a more egalitarian society. The chapter explains that the legal claims of vegans are assessed not only as matters in exclusive human rights, but also as matters that present the suffering of other animals in terms of a personal and private conscience despite the vulnerability and suffering of other animals being a significant concern to the human community.

THE DEFINITION OF VEGANISM

Veganism has no deity and no official definition for the purposes of law.[1] As noted in the Introduction, the definition promoted by The Vegan Society is that veganism is:

> a 'philosophy and way of living which seeks to exclude—as far as is possible and practicable—all forms of exploitation of, and cruelty to, animals for food, clothing or any other purpose; and by extension, promotes the development and use of animal-free alternatives for the benefit of humans, animals and the environment. In dietary terms it denotes the practice of dispensing with all products derived wholly or partly from animals.' [2]

This definition emphasises that veganism is a response to the exploitation and cruelty inflicted on other animals. It builds on the original ideas about what veganism meant to early advocates. In the 1940s, veganism was explained as '[t]he principle of the emancipation of animals from exploitation by man,' which was later clarified as a way of life that sought 'an end to the use of animals by man for food, commodities, work, hunting, vivisection, and by all other uses involving exploitation of animal life by man.'[3]

The current definition of veganism suggests that it is a philosophy that deals with intersecting issues regarding benefits to humans, animals, and the environment. Suggesting a relationship between these broad issues locates veganism as a critical perspective on the status of nonhuman animals and social justice. The definition denounces the exploitation of nonhumans and, at the same time, relates exploitation of nonhuman animals to human well-being and the health of the natural environment.[4]

THE EVOLUTION OF VEGANISM

Reports indicate that in 1944, The Vegan Society was founded in Leicestershire by Donald Watson, Sally Shrigley, and a small number of others.[5] It emerged from a small group of non-dairy vegetarians whose aim was to 'state a case for a reform that . . . is moral, safe and logical.'[6] The term 'vegan' was a contraction of the word 'vegetarian.'[7] It was suggested by Donald Watson, as an interim description of the beliefs of a non-dairy-eating vegetarian. This short word has been described as meaningful, purposeful, and steadfast.[8]

The evolution of veganism, as distinct from vegetarianism, stems from a rift in ethical values concerning the use of other animals for human consumption.[9] In the 1940s, it appears that some pure vegetarians were open to the use of nonhuman animals for food if they were not killed. This rift was, apparently, the impetus for Donald Watson and likeminded strict vegetarians to establish The Vegan Society in the UK.[10]

This break-away group of strict vegetarians aimed for a broad approach to practising moral responsibility to nonhuman animals. The newly formed Vegan Society emphasised the suffering of living animals as important in dietary ethics, citing 'very strong evidence' that the production of dairy products involved 'much cruel exploitation and slaughter of highly sentient life.'[11] While generally, vegetarianism remained concerned with the immorality of killing only, veganism identified the injurious practices associated with producing 'food' from living animals and promoted an enhanced concept of ethical responsibility to them.

The overriding sentiment was that to subject nonhuman animals to a life of confinement, in which they would endure constant suffering, was regarded to be unethical and abhorrent to humanity. This rationale, which I will refer to as the 'suffering' narrative of veganism, is supported by the 1965 Brambell Report, that observes the sentiency of animals used in the dairy industry.[12] This report documents that the process of producing and taking milk from cows for humans requires the separation of the mother and baby cow, which is likely to be traumatic due to their close bond.[13]

Donald Watson believed that 'our present civilisation is built on the exploitation of animals just as pre-civilisations were built on the exploitation of slaves,'[14] and that 'the spiritual destiny of man is such that in time he will view with abhorrence the idea that men once fed on the products of animals' bodies.'[15] Vegetarianism was regarded as a 'half-way house' and was distinguished from what was perceived to be the 'truly human, civilised diet' of veganism.[16]

Veganism, thus, emerges as a philosophy and a way of life that revolves around compassion, responsibility, and duty in the face of animal suffering. The philosophy of The Vegan Society resonated widely and inspired a global movement.

In 2011, the growing culture of veganism had coordinators, groups, and societies in 49 countries.[17] Following the formation of The Vegan Society in the UK in 1944, the first overseas vegan society was formed in California in 1948. In 1960, the American Vegan Society was established.[18] Though accurate statistics are difficult to ascertain, it is estimated that in 2007 there were around 180,000 vegans living in the UK.[19] In 2016, a Mori Poll commissioned by The Vegan Society indicated that 542,000 people in the UK were vegan, and half of these are in the age range 15–34.[20] In the US, available statistics indicate that around 1 percent of the population could be following a vegan diet.[21] A speculative estimate in 2013 suggested that 55 percent of the UK population could be vegan by 2020,[22] while in 2019, UK Supermarket Sainsbury's reported a 24 percent increase in online searches for 'vegan' products and a 65 percent year-on-year increase in the demand for plant-based foods.[23]

THE CHARACTERISTICS OF VEGANS

At the outset of the research that forms the basis for this book, studies about veganism or the vegan lifestyle were few in number.[24] The recent growth in the popularity of veganism has subsequently inspired a plethora of papers on both new and enduring streams of thought.[25]

Historically, veganism has been promoted as an 'extended code of ethics' that transcends what would ordinarily be conferred by human beings upon other human beings and selected species of other animals.[26] It has been said that the vegan code of ethics revolves around reverence and respect for all life, recognises the interconnected nature of life on Earth and that living beings have instincts, abilities, and desires to fulfil and have purpose in the context of interconnected oneness.[27] Vegans are also said to share a worldview in which other animals are not regarded as sources of food, and where '[v]egans see themselves as a part of the natural world, rather than its owners or its masters.'[28] Veganism has been described as a culture in the context of an 'ethos of enlightened morality,' through which the vegan lives a life of 'ethics in practice.'[29] It is said to be a philosophy of life, rather than a religion, in which 'vegan principles influence every aspect of daily living in very constructive and pragmatic ways.'[30]

Other research suggests that a vegan lifestyle is adopted following conscious and purposeful, logical, rational thought.[31] Larsson, Ronnlund, Johansson and Dahlgren state that the conscientious and reflexive decision to become vegan is seriously evaluated and constitutes a crucial part of what Giddens labels a 'life project.'[32]

Living a vegan lifestyle is believed by vegans to enhance health, contentment, and productivity.[33] Vegans are 'self-directed, goal-directed learners'[34] and are said to share an inner knowledge of the rightness of veganism, despite potentially sharing no other common characteristics in their background or life circumstances.[35] Vegans are also 'convinced of the moral rightness of their direction.'[36] Rather than being oversentimental and emotional about other animals, vegans have been found to be moralistically oriented and opposed to all forms of exploitation of other animals, and to embody genuine philosophical concern for all sentient life; a concern unrelated to the more common humanistic affection for other animals.[37] This view of veganism is said to explain what separates vegans from 'animal lovers.'[38]

Writers commenting on the characteristics of vegans support the idea, therefore, of a human identity predisposed to an asymmetrical, compassionate consideration for the suffering of other-than-human life. Their combined comments suggest a human identity capable of perceiving a cross-species ethics of compassion that is extended to nonhuman animals beyond typical and normative behaviours (such as those concerning 'owning' and loving pets). On this view, vegan ethics appear to operate at a posthuman level of moral indistinction.

VEGANISM AS A MORAL BASELINE IF ANIMALS MATTER MORALLY

Veganism gives expression to the moral imperative to attend to the suffering of nonhuman animals. A primary concern of vegans is that sentient, nonhuman animals should be liberated from human exploitation.[39] This paramount principle grounds Gary Francione's view that if other animals matter morally, then ethical veganism is the moral baseline for animal rights.[40] Francione's abolitionist perspective has global appeal for so-called 'ethical vegans,' who agree that veganism is a moral imperative[41] and that there are no justifiable grounds for the commodification and exploitation of nonhuman animals. The abolitionist view grounds the moral standing of animals in their sentiency and rejects the idea that the rights of animals are dependent on observable, humanlike, cognitive abilities.[42] Abolitionist vegans are opposed to the killing of other animals, and causing suffering for human gains, object to the property status of other animals, and do not believe in welfare reforms to justify their continued exploitation. They demand total emancipation and believe that sentiency alone is sufficient for moral and legal standing.[43] Abolitionist logic challenges a willing participation in animal exploitation in the contest of a claim to care about suffering.

THE SUFFERING NARRATIVE OF VEGANISM

From the outset, veganism has been associated with the suffering of nonhuman animals. A primary concern of early The Vegan Society was animal suffering and dietary ethics, which already had a long-established history. Literature indicates, for example, that the Ancient Greeks were aware that a vegetarian diet could sustain healthy human life.[44] Medical professionals in the nineteenth century were aware of the benefits of avoiding foods derived from nonhuman animals,[45] and it was well-known that a longstanding issue of importance for social reformers was the suffering of animals raised and slaughtered for food. In this regard, Howard Williams notes that Ghandi, Tolstoy, and Henry Salt were among those who supported dietary reform.[46] It is also documented that Percy Bysshe Shelley advocated 'veganism' on the basis that '[t]he advantage of a reform diet is obviously greater than any. It strikes at the root of evil.'[47] John Davis also notes that Shelley had joined a 'vegan' commune in 1813.[48] Historical literature on dietary ethics concerns the need for a more humane society in response to the visual experience of suffering, which resonates with philosopher Gary Francione's view of veganism in the twenty-first century: 'Being vegan provides us with the peace of knowing that we are no longer participants in the hideous violence that is animal exploitation.'[49]

MORAL FEELING AND CONCEALING SUFFERING

The dietary element of veganism is supported by a range of sources. Both the British and the American Dietetic Associations show support for the vegan diet and also refer, in their literature, to the serious disadvantages of eating meat.[50] In addition, problems resulting from farming other animals and the cost to the environment and human health are noted by many authors and incorporated into official reports published by the United Nations (UN).[51] Some authors conclude that the vegan diet is the only sensible, viable option for human health and for the preservation of human societies.[52]

In the introduction to Williams' *The Ethics of Diet*, Leo Tolstoy recounts the sickening witness accounts of the treatment and slaughter of nonhumans for food.[53] He argues that we cannot pretend not to know the 'horribly revolting' details of the suffering of those mercilessly butchered, nor the greed, social conditioning, and justification by religion or by simple habit that accompanies it.[54] For Tolstoy and many other reform thinkers, killing nonhumans for food involves an act that is contrary to the moral feeling[55] and is a practice that will be regarded by 'an age more enlightened and more refined' with 'astonishment and horror.'[56]

For these early thinkers, the daily visibility of nonhuman suffering, caused by the butchering hands of humans, inspired debates about the essence of humanity. Leo Tolstoy remarks that the immorality of eating nonhuman animals was known long ago and that it survives simply because 'we refuse to look at what we do not wish to see.'[57] Dietary reform, Williams argues, is deeply founded upon (*inter alia*) '[h]umaneness, in the two-fold meaning of Refinement of Living and of what is commonly called "Humanity."'[58]

Williams argues that attempts to 'reclaim humanity' from the diet of 'slaughter and foul living' dates back as far as the eighth century BC.[59] For Williams, abstinence was a selfless act of revolt in the interests of the 'irrefragable principles of Justice and Compassion—universal Justice and universal Compassion—the two principles most essential in any system of ethics worthy of the name.'[60]

During the many decades since these early accounts of the brutal treatment and suffering of animals, human sentiment towards nonhuman animals has encouraged a plethora of welfare measures, at least within Europe.[61] The sight of suffering of animals being killed has also become obscured from public view in contemporary society. Slaughterhouses are predominantly built in remote locations and, similarly, butchery, to a large extent, is no longer carried out in public view. [62]

Despite these developments and the prevalence of sentiment for other animals, there remain many accounts of hidden suffering. In October 2011, in the UK, Animal Aid reported that their ninth undercover slaughterhouse investigation found continuing, brutal, deliberate cruelty. Images recorded on CCTV cameras include: slaughterhouse workers stubbing cigarettes into the faces of pigs; pigs being beaten, kicked, and punched; pigs being dragged along by their ears; and stunning tongs used in a callous and incompetent manner so that the pigs suffered painful electric shock and fell to the ground screaming.[63] In 2017, further Animal Aid video footage highlights the suffering nonhuman animals are forced to endure immediately prior to their death.

> A slaughterman is shown in one clip picking up a frightened sheep by her fleece and physically throwing her over a gate. The animal was so terrified that she attempted to escape through a blood gully, only to be discovered cowering behind the bleeding-out bodies of her strung-up peers. The slaughterman also attempted to subdue a frantic sheep by deliberately placing electrical stunning tongs around the animal's abdomen. Other incidents caught on camera include a lamb, who was hiding behind a mechanical arm, being dragged out by the hind legs. One animal was pushed with such force that they were overturned and left in this situation for some time.[64]

THE EXTENT OF SUFFERING

The scale of suffering in modern industrialised farming is documented by Gail Eisnitz. Eisnitz explains how, in 1997, 420,000 hogs died on one Oklahoma farm. Eisnitz calculates that, during this year, 48 hogs died every hour from stressful industry conditions. In the interests of bearing witness and in the context of expressing a suffering narrative of veganism, the following extract is unedited. As such, the reader is cautioned to expect graphic details:

> These and millions of other hogs on corporate factory farms didn't die naturally. They died as a result of the hostile, stressful, disease-promoting conditions inside these massive factories. Or they died because, in a business where product uniformity is more important than anything else, they didn't make weight. Or they died because after permanent immobilization inside tiny crates for years, they could no longer stand. Unable to reach their food troughs, they starved to death. And many died violently. Thousands of piglets that were sick or didn't grow fast enough were beaten to death. The industry calls this thumping or PACing: the industry acronym for 'Pound Against Concrete.' Others were flushed alive from waste pits into manure lagoons. Pregnant sows were beaten

with gate rods, wrenches, and hammers; others had their throats cut while they were still alive, some had cesarians performed on them while they were still alive and fully conscious. And thousands, unable to walk, were dragged by their ears and feet and deposited in piles, where they were simply left to die slowly of starvation or dehydration.

'We've thumped as many as 120 pigs in one day. We just swing them, thump them, then toss them aside. Then, after you've thumped ten, twelve, fourteen of them, you take them to the chute room and stack them up for the dead truck. And if you go in the chute room and some are still alive, then you have to do this whole procedure all over again. There've been times I've walked in that room and pigs would be running around with an eyeball hanging down the side of their face, just bleeding like crazy, or their jaw would be broken. I've seen them with broken backs, where they've been knocked unconscious for a few minutes, but then they're trying to get up again.'

'Some of those guys thump them, then they just stand on top of their throats. Whether it's to keep them from moving or to suffocate them, they stand on top of their throats and wait til they die. They break their jaws and everything while they're doing it.'

'You can't really swing the bigger pigs. One time I walked in and the guys were using two by fours and hammers and gate rods and everything else to kill them pigs.'

'We had a total of 138 one day,' said a woman at another farm. 'And the guys who were supposed to thump them didn't kill them all. I went back in that room after they'd left, because I was supposed to pick up all the dead bodies, and there were pigs with blood just running down their heads. And they were up walking around. Here these animals had the courage to make it through the first thumping, and here I have to go and thump them again.'[65]

MUTUAL SUFFERING

A body of research identifies that the super exploited status and oppression of nonhuman animals are fundamentally tied up with human suffering. This literature explains the interlinked nature of oppression. Hooley and Nobis, for example, highlight that the suffering imposed on nonhuman animals has direct consequences for human beings citing animal agriculture as causing asthma and depression in humans, and that the conditions in which nonhuman animals are raised cause bacteria and superbugs that ultimately cause harm to human society.[66] These sorts of problems were also well-known in the 1970s, as Jon Wynne-Tyson observes.[67]

Nibert and Winders analysed intersecting harm in 2004 and highlighted that as technological advances speeded up the processing of the bodies of nonhumans, the conditions for workers worsened.[68] Bob Torres is particularly concerned with capitalist commodification and the processes of production of other animals. He argues that the process of production in capitalist enterprise is not simply about human food needs.[69] Rather, commodification and the process of production is 'tied into politics, gender, technology, and environmental quality' and depends on oppressive layers inherent in social relationships.[70] In this system of commodification and production of nonhuman bodies, the prevalence of human suffering is confirmed by Schlosser[71] and Human Rights Watch.[72] Schlosser comments that 'nothing stands in the way of production.' Workers have accidents and 'lie unconscious on the floor as dripping carcasses sway past them, and the chain never stops.'[73]

Nibert makes the point that 'the oppression of other animals has been devastating for the cultural, spiritual, and economic well-being of the vast majority of humans,' a view supported by the research of Eisnitz,[74] Fitzgerald, Kalof and Dietz,[75] theologian Professor Andrew Linzey, [76] and is even evidenced at the Federal Bureau of Investigation (FBI). [77] Nibert continues 'what is more, the oppression of devalued groups of humans has been, and remains, disastrous for other animals.'[78]

SUFFERING IN THE PRODUCTION OF 'FOOD'

In the latter part of the twentieth century, Jim Mason explained that the methods used in the processing of nonhuman animals for food vary from species to species, but that the principles were the same. The objective, he maintained, was to keep costs to a minimum and maximise profit.

Maximum profit was achieved, in part, by using innovative techniques to ensure optimum productivity. This meant that the reality for nonhuman animals used for the production of food was that they existed in crowded, barren, restricted, and unnatural environments, that they were stressed and frustrated and that they were fed additive-laced, unnatural diets. Mason cites the condition for veal calves as an example of the harsh conditions newborn babies had to endure. These newborn calves, born surplus to the dairy industry, were taken from their mothers and 'turned into anaemic neurotic animals to provide the luxury-grade "milk-fed veal."'[79] In fact, the calves suffered intense distress caused by separation from their mothers, were tied in small confined spaces to restrict movement, and were fed a replacement diet of dried milk, starch, fats, sugar, antibiotics, and other additives. This replacement diet was deficient in iron to facilitate the necessary white flesh that is caused by anaemia. White flesh was most profitable.

Peter Singer also maintains that in the late twentieth century, it was not possible to rear animals for food without inflicting suffering. He observes that at the time of writing in the later part of the twentieth century, food production methods meant that nonhuman animals suffered from being castrated, from having their herds broken up, from being branded, and from being transported to slaughterhouses. In one example, he explains, the more sinister details of the conditions for chickens who are highly sociable creatures with a need for a specific social order. In crowded conditions they suffered light and space deprivation, causing them to attack and kill each other. In an attempt to limit the impact of their confined conditions, the birds underwent a process of 'debeaking.' In this procedure, Singer explains that the chick's head was inserted into a machine that slices off a portion of the beak. According to Professor Brambell, this process causes severe pain because it cuts through bone and sensitive tissue resembling the 'quick' of a human nail.[80] In these conditions, the birds also suffer sores and abscesses. In addition, being naturally timid and nervous, they also suffocate in 'piling' caused by crowding in fear, on top of one another in a corner of their housing. Singer argues that food producers were aware that the conditions in which the birds were kept were responsible for causing their suffering but that market forces prevented them from offering the birds better living environments.

There is overwhelming evidence that Mason's and Singer's historical observations remain prevalent in food production. Current farming practices show that animals continue to suffer cramped, confined conditions and suffer physical and psychological harm in the high-yield, low-cost food production business.[81] The harms cited, and many more brutal procedures, remain norms in the industrial production of nonhumans whose fate is to exist as marketplace commodities.[82]

Bill Winders and David Nibert confirm these conditions in which nonhumans exist as commodified resources in a capitalist economy that is driven by efficiency and profit. They speak of exceedingly painful, brutal, and gruesome deaths, factory farm horrors, miserable deprivations, grotesque deformities, and rough handling. They explain that it is not uncommon for nonhuman animals to arrive at the slaughterhouse in pitiful conditions: for example, 30 to 40 percent of chickens that reach the slaughterhouse already suffer with broken bones. They point out that in the profit-driven economic system in which they exist, the life-span of other animals is of no significance: in the case of chickens, living just one-seventh of their natural life expectancy is not unusual. They report that the feelings of other animals and their urges and instincts to care for their young are disregarded and that birth mothers are traumatised from being removed from their offspring, which often occurs within hours of giving birth. Generally, in the modern food-processing industry, a wide range of nonhumans suffer violence on an unprecedented scale.[83]

Suffering is, thus, cited as a natural consequence of processing nonhuman animals for food —but literature also highlights that permitted cruel and painful practices do not relate to any notion of human need. Bill Winders, David Nibert, and Bob Torres, for example, argue that the conditions nonhumans endure are directly related to their subjugated status and their commodification in a capitalist economy that has encouraged the consumption of them as resources through progressive advances in mechanised, industrial modes of production. Rather than being a necessity for human survival, the suffering of other animals is related to capitalist commodification that has exploited entrenched prejudice. For these authors, it is these social conditions that ground the normative, violent practices that inflict immense suffering.[84] For Hooley and Nobis, harming is standard practice despite suffering being clearly obvious, its identification being a matter of common sense and it being unequivocally evidenced by overwhelming scientific research on the cognitive, emotional, and social lives of other animals.[85] David Thomas, solicitor and former director of UK The Association of Lawyers for Animal Welfare, argues that the outlook for nonhumans caught up in this system is bleak. He also observes a deeply entrenched, institutional, oppressive force in his claim that governments are more concerned to protect commercial interests than animals.[86] Nibert concurs: nonhuman animals suffer because 'it is not in the nature of capitalism'[87] to reduce oppressive gaps; capitalism depends on a false naturalisation and rationalisation that protects the invisibility of oppression and nonhuman pain and suffering.[88]

SUFFERING AND THE SCOPE OF COMMODIFICATION

Sociologist Bob Torres describes how an oppressive social hierarchy, built upon domination of and prejudice against other animals, is responsible for the suffering inflicted upon them, and he notes that their suffering is on a massive scale. He argues that prejudice towards nonhumans has ruthlessly commoditised, in capitalist enterprise, numerous species of other animals.[89] Using the term speciesism, first explained by Richard Ryder[90] as a way of drawing attention to prejudicial attitudes towards animals, Torres explains that it grounds a particularly offensive and rapacious oppressive practice that supports a broad-based capitalist economy. For Torres, it is not only food production that causes suffering. Torres argues that the prejudice against nonhuman animals is directly responsible for society being suffused with other animals as marketable, non-food products and by-products. This observation also has historical roots. In 1980, John Berger in *Why Look at Animals* remarked 'in the so-called post-industrial societies, they [animals] are treated as raw material.'[91]

Products derived from other animals, for humans to either eat, wear or use, are certainly well-known and widely available for purchase. Some, such as those bearing the labels 'veal,' 'genuine leather,' 'pure silk,' or 'fine bone china,' are regarded as 'luxuries.' The extent of uses found for derivatives of dead or living animals is not well-known, but—as documented by The Vegan Society—various commodified extracts of animal bodies find their way into artists' materials, tattoo dyes, glue, hairspray, photographic paper, tableware, soap, and an endless range of cosmetics, household products, and medications.[92] These range from the obvious, such as furniture wax made from beeswax, to the bizarre: for example, a Starbucks Frappuccino contains thousands of dead insects that have been commodified as a food colouring.[93] The particular product in this case is a red liquid dye made by crushing to death and liquidising thousands of cochineal insects. It is a well-used product, prevalent in a wide range of consumables from yoghurts to lipsticks, but it appears with different names and no explanation of its origin.[94]

VEGANISM IN WIDER LITERATURE

In the last few years, academic interest in the culture of veganism has seen significant traction[95] in the expansion of topics under the umbrella term Animal Ethics and developments in Animal and Critical Animal Studies.[96] In 2016, vegan scholars at Oxford University held the first 'Towards a Vegan Theory' conference that posed questions about vegan identity, culture, politics, and coherence, the way veganism challenges the animal/human binary and how veganism challenges current theoretical practices. The Oxford conference description illustrates the growing academic interest in veganism, as well as a contemporary self-reflexive evaluation of veganism itself. In 2019, The Vegan Society held its first ever 'research day,' showcasing a broad range of scholarly research now relevant in the Academy. [97]

This growth of interest in veganism includes a body of critical discourse that promotes the idea that veganism is a form of ethical, human identity that challenges current anthropocentric dominance. Philosopher Matthew Calarco has described veganism as moral indistinction because, in his view, veganism is a way of life through which moral responsibility to both human and nonhuman animals is enacted in practice.[98] Sociologist Bob Torres describes veganism as the 'daily lived expression of ethical commitment and of protest' because it responds to intersecting oppressions that are maintained in the interests of a capitalist economy that exploits entrenched prejudice against nonhuman animals.[99] Adopting a cultural movement perspective, Breeze Harper argues that '[v]eganism is not just about the abstinence of animal *consump-*

tion; it is about the ongoing struggle to produce *socio-spatial epistemologies* of consumption that lead to *cultural* and *spatial* change.'[100] These views conceptualise veganism as educational and an issue concerning social justice.

VEGANISM AS SOCIAL JUSTICE

Veganism remains grounded in objection to the exploitation of nonhuman animals, but has also evolved to become conceptually and strategically important as a means of dealing with broader oppression and social injustice and also includes environmental issues. The sentient status of nonhuman animals is registered as relevant to the foundations of ethical justice, and positive social progress is argued to rely on exposing the relationship between animal suffering and the imposition of arbitrary power and oppression—and on recognising the broad social ramifications of this relationship. Veganism is cited in the disciplines of medicine, nutrition, economics, politics, ethics, philosophy, health, environmental studies, intersectional theory, and queer studies as having social and political significance.[101] It is argued by human rights Professor Gary Francione as being the 'moral baseline'[102] of the movement for animal rights because it 'represents a rejection of the commodity status of nonhumans and recognition of their inherent value.'[103] It has been cited, since at least the mid-1970s, as a positive response to intersecting oppressions of capitalism,[104] and is relevant in historical philosophical comment on the wrongs of eating other beings.[105]

Veganism is also represented in feminist thinking on social justice.[106] The ground-breaking work of Carol J Adams in 1990 analysed the relationship between meat-eating and patriarchy.[107] Adams has also referenced interlinked oppression and suffering, explaining the 'filthy working conditions, sexual harassment and ignored or poorly treated employee injuries' in meat-packing industry employment.[108] In her thesis, five years later, Adams comments that 'the vegan diet is becoming increasingly popular because of the intersection of health and ethics.'[109] Marti Kheel also argued during this time that the oppressive pressure to comply with the norm of meat-eating is managed and maintained by force in patriarchal society.[110] By 2008, the ecofeminist branch of feminist discourse had established that veganism was most relevant to an examination of the root causes of social problems. In the context of theory on the patriarchal marginalisation of veganism, Kheel queries the tendency within our culture to ask: 'Why are you vegan?' rather than: 'Why do you eat other animals?'[111]

The historical ecofeminist search for an explanation of female oppression in patriarchy includes the idea that a naturally compassionate human identity is subjugated under patriarchal rationalism and its creation of dualisms. For at least three decades, feminists have argued that care and compassion for others are intrinsic to human nature but are denied in a patriarchal distinction between reason and emotion. The feminist objection to rationalism inspired Val Plumwood's attempt to articulate a notion of human identity that was on a continuum with nature. It led her to suggest the naturalness of compassion as a manifestation of identifying with others at the level of responsibility.[112] This idea remains significant in current ecofeminist theory. Recently, Deane Curtin has argued that compassion grows out of insight into the connectedness of self and others, including nonhuman animals.[113] He argues that we could not be human, social or moral, without the basic ability to identify others and develop a sense of shared, meaningful experience. For Curtin, compassion is intrinsic to being social and demands nothing less than a paradigm shift in dominant food practice norms in the interest of liberating humans and animals from intersecting oppression. For Richard Twine, ecofeminist discourse challenges anthropocentric thought.[114]

Veganism is, thus, presented in literature as an important culture in opposition to the dominant and normative consumption of nonhuman animals. It recognises the moral standing of other animals, is argued to express an interconnection with nature and as presenting a challenge to patriarchy and anthropocentrism. Its dietary norms are regarded to be healthy and environmentally friendly and is explained as the lived response to ethical responsibility.

These ideas are used to argue that veganism is an anti-oppressive, ethical practice for social justice. In 2016, the ideas were central to the first pro-intersectional vegan conference that explored the intersectionality of abuse of power and the politics and utility of veganism.[115] Topics included the relationship of speciesism to feminism, racism, ageism, classism, and the issues of the LGBTQI+? community.[116]

What these strands of discourse have in common is that they all recognise the oppression of nonhumans and a disregard for their suffering as fundamentally linked to wider social injustices.[117] They recognise that veganism is resistance against oppression and that it speaks to duty and responsibility in the face of vulnerability, oppression, and suffering.

THE IMPORTANCE OF VEGANISM IN LAW

Clearly, veganism is a response to suffering and a culture concerned with ethical social justice. It centres on respect for nonhuman animals and is argued to be relevant to addressing wider oppressive forces within a framework of intersection. At its root, veganism re-presents nonhuman animals as sentient beings in community, and the abolition of harmful practices that cause their suffering.

What is implicit in the idea that veganism can contribute to anti-oppressive social relationships and has restorative value for social harmony, is the suggestion that human nature is, essentially, compassionate and caring, and that a non-oppressive ethical justice concerns compassionate respect and regard for both human and nonhuman animals. This value of veganism is captured by philosopher Stanley M Sapon.[118]

> [v]eganism acknowledges the intrinsic legitimacy of all life. It rejects any hierarchy of acceptable suffering among sentient creatures. . . . Vegan ideals encompass much more than advocacy of a diet free of animal products, or a fervent defense [sic] of animal rights. Veganism excludes no sentient being—animal or human—from its commitment to compassionate, gentle benevolence.[119]

To address mutual suffering, Nibert and Winders argue that those interested in securing a better status for other animals need to understand the broad framework in which the oppression of others operates and to rationalise and promote an alternative ethical system of social organisation.[120] For Nibert, the dealing with oppression necessarily depends upon the development of a more egalitarian system that includes nonhuman animals. In this regard, Nibert cites the utility of veganism in his theory of social justice. He agrees with longstanding abolitionist Gary Francione, who has historically campaigned for the prohibition of the property status of nonhuman animals. Both Nibert and Francione believe that a paradigm shift in social justice is possible 'through prohibitions that recognise that animals have non-tradable interests and where those prohibitions do not substitute alternative forms of exploitation.'[121]

For Nibert, justice requires that the 'social positions humans occupy neither compel violence, nor encourage passive complicity in oppressive practices and arrangements.'[122] In this endeavour, veganism is promoted as a starting point on the grounds that it counters the power of the oppressive, structural forces of social hierarchy, domination, and prejudice.

In the context of wider intersectional oppression, veganism and the recognised and accommodated human rights demands of vegans to be free to practice veganism in recognition of animal suffering raise a number of issues. Not only about the justification for exclusive protective rights, but also the essence of human identity entrenched in the idea of rights and whether human identity is subjugated by socio-political arrangements, including by the rationale for exclusive human rights. To deal with these issues, it is necessary to register the struggle vegans themselves face in their attempts to manifest compassionate responsibility to other animals.[123] Moreover, it is critical to consider the relationship of vegan rights to the idea of exclusive human rights, and bring the subject of the rights claims of vegans to a discussion in which law itself is framed as a possible mechanism of suffering and oppression. Including the human rights claims of vegans in such a discussion is relevant to the aforementioned proposal to understand more about the existing paradigm, and rationalise a paradigm shift to an alternative ethical system of social organisation where the social positions humans occupy neither compel violence, nor encourage passive complicity in oppressive practices and arrangements.

The following section considers the general social conditions in which vegans make rights and equality demands for the right to practice ethical responsibility to nonhuman others. It notes the illogical manifestation of moral regard for other animals, and how attempts to live practically according to the moral conviction that animals matter are compromised by the human right to freedom of conscience.

THE SOCIO-POLITICAL CONTEXT FOR THE DEMANDS AND LEGAL CLAIMS OF VEGANS

The legal claims of vegans to be free to avoid participating in animal exploitation present the moral standing of and aim to protect other animals. Where vegans experience discrimination or feel that their practice is being restricted, they speak with and for suffering animals and look to law for support.

The claims of vegans are set against a backdrop of entrenched prejudice directed towards other animals and their exclusion from the protective rights enterprise. The claims of vegans also arise, however, in the context of a widespread general societal feeling of responsibility and compassionate regard for suffering nonhuman animals: not harming animals is an acknowledged social good. In this regard, there are cases that strongly express the immorality of cruelty to nonhumans.[124] The European Court of Human Rights (ECtHR) has protected the right to freedom of expression concerning the expression of compassionate responsibility and duty to other animals,[125] and rejected an application for a right to hunt foxes with hounds under the human right to freedom of conscience.[126]

In wider society and in law, animals are not regarded as objects, and many regional constitutions provide general protection for animals.[127] Protection for animals exists at the level of the UN and the European Union;[128] animals are regarded as individual living beings capable of experiencing pain and fear and, as such, are regarded to be sapient as well as sentient.[129] These circumstances reflect the uncontested empirical human concern for nonhuman animals and correlate to the development of positive law that supports vegan convictions; such as accommodating the belief in moral duty to other animals in human rights law and progressing developments within the European Union for clear food labelling so that consumers can avoid participating in the exploitation of other animals.[130]

There are also other areas of everyday social life that reflect the human concern with nonhuman animals. For example, the Royal Society for the Protection of Animals (RSPCA) reports that in 2018, it received 1,175,193 phone calls about animal welfare. On average, this amounts to one telephone call every 30 seconds. In the same year, the RSPCA investigated 130,700 complaints of cruelty and secured 1,678 convictions by private prosecution.[131] It is also estimated that in Europe, humans spend 15 billion Euros on purchasing products and services for companion animals.[132] In 2016, hundreds of well-wishers with their dogs in Cornwall accompanied a dog named 'Walnut' and his carer on a final outing prior to his passing by compassionately motivated euthanasia on medical grounds. As they did, thousands more around the globe walked their companion dogs at the same time as a gesture of compassionate support.[133]

In this context of widespread care and regard for nonhumans, activists have secured legal rights for a chimpanzee,[134] city councils have banned the sale of fur,[135] the dietary element of veganism has been validated as beneficial by dietetic and health care organisations,[136] legislation now exists on the right to be provided with vegan food in public institutions,[137] schools are providing completely plant-based food,[138] sports personalities are speaking out against the use of animal derivatives in equipment,[139] and, of course, as noted earlier, veganism has been confirmed to be within the legal meaning for protection under the ECHR and under equality law in Great Britain on the basis that the belief is: genuinely held, is a qualifying belief rather than an opinion or point of view, a weighty and substantial aspect of human life and behaviour, cogent, serious, important, cohesive, worthy of respect in a democracy, not incompatible with human dignity, and does not conflict with the rights of others.

The confused social and political conditions in which other animals exist in human societal arrangements clearly feature in responses to the legal demands of veganism. *Casamitjana* confirmed that vegans are moralistically orientated, opposed to all forms of exploitation of all animals and embody genuine concern for all sentient life. However, responses to the UK to this case were very mixed and included a request from Lord Blencathra that the Government review the scope of the relevant equality provision because, in his view, the tribunal decision was 'idiotic,' 'nonsense,' and 'crazy.'[140] This view reflects the earlier resistance to the inclusion of protection for vegans noted in Parliamentary debates in 2010.[141] Italian Carlo Prisco notes that, generally, vegans can also expect prejudice in the courtroom and that where, in specific cases, a vegan diet requires a defence, this is unlikely to be provided by attorneys. He generalises that attorneys are scared to defend (and first to condemn) the dietary element of veganism.[142]

A manifestation of the social good not to harm other animals is veganism. The concerns of vegans that lead them to make equality and rights demands represent the moral imperative to respond positively to nonhuman suffering. Vegans do not wish to be associated with animal exploitation or be compelled to assimilate into a culture of prejudice towards other animals by being required to participate in speciesist practices. They wish to practice a way of life that gives effect to the recognition that animals matter and should be included in social justice.

As already noted, vegans can expect to be protected under the ECHR and equality law in Great Britain. The re-presentation of other animals and duty to them is uncontentious in court, there is no lengthy discussion to the contrary, and existing supportive summary judgements are short. However, there are forces at work in the administration of justice of human rights and equality law that function to deny the existing, socially recognised duty to other animals. The following section explains this by examining how, in 1993, the ECtHR dealt with a case presented by a vegan.

ANIMAL SUFFERING: LEGAL CLAIMS OF PERSONAL AND PRIVATE CONSCIENCE

In 1993, the ECtHR considered a case presented by a vegan prisoner who complained that the UK Government unlawfully interfered with his Article 9 (ECHR) right to freedom of conscience.[143] The applicant, *H*, objected (inter alia) to a requirement to work in the prison printing facility because he wished to live according to the (widespread) belief that other animals matter, and he did not want to participate in their exploitation. He complained that if he were to work in the prison print facility, he would come into contact with dyes that had been tested for safety on the bodies of nonhuman animals.[144] *H* felt that this requirement contravened ethical responsibility and, thus, his dutiful practice.

The ECtHR upholds the European Convention on Human Rights. Article 9 provides that:

1. Everyone has the right to freedom of thought, conscience and religion; this right includes freedom to change his religion or belief and freedom, either

alone or in community with others and in public or private, to manifest his religion or belief, in worship, teaching, practice and observance.

2. Freedom to manifest one's religion or beliefs shall be subject only to such limitations as are prescribed by law and are necessary in a democratic society in the interests of public safety, for the protection of public order, health or morals, or for the protection of the rights and freedoms of others.

The Commission of the Court (as it was then), apparently without extensive discussion, observed that the UK had not contested that the applicant's convictions for suffering animals were a matter for the right to freedom of conscience, and found in principle that vegan convictions, with regard to animal products, do indeed come within the scope of Article 9 right to freedom of conscience under the Convention.

The court observed that this provision protects 'private and personal beliefs, and the acts which are intimately linked with these attitudes.' However, the Commission deemed *H*'s case inadmissible stating that even if under 9(2) there was interference with his freedom to manifest his beliefs, interference was lawful because it was prescribed by law and therefore justified: the UK Prison Rules were required to maintain order in the prison and the requirement to work in the facility was proportionate to that endeavour.

This case confirms the normative understanding that animals matter morally: the Commission immediately acknowledged the legitimacy of the belief that it is morally wrong to exploit other animals. The Commission accepted the credibility of such convictions in principle but applied the standard test of proportional limitation of personal and private beliefs of conscience and did not allow *H* the right to manifest logical ethical responsibility to suffering animals.

H's claim for the moral standing of other animals was decided in the context of the centrality of the human individual in human rights and his practice was denied on the grounds that there was an overriding interest (a valid law, required for a very good reason which, when applied, would cause no more than proportional interference with 'individual' beliefs).

This case illustrates the primary function of the human right to freedom of conscience to protect the autonomous agency of individuals to live according to individually held moral convictions. Under the right to freedom of conscience, law effectively frames the moral convictions of vegans to suffering animals to be a matter of only the autonomous private and personal conscience of individual claimants. The claims of vegans, however, that animal suffering matters are a recognised social value and the context in which vegans look to law for protection. The rights claims of vegans are motivated not as matters of personal and private conscience, but by the already recognised and acknowledged suffering of others their claims re-present.

There is clearly a need to delve deeper into the system of exclusive human rights to understand more about its role in the oppression of other animals. Consideration needs to be given to the foundation of exclusive human rights, the principles that allow for the accommodation of vegans in human rights, and, given that vegans qualify for protection in human rights but have limited rights to practice, how the idea and practice of human rights can be understood in terms of perpetuating exclusion and oppression. Opening up a discussion about these matters is important in the required search for a paradigm shift to ethical justice.

To start dealing with these issues, the next chapter examines the idea in the groundwork of human rights. It explains that human rights are conceived in a community of others (the human family) but are oriented towards the primacy of autonomous human reason that centres the importance of protection for human individuality. It explains that the primacy of human autonomy in human rights is a value through which vegans have brought the moral standing of other animals to feature in and bear upon human rights, but problematises the orthodoxy of autonomy to start a necessary discussion about the very mission of protective rights to emancipate from suffering and promote moral duty in community.

The chapter closes by suggesting that there is another way to think about human rights that recognises duty to suffering rather than individual autonomy, and that this way of thinking about human rights has value in the search for a paradigm shift to a social, political and legal justice that recognises duty to other animals and vegan values.

NOTES

1. Although, in terms of legal recognition, there is an ongoing attempt to secure Europe-wide rules on food labelling that consider the needs of the vegan community. See European Commission, 'Regulatory fitness and performance programme -refit scoreboard summary' (14 October 2017) <https://ec.europa.eu/info/sites/info/files/regulatory-fitness-and-performance-programme-refit-scoreboard-summary_en_3.pdf> accessed 24 April 2020. In the UK, historic Food Standards Agency guidance advises that '[t]he term 'vegan' should not be applied to foods that are, or are made from or with the aid of, animals or animal products (including products from living animals).' It also recommends notifying consumers about possible cross-contamination: 'Manufacturers, retailers and caterers should be able to demonstrate that foods presented as 'vegetarian' or 'vegan' have not been contaminated with non-vegetarian or non-vegan foods during storage, preparation, cooking or display.' See <https://webarchive.nationalarchives.gov.uk/20100720141723/http://www.food.gov.uk/foodindustry/guidancenotes/labelregsguidance/vegiguidancenotes> and <https://webarchive.nationalarchives.

gov.uk/20150904100120/http://guidanceanddata.defra.gov.uk/vegetarian-vegan-food-labelling/plans-for-future-content/> accessed 24 April 2020.

2. Current definition available at The Vegan Society, 'Definition of veganism' <www.vegansociety.com/go-vegan/definition-veganism> accessed 5 May 2019.

3. The Vegan Society, 'History' <https://www.vegansociety.com/go-vegan/definition-veganism> accessed 5 May 2019.

4. This is my personal view and I do not imply that it is the expressed view of The Vegan Society.

5. Donald Watson is globally recognised as a pioneer of the modern vegan movement. For an insight into his life and thoughts, see George D Rodger, 'Interview with Donald Watson On Sunday 15 December 2002' <www.vegansociety.com/sites/default/files/DW_Interview_2002_Unabridged_Transcript.pdf> accessed 5 May 2016. For information about the contribution of Elsie B. Shrigley (Sally) 1899–1978, see Veggievision. (2018). 'In search of Sally – The Lesser Known Founder of The Vegan Society with Donald Watson' <http://www.veggievision.tv/2016/04/27/in-search-of-sally-2/> accessed 20 October 2019.

6. Donald Watson, 'The Vegan News' (*The Vegan Society*, November 1944 No 1, para 10) <https://issuu.com/vegan_society/docs/the_vegan_news_1944> accessed 5 May 2016.

7. Watson (1944) para 9.

8. Fay K Henderson, 'Vegan Values' (International Vegetarian Union [IVU]. *The Vegetarian*, Winter 1947 No 4, 29–30) <www.ivu.org/history/world-forum/1947vegan.html> Additionally, psycholinguist and philosopher Stanley Sapon (1924-2010) has noted a degree of 'linguistic chaos' and 'crippling ambiguity' regarding the definition of vegetarianism as a moral statement. The word 'veganism' produces fewer ambiguities, although it may indicate differences in motivation or strategy. Sapon emphasises that a clear definition of vegetarianism or veganism ought to indicate much more than what popular culture currently promotes, and that the ethical movement for compassionate living may be adversely affected by popular notions of veg*ism and dietary fads circulated in popular media. Cited in Karen Iacobbo and Michael Iacobbo, *Vegetarians and Vegans in America Today* (Praeger Publishers 2006) 182–183.

9. John Davis, 'The History of Vegetarianism' (Public Lecture. West Midlands Vegan Festival Wolverhampton October 29 2011).

10. Watson (1944) para 10. But see also, Leah Leneman's research extract, 'No Animal Food: The Road to Veganism in Britain, 1909-1944' (The White Horse Press, 1999) <http://vegansociety.today/img/ar-road.pdf> accessed 15 March 2020.

11. Watson (1944) para 1.

12. Francis W R Brambell, Technical Committee to Enquire into the Welfare of Animals kept under Intensive Livestock Husbandry Systems. 'Report of the Technical Committee to Enquire into the Welfare of Animals Kept under Intensive Livestock Husbandry Systems' (Her Majesty's Stationery Office [ca. 1965]).

13. Cows are continually impregnated to maintain milk production. Following birthing, their calves are removed and killed within three days. The natural lifespan of a cow is around thirty years, but they are typically diseased, lame and rendered

useless at around six years of age. They are then killed and processed in food production. More detailed information on the commodification and production of cows can be found at Compassion in World Farming, 'The Life of: Dairy Cows' <www.ciwf.org.uk/media/5235185/the-life-of-dairy-cows.pdf> accessed 5 May 2016.

14. Watson (1944) para 1.

15. Watson (1944) para 4.

16. Watson (1944) para 3.

17. Vegan World Network <www.vegansworldnetwork.org/world_vegan_directory_vcountries.php> accessed 3 November 2011.

18. American Vegan Society, 'History' (para 4) <www.americanvegan.org/history.htm> accessed 12 October 2011. This website has now changed https://americanvegan.org/about-avs/ accessed 5 October 2019.

19. Imaner Consultants (b), 'Vegan Statistics' <www.imaner.net/panel/statistics.htm#reveal> accessed 5 May 2016.

20. The Vegan Society, 'There are three and [a] half times as many vegans as there were in 2006, making it the fastest growing lifestyle movement' (*The Vegan Society*, 17 May 2016) <https://www.vegansociety.com/whats-new/news/find-out-how-many-vegans-are-great-britain> accessed 1 June 2016. For more information see Ipsos MORI:<https://www.ipsos.com/ipsos-mori/en-uk/vegan-society-poll> accessed 3 January 2020.

21. Imaner Consultants (b), 'Vegan Statistics' <www.imaner.net/panel/statistics.htm#reveal> accessed 5 May 2016.

22. Rushprnews, 'Statistics: 55% of Population on Mainly Vegan Diet by 2020 Predict Vegfest UK' (*rushprnews* 25 April 2013) <rushprnews.com/2013/04/25/statistics-55-of-population-on-mainly-vegan-diet-by-2020-predict-vegfest-uk> accessed 12 May 2016.

23. Sainsbury's, 'Future of Food Report' (Sainsubry's 2019) <https://www.about.sainsburys.co.uk/~/media/Files/S/Sainsburys/pdf-downloads/future-of-food-08.pdf> accessed 15 March 2020.

24. This was also noted by: Barbara McDonald, 'Once You Know Something, You Can't Not Know It: An Empirical Look At Becoming Vegan' (2000) 8 (1), 1 Society & Animals; Matthew Cole and Karen Morgan, 'Vegaphobia: Derogatory Discourse of Veganism and the Reproduction of Speciesism in UK National Newspapers' (2011) 62 (1), 134 The British Journal of Sociology; and Rachel MacNair, 'McDonald's 'Empirical Look At Becoming Vegan'' (2001) 9 (1), 63 Society & Animals.

25. The growing popularity of veganism inspired a specific 'Vegan Theory,' formally introduced to the Academy by 'Towards a Vegan Theory' Conference held at Oxford University in May 2016 <https://vegantheory.org/> accessed 1 June 2016. For recent developments in the growth of research see<https://www.vegansociety.com/get-involved/research/research-news>accessed 24 April 2020.

26. Victoria Moran, *Compassion, The Ultimate Ethic: An Exploration of Veganism* (3rd edn, The American Vegan Society 1991) 13.

27. Stanley M Sapon, 'Vegan values: a philosophy of vegan values' (2007-2009) <https://eugeneveg.org/NewsBlog_600.html> accessed 18 October 2019.

28. McDonald (2000) 7.

29. Moran (1991) 14.

30. J Stepaniak, *Being Vegan: Living With Conscience, Conviction and Compassion*. (Lowell House, a division of NTC Contemporary Publishing Group Inc. 2000) 12.

31. McDonald (2000).

32. C L Larsson, U Ronnlund, G Johansson and L Dahlgren, 'Veganism as a status passage: the process of becoming a vegan among youths in Sweden' (2003) 41 Appetite 61, 66. Giddens is known for his sociological work on the nature of self-identity and agency.

33. Moran (1991) 14.

34. McDonald (2000) 12.

35. Moran (1991) 15.

36. McDonald (2000) 12.

37. Steven Kellert, 'Attitudes Towards Animals' (*Vegetarian Times*, Sept-Oct 1978, 15). Vegans were not separated from vegetarians in this three-year study. Similar views about veganism were recognised in 2020 by a UK employment tribunal in the case of Jordi Casamitjana.

38. Wynne-Tyson cited in Moran (1991) 39.

39. A vision of The Vegan Society is 'a world in which humans do not exploit other animals.' The Vegan Society 70 Anniversary, 'Ripened by Human Determination' (*The Vegan Society*, 2014) <http://www.vegansociety.com/sites/default/files/uploads/Ripened%20by%20human%20determination.pdf> accessed 7 October 2016.

40. US Human Rights Professor, Gary Francione. For details of this approach, see Professor Francione's comprehensive website: http://www.abolitionistapproach.com/.

41. The term 'abolition' is used widely in the animal rights movement, apparently in the same way as it was during the anti-slavery campaigns. It is the perspective adopted by those who campaign for a total abolition of the use of nonhumans by human beings. The use of the word 'abolition' is contentious to some vegans because of its relationship with the anti-slavery movement.

42. As is the strategy of the Nonhuman Rights Project. See http://www.nonhumanrightsproject.org/.

43. Gary Francione's version of abolitionist animal rights does not advocate human intervention to prevent harm to animals from other animals, or to prevent harm to animals from other sources. This limitation of duty is based on the idea that law does not impose a duty on individuals to prevent harm to human others and is a principle that can also be applied to a consideration of human obligations to nonhumans. This view is contested by a growing number of vegans who believe humans owe a duty to assist and support nonhumans. The issue has recently become a topic of considerable debate that extends to the idea that wild animals are owed a human duty to assist. For example, Julius Kapembwa (former doctoral researcher at the University of Reading) maintains that duties are not required, whilst Catia Faria (post-doctoral researcher at Pompeu Fabra University, Barcelona, Spain) and Alasdair Cochrane argue that duties do exist, that humans already assist some animals and that some welfare intervention already takes place. The problem, they argue, is that beneficial, positive intervention is speciesist and, therefore, inconsistently applied. For discussion, see Alasdair

Cochrane, *Animal Rights Without Liberation: Applied Ethics and Human Obligations* (Columbia University Press 2012).

44. See for example, Plato, *The Republic* (380BC Desmond Lee tr, 2nd edn, Penguin 1987) 123–124.

45. Dr William Lambe, quoted in John Davis, 'Veganism from 1806' (Vegsource 2011, para 2) <www.vegsource.com/john-davis/veganism-from-1806.html> accessed 6 May 2016. Dr Lambe is presented as a fervent campaigner for the adoption of a plant-based diet and publisher of positive reports on the benefits for good health, including the beneficial effects on cancers. See Howard Williams, *The Ethics Of Diet: A Catena of Authorities Deprecatory Of The Practice of Flesh Eating* (University of Illinois Press 1883/2003).

46. Others include Mark Twain, Queen Victoria, Jung, and C S Lewis. See Jon Wynne-Tyson, *The Extended Circle: An Anthology of Humane Thought* (3rd edn, Sphere Books Ltd 1990).

47. Percy Bysshe Shelley, cited in Williams (1883/2003) 228. Interestingly, Williams notes the friendship between P B Shelley, Dr Lambe, J F Newton (whose children 'scarcely touched animal food' (Williams 202)) and Lord Erskine. Lord Erskine went on to present the Cruelty to Animals Bill to Parliament: *HL Deb 15 May 1809 vol 14 cc553-71.*

48. Davis (2011) para 4.

49. Gary Francione, Animal Rights: The Abolitionist Approach . . . and abolition means veganism <http://www.abolitionistapproach.com/quotes/> accessed 15 August 2015.

50. The American Dietetic Association has now changed its name to Eat Right: Academy of Nutrition and Dietetics.

See for example, Alexandra Caspero, 'Building a Healthy Vegetarian Meal: Myths and Facts' (*Eat Right: Academy of Nutrition and Dietetics* 28 January 2014) <www.eatright.org/resource/food/nutrition/vegetarian-and-special-diets/building-a-healthy-vegetarian-meal-myths-and-facts> accessed 13 September 2019; and the British Dietetic Association, 'Complimentary Feeding (weaning)' <https://www.bda.uk.com/foodfacts/WeaningYourChild.pdf> accessed 13 September 2019.

51. See, for example, Professor Richard Lacey, *Unfit for Human Consumption: Food in Crisis: The Consequences of Putting Profit Before Safety* (Souvenir Press 1991); Peter Singer and Jim Mason, *The Ethics of What We Eat: Why Our Food Choices Matter* (Rodale Inc 2006); and United Nations Food and Agriculture Organisation, 'Livestock's Long Shadow – Environmental Issues and Options' (United Nations FAO Corporate Document Repository 2006); Damian Carrington, 'Avoiding meat and dairy is 'single biggest way' to reduce your impact on Earth' (*The Guardian*, 31 May 2018) <https://www.theguardian.com/environment/2018/may/31/avoiding-meat-and-dairy-is-single-biggest-way-to-reduce-your-impact-on-earth>accessed 17 August 2019, and University of Oxford, Oxford Martin School, 'Plant-based diets could save millions of lives and dramatically cut greenhouse gas emissions' (21 March 2016) <https://www.oxfordmartin.ox.ac.uk/news/201603-plant-based-diets/> accessed 24 October 2019.

52. Jon Wynne-Tyson, *Food For a Future* (Davis-Poynter Ltd 1975); Erik Marcus, *Meat Market* (Brio Press 2005) and Michael Klaper, 'Plant-only medicine man' (*Vegsource.com* 2010 video clip) <www.vegsource.com/news/2011/09/dr-klaper---plant-only-medicine-man-video.html > accessed 13 September 2019.

53. Leo Tolstoy, 'Introduction – The First Step' in Howard Williams *The Ethics of Diet: An Anthology of Vegetarian Thought* (White Crow Books 2009).

54. Tolstoy (2009) 39–44.

55. Tolstoy (2009) 45. Tolstoy also alludes to a gender issue being significant in this act that is contrary to moral feeling. See the details regarding killing and the 'kind, refined lady' in Leo Tolstoy, 'Introduction – The First Step' in Williams (2009) 44.

56. Williams (1883/2003) xxv.

57. Williams (2009) 45.

58. Williams (1883/2003) xxvii.

59. Williams (2009) 47.

60. Williams (1883/2003) xxx. Imaner Consultants (a) record that 87 percent of all vegans, 90 percent of UK vegans and 77 percent of American vegans are vegan for ethical or moral reasons. Imaner Consultants [b]) 'Vegan Profile' <www.imaner.net/panel/profile.htm> accessed 12 May 2016.

61. For example, see Michael Hass, *International Human Rights: A Comprehensive Introduction* (2nd edn, Routledge 2014). For a critical perspective on the utility of welfare measures see Paola Sobbrio, 'The Relationship Between Humans and Other Animals in European Animal Welfare Legislation' (2013) 1 (1) Relations: Beyond Anthropocentrism doi: 10.7358/rela-2013-001-sobb. Sobbrio argues that all welfare measures serve only to ensure the continued exploitation of animals. Other critics also argue that welfare measures are inadequate and create the false impression that animals raised for food are happy. The expression 'happy meat' has emerged in this context.

62. The industrial processing of the bodies of animals takes place out of sight, usually in remote locations. Early work in this area includes Noelle Vialles, *Animal to Edible* (Cambridge University Press 1994). For more contemporary research, see various works by Francesco Buscemi.

63. Animal Aid, 'You can help stop this suffering' (2011) 165 Outrage supplement Winter 2011. In science that seeks to locate 'intelligence' in other-than-human species, pigs are known to be in possession of complex abilities: Lori Marino and Christina M Colvin, 'Thinking Pigs: A Comparative Review of Cognition, Emotion, and Personality in Sus Domesticus' (2015) International Journal of Comparative Psychology 28 available at <http://animalstudiesrepository.org/cgi/viewcontent.cgi?article=1042&context=acwp_asie> accessed 12 May 2016.

64. Animal Aid, 'Calls for Tough Action Against Cruelty in Stockport Slaughterhouse' (*Animal Aid*, 9 May 2017) <https://www.animalaid.org.uk/calls-tough-action-cruelty-stockport-slaughterhouse/> accessed 15 May 2017.

65. Gail Eisnitz, 'From Farm to Fork: Presentation by Gail Eisnitz' (*Compassion Action for Animals,* 1999) <www.exploreveg.org/issues/farmtofork.html> accessed 23

November 2011. This source appears to have been moved. A version is available at <www.animalliberationfront.com/Practical/FactoryFarm/From%20Farm%20to%20Fork.htm> accessed 3 May 2016. For additional accounts of animal suffering, see also Compassionate Action for Animals, 'Embrace Your Empathy' <www.exploreveg.org/stories/> accessed 17 October 2016. A brief search of social media also confirms that suffering exists on a huge scale. Bill Winders and David Nibert say that 'some of the worst forms of mistreatment of other animals in agriculture have been ameliorated somewhat by reforms in Europe. . . .' Bill Winders and David Nibert, 'Consuming the Surplus: Expanding 'Meat' Consumption and Animal Oppression' (2004) 24 (9) International Journal of Sociology and Social Policy 76, 91. For a critical discussion of welfare measures, see Sobbrio (2013).

66. Dan Hooley and Nathan Nobis, 'A Moral Argument for Veganism' in Andrew Chignell, Terence Cunio and Matthew C Halteman (eds), *Philosophy Comes to Dinner: Arguments about the Ethics of Eating* (Routledge 2016).

67. Wynne-Tyson (1975).

68. Winders and Nibert (2004).

69. Bob Torres, *Making A Killing: The Political Economy of Animal Rights* (AK Press 2007).

70. Torres (2007) 15.

71. Eric Schlosser, 'The Chain Never Stops' Mother Jones (July/August 2001) para 12 <http://motherjones.com/politics/2001/07/chain-never-stops> accessed 17 March 2020.

72. Human Rights Watch, 'Blood, Sweat, and Fear: Workers' Rights in U.S. Meat And Poultry Plants' (*Human Rights Watch*, January 2005) <www.hrw.org/node/11869/section/2 Blood Sweat and Fear> accessed 17 March 20120.

73. Schlosser (2001) para 12.

74. Gail Eisnitz, *Slaughterhouse: The Shocking Story of Greed, Neglect, And Inhumane Treatment Inside the U.S. Meat Industry* (Prometheus Books 1997/2007).

75. Amy J Fitzgerald, Linda Kalof and Thomas Dietz, 'Slaughterhouses and Increased Crime Rates: An Empirical Analysis of Spillover from 'The Jungle' into the Surrounding Community' (2009) 22 Organization and Environment 158.

76. Andrew Linzey, 'Does Animal Abuse Really Benefit Us?' in Andrew Linzey (ed), *The Link Between Animal Abuse and Human Violence* (Sussex Academic Press 2009) 1.

77. Linzey (2009).

78. Nibert (2002) xiii.

79. Jim Mason, 'Brave New Farm' in Peter Singer (ed), *In Defence of Animals* (Blackwell 1985) 94.

80. Brambell (1965).

81. See, for example, the short video at Animals Australia: The Voice for Animals (*Animals Australia,* nd) <http://www.animalsaustralia.org/media/videos.php?vid=factoryfarming> accessed 16 February 2017.

82. See, for example, the current website of United Poultry Concerns <http://www.upc-online.org/> accessed 16 February 2017.

83. Winders and Nibert (2004).

84. Torres (2007).
85. Hooley and Nobis (2016).
86. David Thomas, The Law and Animals (2005) 149 (7) Solicitors Journal <www.alaw.org.uk/articles/thelawandanimals.pdf> accessed 12 May 2016.
87. Nibert (2002) 130.
88. Nibert (2002) 253.
89. Torres (2007).
90. Richard D Ryder, *Victims of Science: The Use of Animals in Research* (Davis-Poynter 1975). The term 'speciesism' refers to prejudice towards nonhumans. It is commonly associated with the philosophy of Peter Singer but was in fact a term coined in the 1970s by Richard Ryder. Singer attributes to Richard Ryder his interest in and use of the concept of speciesism as prejudice towards nonhumans in Singer (1983) 27, n 4. See also, Richard Ryder, 'Speciesism Revisited' (*Think*, 2nd June 2004) 83–92, doi 10.1017/S1477175600002840; and Richard Ryder, *The Political Animal: The Conquest of Speciesism* (McFarland Jefferson 1998).
91. John Berger, *About Looking* (Pantheon Books 1980) 23.
92. The Vegan Society, *Animal Free Shopper* (8th edn, The Vegan Society 2008).
93. Kim Bhasin and Noelia de la Cruz, 'Here's What You Need To Know About The Ground-Up Insects Starbucks Puts in Your Frappuccino' (*Business Insider*, 29 March 2012) <www.businessinsider.com/how-cochineal-insects-color-your-food-and-drinks-2012-3?IR=T> accessed 11 May 2016. This insect is called cochineal (food additive known as cochineal extract, carmine or E120). It is widely used in the food and cosmetic industry to colour products red. It is obtained by harvesting thousands of insects and crushing their whole bodies. The red liquid that remains is what is used as a colouring. In response to reports of severe allergic reactions to the product, in 2011 the Food and Drug Administration of the United States of America required accurate labelling to enable consumers to make an informed choice. See Food and Drug Administration, HHS, 'Listing of Color Additives Exempt From Certification; Food, Drug, and Cosmetic Labelling: Cochineal Extract and Carmine Declaration' (1 May 2009) <www.fda.gov/OHRMS/DOCKETS/98fr/FDA-1998-D-0032-nfr.pdf> accessed 11 May 2016.
94. Often called 'carmine' or E120.
95. There is now easy access to sustained academic interest in veganism with research and references in many academic disciplines. For an example of very early work see F R Ellis and T A B Sanders, 'Angina and Vegan Diet' (June 1977) 93, (6) American Heart Journal 803.
96. For example, the Palgrave Macmillan Animal Ethics Series extended its range with the publication of *Critical Perspectives on Veganism*. See Jodey Castricano and Rasmus R Simonsen (eds), *Critical Perspectives on Veganism* (Palgrave Macmillan 2016).
97. Towards a Vegan Theory: An Interdisciplinary Humanities Conference (CFP description posted by Louise Squires 4th December 2015) <http://asle.org.uk/cfp-towards-a-vegan-theory-university-of-oxford-may-2016-call-deadline-14-feb-2016/> accessed 27 May 2016. NB This link appears to be no longer available. An alternative website that explains the conference is Torch: The Oxford Research Centre in the

Humanities <https://torch.ox.ac.uk/article/running-an-interdisciplinary-conference-towards-a-vegan-theory> accessed 24 October 2019. See also, The Vegan Society https://www.vegansociety.com/about-us/research/research-news/vegan-society-research-day-2019 accessed 20 October 2019.

98. Matthew Calarco, 'We Are Made Of Meat: Interview With Matthew Calarco' (Interviewer Caffo L 2013) 1 (2) Relations: Beyond Anthropocentrism <www.ledonline.it/index.php/Relations/issue/view/3> accessed 18 September 2015.

99. Torres (2007) 134.

100. Amie B Harper, 'Race as a 'Feeble Matter' in Veganism: Interrogating Whiteness, Geopolitical Privilege, and Consumption Philosophy of 'Cruelty-Free' Products' (2010) 8(3) Journal for Critical Animal Studies 5.

101. These streams of thought were certainly indicated in vegan literature by 1991. See Kathleen Jannaway, 'Abundant Living in the Coming Age of the Tree' (*Movement for Compassionate Living*, 1991) <www.mclveganway.org.uk/Publications/Abundant_Living.pdf> accessed 6 May 2016.

102. Gary Francione, *Animals as Persons: Essays on the Abolition of Animal Exploitation* (Columbia University Press 2008) 234.

103. Francione (2008) 109.

104. For example, Jon Wynne-Tyson (1975).

105. Prisco (2017).

106. A range of insights are available in Carol J Adams and Lori Gruen (eds), *Ecofeminism: Feminist Interactions with Other Animals & the Earth* (Bloomsbury 2014).

107. Carol J Adams, *The Sexual Politics of Meat* (Polity Press 1990).

108. Adams (1995) 81–82.

109. Carol J Adams, *Neither Man nor Beast: Feminism and the Defence of Animals* (The Continuum Publishing Company 1995) 219, n20.

110. Marti Kheel, 'From Heroic to Holistic Ethics: The Ecofeminist Challenge' in Gretta Gaard (ed), *Ecofeminism: Women, Animals, Nature* (Temple University Press 1993).

111. Marti Kheel, 'Toppling Patriarchy With a Fork – The Radical Potential of Veganism, Lecture by Marti Kheel; Part 2 - Why Aren't More People Vegan?' ([video clip] Internet Archive Community Video website 2008b) <www.archive.org/details/toppling_patriarchy_part_2_of_8> accessed 22 OCtober 2019.

112. Val Plumwood, 'Nature, Self, and Gender: Feminism, Environmental Philosophy, and the Critique of Rationalism' in Robert Elliot (ed), *Environmental Ethics* (Oxford University Press 1995).

113. Deane Curtin, 'Compassion and Being Human' in Carol J Adams and Lori Gruen (eds), *Ecofeminism: Feminist Interactions with Other Animals & the Earth* (Bloomsbury 2014) 39.

114. Richard Twine, 'Ecofeminism and Veganism: Revisiting the Question of Universalism' in Carol J Adams and Lori Gruen (eds), *Ecofeminism: Feminist Interactions with Other Animals & the Earth* (Bloomsbury 2014). Twine's intersectional perspective is comprehensive. Spearheading the recent return to explore intersecting oppression through the use of Barbara Noske's 'Animal Industrial Complex,' Twine observes a 'partially opaque network of relations between governments, public and

private science, and the corporate agricultural sector. Within the three nodes of the complex are multiple intersecting levels and it is sustained by an ideology that naturalises the human as a consumer of other animals. It encompasses an extraordinary wide range of practices, technologies, identities and markets.' See Richard Twine, 'The Industrialisation of Animals: What Happened to Ethics?' (*The Scavenger*, 12 December 2010) <www.thescavenger.net/social-justice-sp-24912/animals/538-the-iindustrialisation-of-animals-where-are-the-ethics-89912.html> accessed 1 June 2016.

115. Vegfest UK <http://london.vegfest.co.uk/intersectional> accessed 17 October 2016.

116. LGBTQI+? is a comprehensively inclusive acronym that refers to the multiplicity of gender identities and possible sexual orientations. It unites lesbian, gay, bisexual, transgender, queer, intersex gender variance and any other gender identity not easily represented by a letter or single word.

117. The symbolic value of veganism is also observed by Cory Lee Wren, 'Human Supremacy, Post-Speciesist Ideology, and the Case for Anti-Colonialist Veganism' in Daniel Moorehead (ed), *Animals in Human Society: Amazing Creatures Who Share Our Planet* (University Press of America 2016).

118. Stanley M Sapon, 'A Philosophy of Vegan Values' (From all-creatures.org Articles Archive) <www.all-creatures.org/articles/sapon.html> accessed 13 October 2019. Stanley Sapon (1924-2010) was Professor Emeritus of Psycholinguistics at the University of Rochester (NY). He was a linguist, ethicist and philosopher. He was elected to the Board of the American Vegan Society.

119. Sapon, 'A Philosophy of Vegan Values' para 7.

120. David Nibert, *Animal Rights Human Rights: Entanglements of Oppression and Liberation* (Rowman & Littlefield Publishers Inc 2002) and Winders and Nibert (2004).

121. Gary Francione, cited in Nibert (2002) 251. Gary Francione promotes abolitionism rather than animal welfare. For a discussion of both perspectives, see Gary Francione and Robert Garner, *The Animal Rights Debate* (Columbia University Press 2010).

122. Nibert (2002) 253.

123. There are a plethora of everyday contexts in which vegans have difficulty practicing their convictions. The Vegan Society has a dedicated advocacy service in the UK to assist vegans, as did the International Vegan Rights Alliance (up to 2019 when it merged with The Vegan Society). The Vegan Prisoners Support Group has been assisting vegan prisoners since 1994 and works with the UK Government National Offender Management Service to ensure that vegans in prison receive adequate and nutritious vegan food as well as vegan clothing, hygiene, and body-care products. In Turkey, prisoner Osman Evcan was reported to have been denied appropriate vegan food. Osman initiated a hunger strike in 2011: ALFSG,'Animal Liberation Front Supporters Group' December 2011 <http://www.alfsg.org.uk/mags/SG_Dec_2011.pdf> accessed 26 July 2016. It should also be noticed that many people involved in the struggle for animal rights have been seriously injured and some have sadly, lost their lives including Mike Hill, RIP, Tom Worby, RIP, Vicki Moore, RIP, and Barry Horne, RIP. For more information and links see 'In memory of Jill Phipps:

Remembering others' <https://www.jillphipps.org/remembering-others-1> accessed 24 May 2020.

124. See, for example, the lengthy discussion on animal cruelty in the 52-page case report of *Let the Animals Live v Hamat Gader* LCA 1684/96. In this case, the Israeli Supreme Court stated that regard for nonhumans concerns our innermost feelings and any abuse disgusts us. It confirmed that we have empathy for vulnerable nonhumans and that there was a moral imperative to protect them. Available at <http://elyon1.court.gov.il/files_eng/96/840/016/g01/96016840.g01.pdf> accessed 13 May 2017.

125. For example, the ECtHR has ensured that dissemination of the explicit brutality and graphic facts of seal hunting are not considered defamatory towards seal hunters because of a 'vital public interest in ensuring an informed public debate over a matter of local and national, as well as international, interest.' See *Bladet Tromsø And Stensaas v Norway* App no 21980/93 (ECtHR, 20th May 1999). It has also confirmed that there is no breach of the peace if blowing a horn to disrupt a fox hunt is not accompanied by any violence or threat. See *Hashman and Harrup v UK* App no 25594/94 (ECtHR, 25th November 1999). It has confirmed that matters concerning nonhuman animal welfare are in the public interest to the extent that restrictions under an Article 10 right to freedom of expression are significantly limited: 'The Court reiterates that there is little scope under Article 10 s 2 of the Convention for restrictions.' See *Verein Gegen Tierfabriken Schweiz (Vgt) V Switzerland* App no 32772/02 (ECtHR, 30 June 2009).

126. See, for example, *Friend, The Countryside Alliance And Others v UK* App no 16072/06 and 27809/08 (ECtHR, 4th November 2009). (Though in the protection of minorities, under the ICCPR, the right to pursue traditional cultural practices may extend to hunting and trapping animals.)

127. For example, the Constitutions of Brazil, India, China and Florida recognise nonhuman animals. International environmental law also emphasises concern for nonhuman animals. Such law is established in the United Nations, Africa, America, Association of Southeast Asian Nations, the World Trade Organisation, the Council of Europe and the European Union. The recognition of animal sentiency in various European states is, to a large extent, related to the inclusion of animals as sentient in the Treaty of Amsterdam Amending the Treaty on European Union (Amsterdam Treaty). Since this Treaty, Germany, Austria, Switzerland, and France have all incorporated the sentient status of animals into their animal welfare legislation. In 2015, New Zealand followed suit, amending its Animal Welfare Act of 1999 primarily to reflect that animals are sentient: New Zealand Parliamentary Council Office, Animal Welfare Amendment Act (No 2) 2015 <http://www.legislation.govt.nz/act/public/2015/0049/latest/DLM5174807.html> accessed 18 June 2016.

128. See, for example, the list of 'animal welfare' and conservation treaties and declarations in Hass (2014).

129. 'Sapience' is a term used to describe the set of abilities organisms have that enable them to act or function according to their specific species and environment.

130. Regulation (EU) No 1169/2011 of the European Parliament and of the Council of 25 October 2011 on the provision of food information to consumers. <https://

eur-lex.europa.eu/legal-content/EN/ALL/?uri=CELEX%3A32011R1169> accessed 3 April 2020.

131. Royal Society for the Prevention of Cruelty to Animals, 'Trustees' Report and Accounts 2018' <https://www.rspca.org.uk/documents/1494939/0/TrusteesReportsAndAccounts+%281%29.pdf/d9beb013-28e1-c7e2-1948-f34bbe484fe3?t=1557490023015> accessed 24 October 2019.

132. The European Pet Food Industry Federation (FEDIAF) 'Fact and Figures 2014' [PDF] <http://www.fediaf.org/facts-figures/> accessed 17 July 2016.

133. Patrick Sawyer, 'Owner 'flabbergasted' as hundreds join Walnut the whippet on his final walk after Facebook invitation' (*The Telegraph*, 12 November 2016) <http://www.telegraph.co.uk/news/2016/11/12/hundreds-join-walnut-the-whippet-on-his-final-walk/> accessed 14 November 2016.

134. Seeker, 'Zoo Chimp Has Legal Rights, says Judge in Argentina (*Seeker*, 7 November 2016) <https://www.seeker.com/zoo-chimp-has-legal-rights-says-judge-in-argentina-2083850453.html> accessed 28 June 2017.

135. Fur Free Alliance, 'City of Berkeley Bans the Sale of Fur' (*Fur Free Alliance*, 10 April 2017) <http://www.furfreealliance.com/city-berkeley-bans-sales-fur/> accessed 28 June 2017. See also PETA <https://www.peta.org/features/fur-bans-fur-free-future/> accessed 24 October 2019.

136. See, for example, British Dietetic Association, 'Food Facts Sheet: Vegetarian Diets' <https://www.bda.uk.com/foodfacts/vegetarianfoodfacts.pdf> accessed 21 July 2016. See also the American Academy of nutrition and dietetics<https://www.eatright.org/food/nutrition/vegetarian-and-special-diets/feeding-vegetarian-and-vegan-infants-and-toddlers> accessed 24 April 2020.

137. Most notably, Portugal has recently introduced legislation to this effect.

138. Admin, 'Daycares in Finland are Going Vegan' (*Ecorazzi*, 18 May 2016) <http://www.ecorazzi.com/2016/05/18/daycares-in-finland-are-going-vegan/> accessed 21 July 2016.

139. Leon Watson, 'Yorkshire's Vegan Cricket Coach Stumps Sponsors after Questioning Use of Leather Balls and Calling for Entire Dairy Industry To Be Shut Down' (*The Telegraph*, 7 June 2016) <http://www.telegraph.co.uk/news/2016/06/07/yorkshires-vegan-cricket-coach-angers-sponsors-after-calling-for/> accessed 21 July 2016. See also former Everton professional footballer Neil Robinson's website <http://veganathletesforpeace.com/about/> accessed 21 July 2016, and that of professional runner Fiona Oakes <http://www.greatveganathletes.com/fiona-oakes-vegan-marathon-runner> accessed 21 July 2016. See also Veg News, <https://vegnews.com/2019/8/british-cricket-club-goes-vegan-ball-and-all> accessed 24 October 2019.

140. HL Deb, 8 January 2020, c275

141. See Parliamentary debate on the Equality Bill 32 March 2010: https://hansard.parliament.uk/Lords/2010-03-23/debates/10032376000529/EqualityBill?highlight=vegan#contribution-10032376000130 "to include cults and other lifestyle choices such as veganism and vegetarianism [under equality law] is to make something of a farce of the debates that we had." See also n5 of the Introduction to this book.

142. Prisco (2017) 114. Prisco emphasises how scientific data from the American Dietetic Association helped him to litigate in the case of a young child expelled from

school because the client could not provide medical certification that the child was in good health and underwent periodic health assessments.

143. *H v UK* (1993) 16 EHRR.

144. The UK Government had denied that the dyes were derived and tested on other animals. The applicant had support from The Vegan Society for the fact that most dyes had, at some stage in their development, been tested on nonhuman animals.

Chapter Two

The Context for Vegan Rights

The Autonomy Orthodoxy of Human Rights

INTRODUCTION

The previous chapter explained that veganism is a response to suffering and that, in all aspects of their daily lives, vegans practice ethical commitment to the moral standing of nonhuman animals. It explained that vegans argue against a requirement to assimilate into the mainstream system of prejudice against animals and have defended their right to respond to nonhuman animal suffering under the human right to freedom of conscience. It was seen, however, that although the vegan concern with nonhuman animal suffering has been recognised in law on account of the immediately recognisable social good not to harm other animals, veganism itself is assessed for its credibility and validity in law, and the ethical convictions of vegans can be lawfully compromised on the grounds that they are deemed private and personal beliefs of individual conscience that must be balanced against competing aims in a democracy.

Crucially, other animals and their suffering are not a feature of this process of justice and proportional interference with the practice of vegans does not consider the ethical duty to protect other animals from suffering. The rights of vegans are, then, considered to be individual moral convictions of the autonomous personal and private conscience of individuals.

The purpose of this chapter is to identify the extent to which the autonomy orthodoxy and emancipation from suffering feature in the values at the heart of human rights. This will give a clearer idea of the relationship of veganism to the idea and practice of human rights.

The chapter firstly outlines the historical development of modern human rights. It observes that the Universal Declaration of Human Rights was created in response to the enormity of suffering witnessed in atrocities of war but that it was developed in the context of tension between the value for human reason and appreciation for the 'conscience of mankind' in the human family.

Attention, thus, turns to how this tension features in the International Bill of Human Rights and its evolution in the European System of Human Rights. The chapter observes that duty in community is an important value, but primacy is given to human autonomy and that this value is represented in the paramount right to freedom of conscience. It finds, however, that despite the exclusive nature of human rights and the relegation of duty to vulnerable others in community, the human right to freedom of conscience is, paradoxically, a vehicle through which the vulnerability and suffering of other animals are raised as a matter of and for human rights. I suggest that the normative acceptance in human rights of a value for protecting vulnerable animals represents the original mission of a protective right enterprise and grounds the exploration of an ethical theory that is better equipped to promote duty-based justice in community.

BACKGROUND

The subjugated status of nonhuman animals is not explicitly written into human rights law. There is no explicit right to kill nonhuman animals or to disregard their suffering. Their subjugated status is, however, the context for exclusive human rights.[1] The human-nonhuman binary in the idea of human rights is supported, for example, by the exclusionary jurisdiction of the ECtHR, which has confirmed that it cannot consider complaints put forward for animal rights because the Convention has no provisions for the rights of animals for it to protect.[2]

International human rights provisions also reflect the resource status of nonhuman animals. For example, Article 27 of the International Covenant on Civil and Political Rights requires states to ensure that minorities are not denied enjoyment of their culture.[3] Under this provision, the Human Rights Committee, in General Comment 23, communicates the status of nonhuman animals as land resources and notes that granting cultural rights may also include protecting, by law, rights (inter alia) to hunting and fishing.[4] This bias of human rights allows herding, trapping, hunting, and killing other animals as human entitlements under the protection of culture.[5] When considering mainstream and the oppositional culture of veganism, this legal opinion is arguably an example of what Heiner Bielefeldt, a former United Nations (UN) special Rapporteur for freedom of religion and belief, describes as a 'prima facie contradiction' between the principle of non-discrimination and the privileging of a particular belief system.[6] If killing, trapping, and hunting are granted as manifestations of human rights that are to be protected by law, questions are raised about how veganism can be protected when its manifestation requires the moral standing of nonhumans to be recognised. In a dominant culture of animal consumption, the neutrality of the current rule of law and its application are, thus, called into question. This is especially so in the case of protection for vegans in the context of entrenched prejudice towards other animals and exclusive human rights.

H v UK[7] confirmed, without debate, that convictions about nonhuman animal suffering are within the scope of human rights protection. This finding was not in recognition that suffering itself was the mission of a rights enterprise, but on the principle that human autonomy of conscience is a paramount concern of human rights, duty to which can be limited on various grounds, none of which include consideration for other animals themselves. Thus, the inclusion of vegans in human rights, the apparent uncontested acknowledgment that animals matter, and the legal principles at play in adjudication reflect a long-recognised ambiguity in human rights. The problem is a tension in human rights between the recognition of a moral imperative to deal with suffering in community, and the orientation of human rights in its prioritisation of protection for individual autonomy. Understanding law's approach to veganism and vegans necessarily starts here.

THE AMBIGUITY OF HUMAN RIGHTS

Confusion surrounds the idea of human rights.[8] Michael J Perry describes the focus on global human rights as the 'dominant morality of our time' and suggests that there is no clear theory of human rights, that the morality of human rights is not well understood but gives expression to an assumed ontology of the essence of human beings.[9] Connor Gearty concurs, arguing that 'the moral obligation apparently inherent in the term 'human rights' is not a moral truth as such; rather it is a kind of mask we assume to help keep us on the right long term path for our species.'[10] Debates in human rights often concern justifications for exclusionary human rights and whether rights are grounded in duty or the primacy of the self-legislating individual.

Referencing exclusionary human rights, Gearty asserts that the main reason why humans became the creators of their own moral superiority in philosophical rights discourse was simply because, at some point in time, the idea of a religious soul gave way to the plausibility of a conscious, autonomous mind. He maintains, however, that the human/animal boundary is accidental.

Gearty puts forward the idea that human rights emerged as an 'emancipatory force against the abuse of power,'[11] and that there was never an explicit intention to exclude the suffering and moral standing of nonhuman others. He maintains that the creation of a species boundary is an inadvertent human construct in the story of a rights discourse initiated by human beings for their own purposes. Gearty also supports the view that the primacy of individual autonomy is insufficient grounds for rights to be afforded to the human species alone as, logically, this would preclude babies and other humans who are unable to assert their autonomy or make conscious, rational, autonomous choices. These and other similar observations concerning the logic of perceptions upon which distinctions are drawn between species are longstanding in the history of philosophical thought regarding the status of other animals in human social organisation. They are documented by Primatt[12] in the mid-1700s and given support by contemporary theorists, such as Cavalieri,[13] Regan,[14] Ryder,[15] Singer,[16] and Cochrane.[17]

The tension regarding whether rights are for autonomous individuals or a means to deal with suffering is clear in the history of human rights discourse. Jeremy Bentham (1748-1832), ardent campaigner against the idea of natural human rights, proclaimed that '[o]ther animals, which, on account of their interests having been neglected by the insensibility of the ancient jurists, stand degraded into the class of *things*.'[18] Further:

> The day has been, I grieve to say in many places it is not yet past, in which the greater part of the species, under the denomination of slaves, have been treated by the law exactly upon the same footing as, in England for example, the inferior races of animals are still. The day may come, when the rest of the animal creation may acquire those rights which never could have been withholden from them but by the hand of tyranny. The French have already discovered that the blackness of the skin is no reason why a human being should be abandoned without redress to the caprice of a tormentor. It may come one day to be recognized, that the number of the legs, the villosity of the skin, or the termination of the *os sacrum*, are reasons equally insufficient for abandoning a sensitive being to the same fate. What else is it that should trace the insuperable line? Is it the faculty of reason, or, perhaps, the faculty of discourse? But a full-grown horse or dog is beyond comparison a more rational, as well as a more conversable, animal than an infant of a day, or a week, or even a month, old. But suppose the case were otherwise, what would it avail? the question is not, Can they *reason*? nor, Can they *talk*? but, Can they *suffer*?[19]

THE IDEA OF HUMAN AUTONOMY IN THE GROUNDWORK OF RIGHTS

A survey of human rights literature reveals that the search for the origins of and justifications for the modern notion of universal human rights is extensive. What is most prominent in this discourse is the lack of attention paid to rights as a response to duty in the face of suffering, in favour of the development of a notion of human rights as the natural rights of self-determining individuals. This notion of human identity is associated with the existence of natural law and has been heavily influenced by a Western liberal view of human nature that became most prominent during the Enlightenment.

The idea that human rights represent the natural rights of self-determining individuals is historical. Michael Hass briefly notes that a relationship between a conception of natural law and the existence of human law can be traced back at least to the Ancient Greeks.[20] Aristotle (384–322 BC), for example, argued that the good governance of a nation would be one that protected human liberty by ensuring the conditions under which individuals could flourish and achieve according to their capabilities.[21] Moving forward in time, the philosophy of the Stoics of the third century AD was that nature revealed a universal truth which would emerge through rational beings respecting each other as equals. Bertrand Russell explains that for the Stoics, human life was inextricably intertwined with nature and God, and each person was thought to be directed by a Divine presence. On this view, human reason is supreme and facilitates the process by which the universal moral law will become known and established. The Stoics believed that an individual has total autonomy of mind and 'perfect freedom' to exercise the Divine virtue they personify.[22]

Into the Middle Ages, this historical narrative of human law is entirely within an understanding of a pre-existing, natural order that concerns a God-given knowledge of Divine natural law. Since God was observed as the creator, awareness of how to live in community with regard for others would be instinctive and universal knowledge. The idea was that the freedom of individuals in community ought not be limited by the state. Since natural law was universal and discoverable through reason, individuals should be left to exercise natural liberty and self-determination to do good and avoid evil.[23]

Contemporary theorist James Griffin notes the historical significance of a perception of a natural law of the universe in the development of human law, but he observes the way in which the established perception of natural law gave way to a new, modern idea of human rights in the Enlightenment period of the eighteenth century.[24] Before this era, as Costas Douzinas explains, there was no concept of enforceable, natural, individual human rights.[25] The social contract philosophies of Rousseau (1712–1778), Thomas Hobbes (1588–1679) and John Locke (1632–1704) were significant in the development of a discourse on the relationship between natural rights and freedom from state interference. Rousseau argued that '[man] is born free; and everywhere he is in chains.'[26] Hobbes argued that individual freedom is relinquished to government only to secure safety, social order, peace and harmony in the otherwise brutal world of unrestrained man in competition with others.[27] John Locke partially agreed with Hobbes but qualified the extent of individual submission to authority, arguing that men have 'a title to perfect freedom and an uncontrolled enjoyment of all the rights and privileges of the law of [n]ature, equally with any other man' and basic natural rights to 'property, life, liberty, and estate.'[28]

These Enlightenment ideas continued the natural rights tradition, observed humanity to be composed of equal rational individuals in community, and argued that state authority was only necessary for protection. Individualised human rights had not yet surfaced, but when they did their orientation to human individuality was established.

THE EMERGENCE OF INDIVIDUALISED HUMAN RIGHTS

Historian Lynn Hunt describes the Enlightenment period as a time preoccupied with the idea of individuals as autonomous agents. She argues that this had significant implications for the socio-political landscape and the development of modern human rights.

The influencing factors cited by Hunt include the demise of God and the emergence of secular ideas, but also the prior American and French revolutions and subsequent declarations that referred to the rights of man. Hunt suggests that the Enlightenment saw the introduction and development of a different notion of human identity and a corresponding notion of 'self-evident' human rights.[29] These were inspired by new ideas about man being 'born free,' rights being 'natural' and people being 'equal,' and about the universal application of these concepts. Hunt argues that during the Enlightenment, the notion of individual human rights emerged.

Hunt notes that English jurist William Blackstone defined the rights of man as 'the natural liberty of mankind, that is, the absolute rights of man, considered as a free agent endowed with discernment, to know good from evil.'[30] This definition reflected the situation of individuals in community and gave the reason for the assumed free agency. Hunt argues that, during the Enlightenment, liberty and rights came to be justified on the basis of 'a set of assumptions about individual autonomy.'[31] This was an assumption thought to guarantee the moral evolution of humanity on the grounds that each individual had within them the ability to know how to conduct themselves in community according to a universal moral law that respected and acknowledged the natural rights of others. These ideas were greatly influenced by the philosophy of the time, not least the work of Immanuel Kant.[32]

For Kant, individual human reason is an a priori characteristic and must not be restrained, since its function is to observe and express universal moral law. Through reason, the moral law is observed according to hypothetical and categorical imperatives. The hypothetical imperative is characterised as advisory thinking about how to achieve a desired end, and the categorical imperative is an obligatory, objective course of action that is required regardless of any end. These innate commands would guide human conduct to facilitate universal human morality. Bertrand Russell explains that Kant believed the categorical imperative to be a priori all subsequent reasoning, and that it was derived from Kant's concept of universal law.[33]

On the basis of objective categorical imperatives, Kant envisaged humanity's moral progress to be designed by universal principles that were accessible through individual human reason. The significance of human beings as independent rational agents was, thus, established. Lynn Hunt observes the importance Kant gave to individual reason. It was the means by which each person would realise their own understanding and think independent moral thoughts to guide the moral will. Hunt also notes, however, that autonomy and moral conduct were tied up with community values, thus confirming the collective importance of a sense of duty towards each other.

Hunt speculates that the new notion of personal autonomy did not displace the centrality of community and each person's awareness of and feelings for each other. The recognition of self-evident human rights was bound up with a common 'interior feeling' of something universal that made social life possible and human rights universal. This feeling was a 'social gravitational force' that brought 'people outside themselves' to manifest a natural disposition to care about others.[34] The assumed a priori nature of human reason was considered only a posteriori to a unifying affectivity. Hunt concludes that the development of universal human rights recognises individual autonomy but only insofar as it represents a prior existing, natural concern for the freedom of the other and a shared awareness of the undesirability of suffering. Hunt clearly alludes to autonomy being less important than the innate human sense of community, a principle of ethical otherness in community and a desire to manifest duty and care in community.

Hunt's understanding of the way 'otherness' or 'a common universal feeling' informed the development of a human rights of the individual is not widely recognised as being explicitly entrenched or reflected in human rights practice.[35] This is perhaps because Kant's philosophy focused much more on the absolute self-governance of the individual in relation to moral conduct rather than on moral conduct in response to suffering, to vulnerability or the precarious mortality of others. A highly influential idea for Kant was the concept of the self-legislating individual that emerged from his concept of human dignity.

In *The Groundwork of the Metaphysics of Morals,* Kant explains that individual autonomy is supreme because it reflects the intrinsic dignity in the command of the obligatory, categorical imperative that facilitates and gives expression to duty.[36] Autonomy, Kant argues, is 'the ground of the dignity of humanity.'[37] It represents the 'inward worth'[38] of the ethical imperatives that are naturally accessible to the rational mind.

On Kant's thesis, individual reason represents dignity on the basis that it gives access to morality. Further, humanity is composed of individuals who are ends in themselves because the will of rational beings is always legislative. These ideas have been given greater prominence and generated what has come to be known as the orthodoxy of autonomy of human rights.

THE IMPLICATIONS OF AUTONOMY FOR HUMAN RIGHTS

Costas Douzinas argues that the importance given to human reason in Kant's thinking does not deny the otherness-in-community of human rights and that '[t]he quest for a rational justification of rights starts here.' He identifies, though, a fundamental problem generated by Kantian autonomy and the idea of innate, categorical imperatives stated to be accessible through individual rationality. Douzinas argues that the philosophy of rights, rather than entrench duty, came to promote self-government and the creation of legal rules that entitled the bearer to seek various personal benefits in pursuit of their own interests. Right-holders became entitled to personalise and privatise their claims, and individuals were enfranchised 'to initiate their public enforcement; by organising their content in accordance with the desires and needs of their holders.' As such, the development of a profound dignity principle for human rights emphasised the importance of individuality and eroded the notion of natural rights as espousing respect for otherness: the basic community value of recognising suffering in the human condition of others. Human rights became derived 'of a law given by the self to itself and for itself.'[39]

For Douzinas, the centrality of Kantian rationality in the ethics of human rights has been instrumental in a counter-intuitive social construction of human identity as espousing self-seeking autonomy. This, he argues, has created an impoverished version of rights and law.[40] Lynn Hunt is of the same opinion. She suggests that the prevalence of a notion of human autonomy meant that individuals moved further and further away from community and became increasingly independent agents, both legally and psychologically. On this view, rooted in the groundwork of human rights, is a denial of the human need for the natural justice of compassion and duty in a community of vulnerable others, and the construction of atomised individuals.

The primacy of autonomy prevails and is a common feature of much rights discourse.[41] Autonomy as 'self-governance—the ability to determine one's own actions and beliefs,'[42] is so entrenched that the idea of autonomous self-direction is now also often used to ground claims for other animals. For example, the legal claims of the Nonhuman Rights Project (NhRP) for the liberty and equality of a number of chimpanzees and other animals.[43] But the special consideration given to human dignity has been strengthened through by the articulation of a further extensive range of human characteristics that, according to James Griffin, help to give a clearer idea of what human rights are and how they are justified.

Stating that a substantive account of current human rights retains strong elements of the Kantian tradition, Griffin shows how the exclusion of other animals is justified in the autonomy orthodoxy of human rights. Being autonomous, human individuals are considered to be free agents who have a conception of themselves, perceive of a past and a future, aim to achieve goals; deliberate, assess, choose, experience desires and aim for a good life. Griffin conceives of human individuals who value their moral and legal standing as autonomous agents and rely on human rights to protect this status. On this view, current human rights protect normative agency by respecting the primacy of autonomy, welfare, and liberty. They confer, for example, the right to life, to security, and to freedom of expression,[44] and the liberty to pursue what Griffin argues to be the most appropriate defence of human rights: freedom and protection in the pursuit of a worthwhile life.[45]

A consequence of this understanding of human rights, as one that speaks to the dignity of human beings and individual autonomy, is the demise of a concept of ethical duty in the context of arbitrary abuse of power, suffering, otherness, and community. The expression of the range of individual characteristics as reasons for rights moves the idea of rights further away from their origins as securing duty in community, fails to recognise ethical regard for suffering, moves the community of others further away from each other, and justifies the exclusion of nonhuman others as beneficiaries of protective basic rights.

EXCLUSIVE HUMAN RIGHTS, AUTONOMY, DIGNITY, AND PERSONHOOD

For Griffin, an interpretation of 'dignity' for the purpose of understanding exclusive human rights is personhood. Griffin retains rights for human individuals who are in pursuit of a worthwhile life. He argues that they are the only beings who can perceive of what is valuable and what is not valuable to achieve such an end. He argues that the notion of autonomy that supports the idea of human rights requires complex language and human beings are the only species that comply with this requirement. He also argues that it is not the uniqueness of each individual that is important to justify human rights, but the fact that the human species alone has the dignity that grounds current human rights. Individual capability is of little significance to Griffin. It does not impact on intrinsic dignity or worth. The specific kind of autonomy Griffin elaborates as a justification for current human rights only depends on the acknowledgement that human beings 'have a capacity to recognize good-making features of human life, both prudential and moral, which can lead to the appropriate motivation and action.'[46] In his account of the ethics of human rights, Griffin retains the dignity principle, grounding it in the autonomous pursuit and realisation of a subjectively valued, worthwhile life to justify the existence of current human rights. His account of current human rights has been well-received by other scholars and is considered to be critical to further discussion of the meaning and value of human rights.

The dignity principle and the notions of autonomy and personhood are, then, the most notable concepts for the centrality of the human individual in the idea of human rights. Support for this idea can also be found in case law. For example, chief justice Aharon Barak of the Israeli Supreme Court promotes human rights on the grounds of dignity and autonomy.[47] In *Academic Center of Law and Business v Minister of Finance*, he argues that 'human dignity is based on the autonomy of the individual will, the freedom of choice and the freedom of action of a human being as a free agent.'[48] In Germany, the Federal Constitutional Court declared that the state has a duty to protect human dignity and that it represents the highest legal value. It is a value 'founded on the conception of man as a spiritual-moral being, that has the potential to determine himself in freedom and develop from within.'[49] But the concepts of dignity, autonomy and personhood do not secure the centrality of the human individual in the idea of rights without controversy. Contesting the validity of exclusive rights and arguing for the personhood of chimpanzees on the basis of their complex cognitive and emotional characteristics, Michael Mountain of the Nonhuman Rights Project states that '[o]ur goal is, very simply, to breach the legal wall that separates all humans from all nonhuman animals.'[50] The concept of dignity is also contested.

Dictionary definitions of dignity refer to the concepts 'worth' and 'value' and it is common to find dignity referred to as '[t]he state or quality of being worthy of honour or respect.'[51] The term 'dignity' is used in many contexts to describe status or value. For example, a person can be a dignitary, and a person can behave in an undignified manner. For Professor Kass, 'the dignity of human *being* and the dignity of being *human*' is absolute.[52] A human being has 'special dignity because he shares in the godlike powers of reason, freedom, judgment, and moral concern, and, as a result, lives a life freighted with moral self-consciousness—a life above and beyond what other animals are capable of.'[53]

Martha Nussbaum has a different view. She starts from a notion of human dignity to develop a model of justice that gives precision to the language of rights.[54] She refers to this as the 'capabilities' approach. In this model, both humans and nonhumans have moral standing because they have needs and abilities that are essential to living a life with dignity. Case law also promotes the dignity of nonhuman animals. In *Let the Animals Live v Hamat Gader*,[55] the Israeli Supreme Court referred to nonhuman animals as knowing how to safeguard their dignity[56] and also said '[a]n animal, like a child, is a defenceless creature. Neither are able to defend themselves, nor can either stand up for their rights, honor and dignity.'[57]

These ideas have, thus far, not created nonhuman beneficiaries of rights, nor have they displaced the centrality of human beings in the idea of universal protective rights. Roberto Adorno notes that human rights instruments and the decisions of national and international courts show that the term 'dignity' plays several different roles and has different functions. Its primary meaning, though 'refers to the intrinsic value of human beings' and its function is to 'provide the deepest justification for human rights.'[58]

The concepts that ground human personhood—dignity and autonomy—also ground further specific, philosophical and socio-political reasoning that justifies the centrality of the human individual autonomy in the idea of human rights. This is most evident in the primacy of the human right to freedom of conscience. It is the development of this universal human right that has enabled vegans to re-present vulnerable nonhuman others to the exclusive system of human rights as a matter of justice.

AUTONOMY AND A PARAMOUNT RIGHT TO FREEDOM OF INDIVIDUAL CONSCIENCE

Following the Enlightenment 'age of reason' and the growth of secularism, the nineteenth century saw the development of further liberal philosophy that emphasised the primacy of autonomy in the context of a perceived historical struggle between individual liberty and state authority. Discussing the legitimacy of power exercised over the individual, John Stuart Mill asserted that 'the inward domain of consciousness' demands nothing more that absolute freedom.[59] This domain, Mill asserts, is that of 'the dignity of thinking beings.'[60] As such, any attempt to deny an individual the development of their own opinions, beliefs and views was absolutely wrong, primarily because no one could claim knowledge of infallible, objective truth.[61] On Mill's view, the liberty of the individual includes a social right to be free to think and be heard, and anything less would constitute a social tyranny whereby a majority view would infuse society and permeate law and legal process. Mill's thesis is widely cited as critical to the importance and development of a right to freedom to express personal views on religious convictions. It remains an important contribution to discourse on individual freedom of expression in the context of the recognition of plurality and diversity.

This modern development of a principle of absolute, individual freedom of conscience remains central to questions about legitimate state interference. In his *Theory of Justice,* John Rawls argues that freedom of conscience is fundamental to justice because it constitutes a primary aspect of human life and denotes personal identity. In Rawls' theory, when individuals contemplate the grounds for justice from, what he refers to as, the 'original position,' 'equal liberty of conscience' is an overriding principle that all will agree on because, he argues, freedom of conscience is critical to each.[62] Rawls argues that the argument for a constitutional equality of conscience is strong. It requires 'a regime guaranteeing moral liberty and freedom of thought and belief, and of religious practice . . . regulated only on the necessary grounds of public order and security.'[63]

Equality of individuality is also central to Ronald Dworkin's foundational legal justice. In a comprehensive analysis of Rawls' theory, Dworkin argues that it is legal equality that must be established prior to a Rawlsian concept of justice. Starting from a principle of legal equality, rather than freedom of conscience, Dworkin's concern, nonetheless, is to promote and support the view that there must be no constraint on individual liberty to decide what constitutes a good life.[64] For Dworkin, this prohibition is strict. Individual rights are political 'trumps' against collective views and state interference. Any such interference must be justified by very special reasons.

The socio-political philosophy of Mill, Rawls and Dworkin supports the general principles of Enlightenment philosophy on autonomy and individual liberty. On their views, the free thinking of rational individuals grounds a requirement for positive law and a great degree of individual autonomy and freedom over which the state has extremely limited authority. Ideas emerging in the Enlightenment regarding self-governance, autonomy, and human dignity are represented in arguments for strong individual rights to reign supreme against state interference with any chosen way of life or religious persuasion. In addition, this discourse has been developed to include an argument for social plurality as a necessary component of a value for autonomy.

For Joseph Raz, autonomy is a concept that expresses the way people shape their destiny by 'fashioning it through successive decisions throughout their lives.'[65] But '[a]utonomy is exercised through choice, and choice requires a variety of options to choose from.'[66] Raz argues, therefore, that 'valuing autonomy leads to the endorsement of moral pluralism.'[67] On this basis, Raz suggests that moral pluralism is the political ideal and justification for the right to individual freedom because it supports and promotes a tolerant society.

Discourse on autonomy, liberty and individual freedom is vast, and the views above represent just a small fraction of literature available. The brief overview presented above cannot do justice to the respective theses, nor can it include a critical appraisal of additional critical discourse on their content and scope. Nevertheless, it sketches out a linear view of the historical justifications given for the existence of the primacy of the individual rights to autonomy and agency, why they are said to be important and their value for wider society.[68]

On the basis of the views presented, the overarching context for the presentation of the human rights claims of vegans is the primacy of individual autonomy that is perceived to be a fundamental value to humanity. It is grounded on the dignity principle that is expressed through the rational and normative agency of each and every person. Autonomy ought not be limited by the state, except for very important reasons, and it gives expression to the morality of pluralism in human society. However, it is clear that the motivation for the claims of vegans is moral duty in an extended community of others, rather than to secure rights for autonomous freedom.

The primacy of the idea of individual autonomy in human rights does not itself necessarily preclude the existence of compassion for others in community, but the extent to which this historical context for human rights has shaped positive human rights law at the expense of moral responsibility to others needs to be assessed.

DUTY IN COMMUNITY AND AUTONOMY IN HUMAN RIGHTS: THE DEVELOPMENT OF THE UNIVERSAL DECLARATION OF HUMAN RIGHTS

The Universal Declaration of Human Rights (UDHR, the Declaration) is one of three legal instruments that make up the International Bill of Rights. The Declaration is formative but does not itself have the force of law. International legal effect is given to its provision in two later Covenants. These are the International Covenant on Civil and Political Rights (ICCPR) and the International Covenant on Economic, Social and Cultural Rights (ICESCR).[69]

Michael Hass notes the influence of previous eras in the incremental developments that led to the modern notion of human rights and the creation of the Universal Declaration of Human Rights that was drafted following World War atrocities.[70] It is fair to say that the immense suffering witnessed shocked the world and motivated a collaborative effort. Professor Upendra Baxi maintains that modern human rights emerged from a context of violence and that it is 'axiomatic that the historic mission of contemporary human rights is to give voice to human suffering, to make it visible, and to ameliorate it.'[71] Baxi is in no doubt that contemporary human rights are the mechanism through which humanity has formalised the fundamental, universal moral value of empathy and compassion for others in its endeavour to alleviate suffering. However, there was widespread agreement that the rights being articulated entrenched traditional philosophy and, perhaps inadvertently as Gearty might agree, the human individual. Human rights were:

> based on the most ancient ideas of the great philosophers and on the concept that the power of the State must rest on the respect for the human person. [The draft] was a concrete expression of that trend of thought which now shaped the conscience of nations.[72]

Exclusive human rights were, thus, conceptualised as ethically grounded in some concept of human individualism, and promoted as necessary to prevent arbitrary state power.

In her discussion of the creation of the Declaration, Mary Ann Glendon also observes the divergent philosophical and ethical traditions that were brought together to inform a notion of universal human rights.[73] She argues that the Declaration recognises the 'common convictions' of humanity and predominantly emphasises that human rights should not be perceived as the rights of individual sole agents but as entitlements that are grounded in the fact that individuals are constituted in community, by and through relationships with others. Though there are references to the free development of individuality and basic individual freedoms, she argues that the historical documents that record the development of the Declaration make it clear that community and duties to each other were to be recognised on the understanding that everyone is mutually dependant.[74]

Glendon is correct in her observations. The final Declaration makes it clear that the individual is not a lone bearer of rights and that the context for rights was the pre-existing fact of a community of others into which everyone is born. Johannes Morsink also observes the attention given to the value for and duty to others in community.[75]

The first sentence of the Preamble to the Declaration speaks of equal rights for all members of *the human family*. The second sentence says that disregard and contempt have led to barbarous acts against the *conscience of mankind*.[76] Article 1 confirms that '[a]ll human beings are born free and equal in dignity and rights. They are endowed with reason and conscience and should act towards one another in a *spirit of brotherhood.*'[77] Article 29(1) provides that *'[e]veryone has duties to the community in which alone the free and full development of his personality is possible.'*

The existence of community is, therefore, the stated backdrop to the rights granted, and these references to the wider community indicate the importance, significance, and necessity of the community setting in which human beings are born, grow and become. Further, the 'otherness' of human rights is undisputable: it cannot be contested that a Declaration of human rights could only have emerged in the context of a community value that the vulnerable mortality and suffering of others matter. The community bore witness to the suffering of others and legislated for duty in and for community: there was, therefore, a clear moral imperative in the human conscience to provide a system of justice that would ensure emancipation from suffering. For Glendon, the expressions 'the human family,' 'conscience of mankind,' and a 'spirit of brotherhood' are evidence that the international community did not wish to reject the significance of the human desire for and duty in community. It appears, thus, that the significance and importance of intersubjective becoming in community were inadequately represented at the drafting stage.

The records of the drafting committee of the Declaration reveal the tension that existed between the acknowledgements of community and the representation of human individuality. It appears that the drafting of the Declaration was fraught with conceptual difficulties regarding individual autonomy and the need to speak of rights in terms of a human family. For example, the Syrian delegation were keen to suggest that human rights were to be defined in terms of the individual because rights and freedoms for individuals gave all an equal chance to develop their capacities and live as men wished to live. This would ensure that men would live in friendship with each other: it would facilitate social justice and a sense of brotherhood.[78]

On the other hand, at a meeting on the day of its proclamation, the Yugoslavian representative commented that the current text of the Declaration was objectionable. He argued that human rights should not focus on individualism but should recognise the interdependence of the individual and his community. He remarked that '[t]he text before the assembly was based on individualistic concepts which considered man to be an isolated individual,' and that '[t]he Declaration was, in certain respects, not based on reality, because it described man as an isolated individual and overlooked the fact that he was also a member of a community.'[79]

The tension between duty in community and individual autonomy does not appear to have been resolved in the Articles of the Declaration that appear to emphasise the primacy of the individual rather than duty to others.

COMMUNITY AND AUTONOMY IN THE UNIVERSAL DECLARATION OF HUMAN RIGHTS

Despite awareness of the significance of human community at the drafting stage, the Declaration is vague about 'duty' in community. But, from the outset, there is clear articulation of the significance of human reason being manifested in a community of others. Article 1 emphasises the nature of human identity as being born free, with the capacity to reason. It states that:

> All human beings are born free and equal in dignity and rights. They are endowed with reason and conscience and should act towards one another in a spirit of brotherhood.[80]

Article 18 deals with the right to freedom of thought, conscience and religion. It emphasises the rational character of human individuals and states:

> Everyone has the right to freedom of thought, conscience and religion; this right includes freedom to change his religion or belief, and freedom, either alone or in community with others and in public or private, to manifest his religion or belief in teaching, practice, worship and observance.

The Declaration clearly entrenches the idea that the ethics of human rights concerns human individuals as rational subjects. Individual human beings are declared free and equal in all respects—including in respect of equality of conscience. Individuals will be equal before the law and will benefit from the principle of non-discrimination. These values are to be upheld through teaching and education, some of which will be compulsory.[81]

The value for freedom of conscience is supported by other Articles and made unequivocal in Article 18. These provisions of the UDHR that benefit individuals are to be restricted only if there is a law that is required for good reasons in a democracy. Article 29(2) states that:

> In the exercise of his rights and freedoms, everyone shall be subject only to such limitations as are determined by law solely for the purpose of securing due recognition and respect for the rights of others and of meeting the just requirements of morality, public order and the general welfare in a democratic society.

The a priori existence of community, individual awareness of and value for it, are recognised in the Declaration, but the emphasis of this primary modern human rights document is, arguably, one that speaks to individual liberty, freedom, and autonomy. Despite recognising the importance of community, the Declaration speaks primarily of rights, rather than duties, for everyone born into the pre-existing community of others.

Explicit and implicit in the beginning of the Declaration, and confirmed in Article 18, is a conception of human identity that recognises autonomy and the historical primacy of human reason. It is presented as the principle defining characteristic of human nature, despite the recognition that before the individual has come the community of others.

From the outset, although the international community was motivated to produce a Declaration following the atrocities of war, it entrenches an ethical orientation based on human capacity for reason. It is apparent that, perhaps inadvertently, the ethical orientation of human rights did not explicitly emphasise an overriding duty to others in community or an ethical orientation towards protection from suffering.

The international community has enunciated further the meaning of provisions contained in the Declaration. These elaborations are worth noting for two reasons: firstly, because they show the way international human rights emphasises autonomy as a central value and, secondly, because international measures can influence regional human right systems as in Europe, where the ECtHR has also declared that it aims to be consistent with accepted principles of international law and developments on common matters.[82]

The Centrality of Autonomy in International Human Rights

As previously explained, the UDHR is one of three legal instruments that make up the International Bill of Rights. It does not itself have the force of law, and legal effect is given to its provision in two later Covenants. These are the International Covenant on Civil and Political Rights (ICCPR) and the International Covenant on Economic, Social and Cultural Rights (ICESCR).

The ICCPR also looks to the importance and significance of the human family in the creation of its provisions for individual rights. It refers to the 'human family' and the duties individual beneficiaries of rights have towards other individuals in community. These references do not, however, articulate a comprehensive understanding of the intersubjective context in which it has given legal force to the civil, political and social rights it contains. What it emphasises more clearly is human self-determination and that human rights are derived from the inherent dignity of the human person.[83] The centrality of human individuality is confirmed in Article 18, which gives legal effect to the right to freedom of conscience. Its development and clarification are clearly associated with the developing orthodoxy of autonomy. Article 18 reads:

1. Everyone shall have the right to freedom of thought, conscience and religion. This right shall include freedom to have or to adopt a religion or belief of his choice, and freedom, either individually or in community with others and in public or private, to manifest his religion or belief in worship, observance, practice and teaching.
2. No one shall be subject to coercion which would impair his freedom to have or to adopt a religion or belief of his choice.
3. Freedom to manifest one's religion or beliefs may be subject only to such limitations as are prescribed by law and are necessary to protect public safety, order, health, or morals or the fundamental rights and freedoms of others.
4. The States Parties to the present Covenant undertake to have respect for the liberty of parents and, when applicable, legal guardians to ensure the religious and moral education of their children in conformity with their own convictions.

Regarding the scope of protection for autonomy, the UN Committee on Human Rights has provided some guidance in General Comment No. 22 of 1993, which states that:

> the terms 'belief' and 'religion' are to be broadly construed. Article 18 is not limited in its application to traditional religions or to religions and beliefs with institutional characteristics or practices analogous to those of traditional religions.[84]

In addition, the freedom to have a belief necessarily requires the freedom to choose one.[85] Outlawed in this context are the use of threat, physical force or penal sanctions to force conversion from one belief to another and, importantly, *any policies or practices* that have the same effect.[86] Under the terms of the ICCPR, this protection is applied to all beliefs—even those which are non-religious in nature.[87] Regarding interference, the UN sets out general legal obligations in General Comment No. 31. In this document, the Human Rights Committee makes it clear that states must demonstrate the necessity of interference and only take such measures as are proportionate to the pursuance of legitimate aims.[88]

From these measures, it is clear that the ethical orientation of human rights rests very firmly on the primacy of individual autonomy. This is confirmed further in the 1981 Declaration on the Elimination of All Forms of Intolerance and of Discrimination Based on Religion or Belief,[89] which is more explicit regarding the scope of autonomy and its manifestation. Referring to the importance of the UDHR, this Declaration states in its introductory Preamble that:

> religion or belief, for anyone who professes either, is one of the fundamental elements in his conception of life and that freedom of religion or belief should be fully respected and guaranteed.

The 1981 Declaration is explicit on the breadth of the meaning of 'belief,' stating, in Article 1, that a person is free to believe 'whatever belief' (he chooses). The Declaration states that the concept of freedom of conscience is vital to eliminate ideologies or practices of colonialism and racial discrimination and to ensure that there is no coercion that would impair the freedom to adopt and hold a belief of choice. These developments on the Universal Declaration highlight the centrality of individual autonomy in the human rights enterprise. Individuals have inherent dignity because they have autonomy of mind, are free thinking and must be allowed to retain absolute control over their inner realm of consciousness.

There is additional evidence that the notion of individual autonomy is deeply entrenched in human rights discourse. This is expressed as the primacy of the inner realm of consciousness, known as the '*forum internum*.'[90] It is argued that it 'cannot be interfered with in any way'[91] and that 'there are no permissible limitations to this right.'[92] Paul Taylor suggests that the absolute element of the right to freedom of conscience is unproblematic. Although interference is declared illegitimate, he suggests that it would actually be impossible to try to attempt to control one's inner realm.[93] Others too assume that this freedom is an 'easy case'[94] because 'states have not considered it difficult to allow their citizens the freedom to think.'[95] Morsink maintains that the result of the right to freedom of conscience is total freedom from a state-sponsored doctrinal position.[96] Former Special Rapporteur Arcot Krishnaswami supports these views, maintaining that freedom of mind is within the inner 'conscience of an individual' and noting that '[v]iewed from this angle, one would assume that any intervention from outside is not only illegitimate but impossible.'[97]

It is clear that the idea of an autonomous *forum internum* and the subsequent primacy of the individual are central to the idea of universal human rights. They are values that ground the validity of rights and inform a paramount human right to freedom of conscience. These values are also entrenched in the European system of human rights, as documented in the European Convention on Human Rights which, according to the overseeing court (ECtHR), provides protection for vegans in their re-presentation of duty to suffering nonhuman others in community. It is, therefore, worth exploring the meaning and application of this human rights provision.

THE EUROPEAN CONVENTION ON HUMAN RIGHTS

The European Convention on Human Rights is a regional human rights treaty that came into force four years after the adoption of the UDHR. It has developed independently of the UN treaties. It states from the outset that it is drafted in direct relation to the UDHR in the interests of the universal recognition of the rights it declares. It aims to promote a common understanding of human rights and observes that the fundamental freedoms outlined are the basis for justice and peace in the world. As such, it lists the basic rights and fundamental freedoms of every person. As a living instrument, its principles and provisions evolve over time through the addition of new Protocols and through Court judgments that develop and clarify the meaning of its Articles.

Unlike the UDHR, the Convention does not refer to the human family, the conscience of mankind or the spirit of brotherhood. Its provisions recognise, primarily, the inherent dignity of human beings and are explicated, almost exclusively, in terms of the rights of individuals.

It is clear from the *Travaux Préparatoires*[98] that the drafters of the Convention considered the centrality of individual, autonomous reason a critical component of European compliance with the principles of the UDHR. The president of the Council of Europe's Consultative Assembly announced that the aim of the Council was to recognise the fundamental principle of individual freedom.[99] Speakers emphasised the need to draw up a list of individual freedoms[100] in respect of the fundamental rights of the human individual.[101] They advised that the Council of Europe should ensure that Europe became a guardian of the individual human being,[102] in recognition of the prize of individual liberty.[103] The Council would ensure a principle of non-interference with individual liberties[104] and commit to the development of individuals.[105] It would comply with a duty to affirm the rights of the human individual[106] and, most significantly, would declare 'without hesitation that we stand for a concept of human rights in which the individual is supreme.' Against the primacy of individual freedom, everything else was considered subordinate.[107]

On behalf of the drafting committee, M. Teitgen explained that the right to autonomous reason is required to protect citizens from state authorities that could 'rob' a person of 'control over his intellectual faculties and of his conscience.'[108] It was described by many speakers as a fundamental right of humanity, a 'fundamental undisputed freedom' and a most 'sacred right' that must not be suppressed.[109]

The centrality of human, individual self-determination in the developing European system of human rights was clearly expressed as the mission of the Convention. Though one or two drafters referred to the history of struggle and suffering in the evolution of human rights, dealing with the eradication of suffering was not a focus, nor was it emphasised as the mission and target of their enterprise. The overriding centrality of individual autonomy was declared essential, particularly for individuals to discover their ethical orientation and live according to their individually worked out convictions. This was expressed in terms of a fundamental right to religious freedom.

The importance of autonomy is represented in the Convention in the areas of free speech, freedom of association and other rights that facilitate individual self-direction. Autonomy of reason is specifically expressed in Article 9. It corresponds to Article 18 of the UDHR and, in principle, was unanimously accepted by the drafters of the Convention. It entrenches the, now established, orthodoxy of autonomy and explains the right to freedom of thought, conscience, and religion as a right with very limited grounds for interference:[110]

> Article 9—Freedom of thought, conscience and religion
>
> 1. Everyone has the right to freedom of thought, conscience and religion; this right includes freedom to change his religion or belief and freedom, either alone or in community with others and in public or private, to manifest his religion or belief, in worship, teaching, practice and observance.
> 2. Freedom to manifest one's religion or beliefs shall be subject only to such limitations as are prescribed by law and are necessary in a democratic society in the interests of public safety, for the protection of public order, health or morals, or for the protection of the rights and freedoms of others.

Article 9, thus, emphasises the primacy given to autonomous human reason as a manifestation of autonomy and provides for an absolute freedom of conscience, the manifestation of which can only be limited in very specific circumstances.

The intention is to recognise and permit absolute freedom of thought on matters of conscience but, in the interests of justice for a wider community, limit its practical manifestation. It is on these grounds that the Commission (as it was then) of the European Court of Human Rights heard and ruled on the case of *H v UK* as a matter concerning the human right to freely determine one's ethical orientation, not as a matter that re-presented duty in a community of suffering others.

THE DEFINITION OF FREEDOM OF CONSCIENCE

The Convention gives general support to the entrenched orthodoxy of autonomy and recognises, specifically, the importance of establishing a protective right to freedom of conscience. Neither the Convention nor its *Travaux Préparatoires* define the terms 'thought,' 'conscience,' 'religion,' or 'belief.' Martin Scheinin quotes the views of Karl Josef Partsch, who sums up the expression as one that covers:

> all possible attitudes of the individual toward the world, toward society, and toward that which determines his fate and the destiny of the world, be it a divinity, some superior being or just reason and rationalism, or chance.[111]

Liskofsky concurs that the use of the expression indicates its broad, inclusive scope.[112]

In the absence of an explicit definition, the interpretation of the meaning of these terms has been left to the ECtHR, which, in line with scholarly opinion, has taken a very broad approach to Article 9(1).[113] Literature notes that the Court is not always consistent in its application of Article 9(2), but that it should be grounded in the orthodoxy of autonomy.[114] The broad approach taken and the principle of limited interference have resulted in the idea that a European right to freedom of conscience allows individuals to believe in anything they want to believe in.[115] Further, as long as there is no harm to society, individuals are able to manifest individual autonomy and self-direction as they wish and do not have to apply for protection to do so.[116]

It is in these circumstances that the Court granted protection to vegans but as noted earlier, unlike some other beliefs that are presented, there is apparently no extensive judicial assessment of the validity of the meaning of other animals, concern for their mortal existence and their capacity to suffer. It is implicit in this absence of discussion of merit, that the widespread regard for other animals extends to the judiciary and grounds the immediate acknowledgement that veganism qualifies for protection. This context for veganism in human rights needs to be explored further.

PROTECTION FOR FREEDOM OF CONSCIENCE

Under the Convention, human rights protection for the practical manifestation of conscience depends on whether the autonomous thought and self-direction presented is judged to be within the scope of Article 9(1). In the absence of a clear definition of terms, the Court uses a set of criteria that has developed from case law to determine whether the belief in question has sufficient gravity to come within the scope of protection offered by the Convention. Important considerations are if the belief is 'important,' 'serious,' 'cogent,' and 'cohesive.' Traditional religious beliefs are well-known to be within the scope of protection, but in the presentation of non-religious philosophical beliefs the Court will assess whether or not they qualify. The convictions of the applicant, for example, must be important, serious, cogent, worthy of respect in a democracy, they should not be incompatible with human dignity, relate to a weighty and substantial aspect of human life and behaviour and reflect the integrity of the person. To qualify for protection under Article 9, a non-religious 'philosophical belief' does not need to prove that it is 'a fully-fledged system of thought' but, conversely, it cannot be a 'matter of insufficient weight or substance.'[117]

Following confirmation that a belief is recognised as being within the scope of Article 9(1), a defence of lawful interference will turn on whether it is for any of the stated reasons given in Article 9(2). Under this sub-section, interference is permissible only if it is on the basis of a necessary, existing law that is required in a democratic society in the interests of public safety, or for the protection of public order, health or morals, or for the protection of the rights and freedoms of others.

Article 9, thus, provides an absolute right to think and a qualified right to practise that takes into account the interests of the wider needs of human community. It is a right that is adjudicated on the principle that any lawful interference must be grounded by a legitimate aim and that lawful interference will only cause the applicant a personal disadvantage that is proportional to the legitimate aim sought.[118] This doctrine of proportionality is particularly important—as an inherent element of the Convention—in the 'search for a fair balance between the demands of the general interest of the community and the requirements of the protection of the individual's fundamental rights.'[119] This process aims to facilitate a fair and neutral application of the rule of law. The neutrality of principles applied is expressed in *C v UK*. Freedom of thought, conscience, and religion:

> primarily protects the sphere of private, personal beliefs, and not every act in the public sphere which is dictated by such convictions. It does not authorise the right to refuse to abide by legislation . . . the operation of which is provided for by the Convention, and which applies neutrally and generally in terms of freedom of conscience.[120]

VEGAN COMPASSIONATE RESPONSIBILITY, PERSONAL DISADVANTAGE, AND THE LIMITS OF THE RIGHT TO FREEDOM OF CONSCIENCE

The European human right to freedom of conscience is a provision that reflects the orthodoxy of autonomy. It exists to protect individual, personal and private conscience and associated practical manifestation. In this system, the application of an assumed fair and neutral rule of law and principles, such as legitimate aim and proportionality, did not support *H*'s vegan presentation of ethical responsibility to nonhuman suffering beyond a mere recognition that *his individual* convictions for the welfare of nonhuman animals came within the scope of protection under the right to freedom of conscience.

This protection is subsequent to the primacy of protection for individual autonomy but reflects the lack of attention given to duty in community and the exclusion of nonhuman others in an extended community of those who suffer. Further, the emphasis, in claims of conscience that present ethical responsibility to the suffering of nonhuman animals, is on the disadvantage experienced by the human applicant in the context of the wider social interest which does not include consideration of the suffering of nonhuman animals represented in the claim.

This approach is also seen in the later cases of *Jakóbski v Poland*[121] and *Vartic v Romania*,[122] that concern consideration for nonhuman suffering and the provision of suitable food for the prisoner applicants. In both of these cases, responsibility to nonhuman animals was not discussed in terms of a moral imperative to attend to suffering but focused on whether the applicants were disadvantaged by the prison regimes and, thus, whether the state exercised unlawful interference with liberties associated with the human right to free conscience.

This avoidance of the moral imperative to attend to suffering as an element of human conscience is also made clear in *Herrmann v Germany*.[123] This was a case also brought (partly) under Article 9 (the human right to freedom of conscience) by an applicant opposed to an official requirement to support the local fox hunt as a means of land maintenance, but was decided by a majority, under a Protocol 1 right to enjoyment of property.[124] In this case, the court relegated the Article 9 part of the claim that presented ethical regard for suffering as a matter for human rights.

In these types of Article 9 claims, the current tools of litigation are, thus, inadequate to accommodate the actual claim presented by the applicants: that the ethical duty to nonhuman suffering extends further than the conception that moral responsibility to other animals is a matter of personal and private conscience. In litigation, animals have no rights, the relevance of community values around suffering are non-existent, the assessment of lawful interference on the grounds of personal disadvantage makes no reference to the moral imperative to attend to suffering presented, and the empirically evident practice of responsibility and compassionate regard for nonhumans that is well-established in the socio-political and public domain in extended community is overlooked at best, and ignored and dismissed at worst.

These cases illustrate that a manifestation of the orthodoxy of autonomy is that the ethical response to suffering in an extended community of others, as registered in the domain of public conscience and in the rights claims of those who seek to defend their right to live with respect for other animals, is registered as a matter of personal and private conscience in human rights. This evidences the inadequacy of the orthodoxy of autonomy to ground empirically valued ethical duties in community. These cases also show how community values and extended community and nonhuman suffering bear heavily on the exclusivity of protective rights. In this regard, the dissenting statement of Judge Pinto of Albuquerque in *Herrmann* is revealing. Pinto's partially dissenting judgment was critical of the Court for not recognising the value of the human right to freedom of conscience as an important provision through which to express convictions around animal suffering. He remarked that dismissing the importance of a claim for nonhuman suffering under Article 9 by prioritising property rights constitutes circumstances that result in a *capitus diminuitio* [125] of the person who is opposed on the basis of conscience, and that this is a situation not tolerable in a democracy.

Though Pinto's view pertains to the established orthodoxy of autonomy, he also made an additional, important point by explaining that the presentation of animals under the Article 9 provision, right to freedom of conscience, is an important constituent part of a clear and uncontested broad trend towards the acceptance of the moral standing of nonhumans. In this regard, he observed that the Convention and the Court offer them some form of protection. Such a statement clearly highlights a paradox of exclusive human rights and the problem of litigating cases that present nonhuman suffering on the grounds of the personal and private convictions of applicants.

Pinto's statement raises questions about the primacy of the orthodoxy of autonomy and the centrality of the human individual of a protective rights enterprise in which human conscience recognises duty to vulnerable nonhuman others, in community.

CONCLUSION

This chapter has explored the centrality of individual, human self-determination central to the autonomy orthodoxy of human rights and concludes that the post-war moral imperative to deal with suffering in community has been displaced by the primacy of rights for the self-legislating individual. The chapter has also drawn attention to the possible inadvertent exclusion of animal others from the protection of basic rights, and the paradox created by the human right to free conscience, under which cases defending the moral imperative to attend to nonhuman animal suffering are presented and acknowledged.

On the above observations, the claims of vegans that are brought under the right to freedom of conscience present the moral standing and suffering of nonhuman animals but cannot be litigated or adjudicated in terms of nonhuman suffering or socially valued compassion in community. They are, instead, dealt with in human rights as matters of personal and private conscience despite a clear interface of human and nonhuman moral standing evident in human rights law and legal opinion in cases that re-present the suffering of nonhuman animals to the wider community. This problematic situation points to the overlooked and inadequate representation of community values around suffering in the formative (human) protective rights documents.

The following chapter presents an assessment of an alternative approach to protective rights. It looks to the work of critical human rights scholars who ground the idea for justice in Emmanuel Levinas's ethics of alterity. Its purpose will be to explain the grounds for duty to others in community and the validity of the moral imperative to deal with suffering as a new approach to thinking about human rights, animal rights, the rights of vegans and all those who re-present suffering animals and defend their right to practice compassionate justice.

NOTES

1. However, note that the Council of Europe is pro-active in facilitating open discussion. It encourages young people to explore various rights in the context of liberty, culture and sustainability in relation to the natural environment. See, for example, Council of Europe, 'Compass: Manual for Human Rights Education with Young People: Makah Whaling' <http://www.coe.int/en/web/compass/makah-whaling> accessed 13 July 2016.

2. In 2008, a committee of the First Chamber at the European Court of Human Rights examined an application for legal personhood, put forward on behalf of an ape (Matthew), by Miss Stibbe (*Stibbe v Austria* App no 26188/08 ECtHR, 4 May 2008). The committee rejected the application on the grounds of incompatibility *ratione materiae*. ('The compatibility *ratione materiae* with the Convention of an application or complaint derives from the Court's substantive jurisdiction. For a complaint to be compatible *ratione materiae* with the Convention, the right relied on by the

applicant must be protected by the Convention and the Protocols thereto that have come into force.') See Council of Europe, European Court of Human Rights, 'Practical Guide on Admissibility Criteria' (2011) <http://www.justitsministeriet.dk/sites/default/files/media/Arbejdsomraader/International/Guide_pratique_ENG.pdf> accessed 18 June 2016. For a news report of this case, see Allan Hall, 'European Court Agrees to Hear Chimp's Plea for Human Rights' (*Mailonline,* 2008) <http://www.dailymail.co.uk/news/article-1020986/European-Court-agrees-hear-chimps-plea-human-rights.html#ixzz4FbLnblNK> accessed 18 June 2016.

3. International Covenant on Civil and Political Rights (adopted 16 December 1966, entered into force 23 March 1976) 999 UNTS 171 (ICCPR).

4. United Nations Human Rights Committee (HRC), 'CCPR General Comment No 23: Article 27 (Rights of Minorities) (8 April 1994) UN Doc CCPR/C/21/Rev.1/Add.5.

5. See, for example, *Chief Bernard Ominayak* and the *Lubicon Lake Band v Canada* Comm no 167/1984 UN Doc CCPR/C/38/D/167/1984, 10 May 1990; *Kitok v Sweden* Comm. no 197/1985, UN Doc CCPR/C/33/D/197/1985 10 August 1988; *Länsman et al v Finland* (no 1) Comm no 511/1992, UN Doc CCPR/C/52/D/511/1992, 8 November 1994; *Länsman et al v Finland* (no 2) Comm no 671/1995, Un Doc CCPR/C/58/D/671/1995, 22 November 1996; *Länsman et al v Finland* (no 3) Comm no 1023/2001, UN Doc CCPR/C/83/D/1023/2001, 15 April 2005. *Angela Poma Poma v Peru* Comm no 1457/2006 UN Doc CCPR/C/95/D/1457/2006 27 March 2009. See also the significance of culture in *Smit NO and Others v King Goodwill Zwelithini Kabhekuzulu and Others* (10237/2009) [2009] ZAKZPHC 75 (4 December 2009). The applicants' attempt to prevent the slaughter of animals at the Zulu Ukweshwama festival through the presentation of facts about grotesque animal suffering was held to be insufficient compared to the cultural significance of the ritual torment and slaughter of a bull. Without the ritual and death of the bull, there would be no symbolic transfer of power to the Zulu king and the Zulu nation would be left with a powerless king.

6. Heiner Bielefeldt, 'Freedom of Religion or Belief: A Human Right Under Pressure' (2012) Oxford Journal of Law and Religion 1(1), 24 doi 10.1093/ojlr/rwr018.

7. (1993) 16 EHRR.

8. James Griffin, *On Human Rights* (Oxford University Press 2008/2013) 1.

9. Michael J Perry, *Toward a Theory of Human Rights: Religion, Law, Courts* (Cambridge University Press 2007) 4.

10. Conor Gearty, 'Can Animals Have Human Rights Too?' (PDF, Conor Gearty, 2007) <http://www.conorgearty.co.uk/pdfs/Animals.pdf> 9.

11. Gearty (2007) 5.

12. Humphrey Primatt, *The Duty of Mercy* (first published 1776; Centaur Press 1992).

13. Paola Cavalieri, *The Animal Question, Why Non-Human Animals Deserve Rights* (Oxford University Press 2005).

14. Regan (1988).

15. Ryder (1998).

16. Peter Singer, *Animal Liberation a New Ethics for Our Treatment of Animals* (Avon Books 1975).

17. Cochrane (2013).

18. Jeremy Bentham, *Introduction to the Principles of Morals and Legislation* (first published 1789, Clarendon Press 1907) ch xv11.6 <http://www.econlib.org/library/Bentham/bnthPML18.html#Chapter XVII, Of the Limits of the Penal Branch of Jurisprudence> accessed 24 January 2013.

19. Bentham (1789) n122.

20. Hass (2014) Chapter 2.

21. Hass (2014) 24.

22. Bertrand Russell, *History of Western Philosophy* (Routledge 1994) 262.

23. In this regard, literature cites the influence of Thomas Aquinas.

24. Griffin, (2008/2013) 9.

25. Costas Douzinas, 'The Poverty of Rights Jurisprudence' in Conor Gearty and Costas Douzinas (eds), *The Cambridge Companion to Human Rights Law* (Cambridge University Press 2012) 60.

26. Jean-Jacques Rousseau, *The Social Contract or Principles of Political Right* (G D H Cole tr, public domain, Foederis æquas Dicamus leges 1762) <https://www.ucc.ie/archive/hdsp/Rousseau_contrat-social.pdf> accessed 3 January 2016.

27. Patrick Hayden, *The Philosophy Of Human Rights* (Paragon House 2001).

28. John Locke, *Two Treatises of Government* Chpt VII (1823, 141 point 87). Available at the McMaster University Archive for the History of Economic Thought <http://socserv2.socsci.mcmaster.ca/econ/ugcm/3ll3/locke/government.pdf> accessed 6 February 2017.

29. Lynn Hunt, *Inventing Human Rights: A History* (W.W. Norton and Company Ltd.) 19.

30. Hunt (2007) 25.

31. Hunt (2007) 27.

32. Kant is widely referred to in human rights literature as providing the philosophical grounds for the idea of modern human rights.

33. Russell (1994) 683.

34. Hunt (2007) 65.

35. Chapter 3 of this book returns to the idea of otherness in human rights and the idea that the target and mission of human rights is to attend to suffering.

36. There are different versions of electronic publications of Kant's *Groundwork Of The Metaphysics Of Morals*. They are also listed with different versions of the title. The version used here is Immanuel Kant, *The Metaphysic of Ethics* (J W Semple tr, Thomas Clarke M.DCCC.XXXVI), available at <http://philosophyfaculty.ucsd.edu/faculty/ctolley/texts/kant.html> accessed 3 February 2017.

37. Kant (M.DCCC.XXXVI) 54.

38. Kant (M.DCCC.XXXVI) 52.

39. Douzinas (2012) 76.

40. Douzinas (2012) 76–77.

41. There is also a branch of discourse that moves away from the search for moral grounds for human rights and cites metaphysical accounts as unhelpful, highly con-

tested ground. This literature focuses instead on the utility of a pragmatic application of human rights. See, for example, Michael Ignatieff, 'II Human Rights As Idolatry: The Tanner Lectures' (Delivered at Princeton University 4–7 April 2000, PDF 320) <http://tannerlectures.utah.edu/_documents/a-to-z/i/Ignatieff_01.pdf> accessed 10 February 2017.

42. Robert M Martin, *The Philosophers Dictionary* (2nd ed, Broadview Press 1994) 29.

43. Nonhuman Rights Project <https://www.nonhumanrightsproject.org/litigation/> accessed 28 June 2016. For a discussion, see Richard L Cupp Jr, 'Focusing on Human Responsibility Rather than Legal Personhood for Nonhuman Animals' (2016) Paper Number 2016/17 Legal Studies Research Paper Series (Pepperdine University School of Law) <http://papers.ssrn.com/sol3/papers.cfm?abstract_id=2784890> accessed 22 July 2016.

44. Griffin (2008/2013) 32-33.

45. Griffin (2008/2013) Ch 8–9.

46. Griffin (2008/2013) 156.

47. Daphne Barak-Erez, 'Israel: Citizenship and Immigration Law in the Vise of Security, Nationality, and Human Rights' (2008) Int J Constitutional Law 6(1) 184.

48. *Academic Center of Law and Business v Minister of Finance* HCJ 2605/05, available at <http://elyon1.court.gov.il/files_eng/05/050/026/n39/05026050.n39.pdf> accessed 28 February 2017.

49. Life Imprisonment Case (1977) 45 BVerfGE 187 (1977). English translation available at <http://www.hrcr.org/safrica/dignity/45bverfge187.html> accessed 28 February 2017.

50. Michael Mountain, 'Lawsuit Filed Today on Behalf of Chimpanzees Seeking Legal Personhood' (*Nonhuman Rights Project*, 2 December 2013) <http://www.nonhumanrightsproject.org/2013/12/02/lawsuitfiled-today-on-behalf-of-chimpanzee-seeking-legal-personhood/ [https://perma.cc/6BDE-85B8]> accessed 12 December 2013. The nonhuman rights project is now very well established. See updated website <https://www.nonhumanrights.org/blog/> accessed 24 October 2019.

51. English Oxford Living Dictionaries, <https://en.oxforddictionaries.com/definition/dignity> accessed 12 December 2016.

52. Leon R Kass, 'Defending Human Dignity' (*Human Dignity and Bioethics: Essays Commissioned by the President's Council on Bioethics* 2008) para 21 <https://bioethicsarchive.georgetown.edu/pcbe/reports/human_dignity/chapter12.html> accessed 12 December 2016.

53. Kass (2008) para 69.

54. Nussbaum (2007) 284.

55. LCA 1684/96, para 41.

56. LCA 1684/96, para 34.

57. LCA 1684/96, para 41.

58. Roberto Adorno, 'Human Dignity and Human Rights as a Common Ground for a Global Bioethics' (2009) 34(3) *Journal of Medicine and Philosophy* 223–240.

59. John Stuart Mill, *On Liberty* (Penguin 1984) 71.

60. Mill (1984) 96.

61. Mill (1984) 77.

62. John Rawls, *A Theory of Justice* (revised ed, Harvard University Press 1971/1999) 181.

63. Rawls (1971/1999) 186.

64. Ronald Dworkin, *Taking Rights Seriously* (Harvard University Press 1978).

65. Joseph Raz, *The Morality of Freedom* (Oxford University Press 1988) 269.

66. Raz (1988) 398.

67. Raz (1988) 399.

68. For additional historical reading, see Maurice Cranston, *What Are Human Rights?* (Bodley Head 1973). For a very good collection on current debates, see Rowan Cruft, S Matthew Liao and Massimo Renzo (eds), *Philosophical Foundations of Human Rights* (Oxford University Press 2015).

69. Universal Declaration of Human Rights (adopted 10 December 1948 UNGA Res 217 A (UDHR), International Covenant on Civil and Political Rights (adopted 16 December 1966, entered into force 23 March 1976) 999 UNTS 171 (ICCPR). International Covenant on Economic, Social and Cultural Rights (adopted on 16 December 1966, entered into force on 3 January 1976) 993 UNTS 3 (CESCR).

70. Hass (2014).

71. Baxi (2009b) 6.

72. Belarmino Austregésilo de Athayde, Ninety-Second Meeting Draft Declaration of Human Rights. A/C.3/SR.92 <https://documents-dds-ny.un.org/doc/UNDOC/GEN/NL4/804/33/PDF/NL480433.pdf?OpenElement> accessed 24 February 2017.

73. Mary Ann Glendon, *A World Made New: Eleanor Roosevelt and the Universal Declaration of Human Rights* (Random House 2002).

74. Available at <http://research.un.org/en/undhr/draftingcommittee/1> accessed 28 June 2017.

75. For discussion regarding evidence that duties and community are overtly and adequately represented in the Declaration, see Johannes Morsink, *The Universal Declaration of Human Rights: Origins, Drafting and Intent* (University of Pennsylvania Press 1999).

76. Historical documents are not gender neutral. Though this is also a matter for analysis of intersecting oppression, it is not within the scope of the present discussion to foreground this beyond a brief mention.

77. Universal Declaration of Human Rights (adopted 10 December 1948 UNGA Res 217 A) (III) (UDHR) Preamble and Article 1.

78. United Nations 'One Hundred and Eighty Third Plenary Meeting. Continuation of the Discussion on the Draft Universal Declaration of Human Rights: Report of the Third Committee (A/777)' A/PV.183, 921-923 <https://documents-dds-ny.un.org/doc/UNDOC/GEN/NL4/812/23/PDF/NL481223.pdf?OpenElement> accessed 24 February 2017.

79. United Nations 'One Hundred and Eighty Third Plenary Meeting. Continuation of the Discussion on the Draft Universal Declaration of Human Rights: Report of the Third Committee (A/777)' A/PV.183, 913–914 <https://documents-dds-ny.un.org/doc/UNDOC/GEN/NL4/812/23/PDF/NL481223.pdf?OpenElement> accessed 24 February 2017.

80. There are references in this Article to Enlightenment ideas concerning Social Contract Theory (Jean-Jacques Rousseau), the French Declaration on the Rights of Man, and Kant's philosophy.

81. Preamble and Article 26.

82. Arts 31–3 of the Vienna Convention on the Law of Treaties (adopted 23 May 1969) 1155 UNTS 331. Though the principle does not have to be applied retrospectively, the ECtHR has applied the principle as enunciating 'in essence generally accepted principles of international law.' See *Golder v UK* (1975) Series A no 18 at 14.

83. International Covenant on Civil and Political Rights (adopted 16 December 1966, entered into force 23 March 1976) 999 UNTS 171 (ICCPR), Preamble.

84. United Nations Human Rights Committee (HRC), 'CCPR General Comment No 22: Article 18 (Freedom of Thought, Conscience and Religion)' (30 July 1993) UN Doc CCPR/C/21/Rev.1/Add.4, para 2.

85. UN General Comment No. 22 para 5.

86. UN General Comment No. 22 para 5.

87. UN General Comment No. 22 para 5.

88. UN Human Rights Committee, General Comment No. 31, para. 6. CCPR/C/21/Rev.1/Add. 1326 May 2004.

89. Declaration on the Elimination of all Forms of Intolerance and Discrimination Based on Religion or Belief, UNGA Res 36/55 (25 November 1981).

90. Bahiyyih G Tahzib, *Freedom of Religion or Belief: Ensuring Effective International Protection* (The Hague, Kluwer Law International 1996) 25–7. Asma Jahangir, *Elimination of all Forms of Religious Intolerance* UN Doc A/60/399 (2005) para 49.

91. Jahangir (2005) para 49.

92. Jahangir (2005) para 49.

93. Taylor (2007) 24.

94. Martin Scheinin, 'Article 18' in Asbjørn Eide and others (eds), *The Universal Declaration of Human Rights: A Commentary* (Scandinavian University Press 1992) 263–264.

95. Scheinin (1993) 263–264.

96. Johannes Morsink, *Inherent Human Rights: Philosophical Roots of the Universal Declaration* (University of Pennsylvania Press 2009) 333.

97. UNCHR (A Krishnaswami, Special Rapporteur of the Sub-Commission on Prevention of Discrimination and Protection of Minorities), 'Study Of Discrimination In The Matter Of Religious Rights And Practices' (1960) UN Doc E/CN.4/Sub.2/200/Rev.1, 16 <http://www.ohchr.org/Documents/Issues/Religion/Krishnaswami_1960.pdf> accessed 30 June 2017.

98. This is a French term meaning the preparatory historical records in the development of conventions and treaties.

99. Council of Europe, *Collected Edition of the 'Travaux Préparatoires' Volume 1: Preparatory Commission of the Council of Europe, Committee of Ministers, Consultative Assembly 11 May-8 September 1949* (Martinus Nijhoff-The Hague 1975) 134.

100. Council of Europe (1975) 44.

101. Council of Europe (1975) 46.
102. Council of Europe (1975) 66.
103. Council of Europe (1975) 78.
104. Council of Europe (1975) 104.
105. Council of Europe (1975) 126.
106. Council of Europe (1975) 134.
107. Council of Europe (1975) 130.
108. Council of Europe (1975) 200.
109. Council of Europe (1975) 62.
110. Part 1 was uncontentious to the drafting committee, and Part 2 was debated.
111. Karl Josef Partsch as cited in Scheinin (2000).
112. Sidney Lifskofsky, 'The UN Declaration on the Elimination of Religious Intolerance and Discrimination: Historical Perspectives' in James E Wood (ed), *Religion and the State: Essays in Honour of Leo Pieffer* (Baylor University Press 1985) 456.
113. In addition to veganism, other non-religious and non-traditional beliefs have been held to be within the scope of Article 9(1). For example, beliefs in Druidism (*Chappell v UK* (1987) 53 DR 241), pacifism (*Arrowsmith v UK* (1978) 19 DR 5) and atheism (*Kokkinakis v Greece* (1994) 17 EHRR 397). For a discussion, see Paul Taylor, '*Freedom of Religion': UN and European Human Rights Law and Practice* (Cambridge University Press 2005). Karon Monaghan QC also has a very readable section on this in *Equality Law* (Oxford University Press 2007). A very accessible and useful, but now dated, resource in terms of cases presented is Carolyn Evans, *Freedom of Religion under the European Convention on Human Rights* (Oxford University Press 2001).
114. Evans (2001) 33.
115. For example, Evans (2001) and Taylor (2005).
116. See, for example, the Church of the Flying Spaghetti Monster and the right to wear a pasta sieve in a photographic image of identity on a driving licence: BBC News, 'Austrian driver allowed 'pastafarian' headgear photo' (*BBC News*, 14 July 2011) <http://www.bbc.co.uk/news/world-europe-14135523> accessed 13 June 2016. The right to wear the sieve has been denied, however, and was the subject of a legal claim. See Henley Jon, 'Documentary follows Pastafarians as they strain for recognition' (*The Guardian,* 18 September 2019) < https://www.theguardian.com/world/2019/sep/18/documentary-follows-pastafarians-strain-for-recognition> accessed 24 October 2019.
117. Discussed in *Campbell and Cossans v UK* (1982) Series A no 48.
118. *National Union of Belgium Police v Belgium* App no 4464/70 (ECtHR, 27 October 1975).
119. *Soering v UK* (1989) 11 EHRR 439. A strict test for proportionality is set out in *Handyside v UK* (1976) Series A no 24.
120. *C v UK* (1983) DR 142.
121. *Jakóbski v Poland* App No 18429/06 (ECtHR, 7 December 2010).

122. *Vartic v Romania* (no 2) App no 14150/08 (ECtHR, 17 March 2014). At the communication stage, Vartic's claim referred to veganism. This explicit ground for the claim seems to have disappeared in later case reports.

Vartic considered a higher threshold of 'significant disadvantage' under an admissibility practice criterion that was introduced by Protocol No. 14. The new criterion entered into force on 1 June 2010 and is incorporated in Article 35 paragraph 3(b) of the Convention. Convention for the Protection of Human Rights and Fundamental Freedoms (European Convention on Human Rights, as amended) (ECHR) Protocol 14 <http://www.echr.coe.int/Documents/Library_Collection_P14_ETS194E_ENG.pdf> accessed 14 July 2016.

123. *Herrmann v Germany* App No 9300/07 (ECtHR, 26th June 2012) case concerning landowners' rights against the local hunt.

124. Convention for the Protection of Human Rights and Fundamental Freedoms (European Convention on Human Rights, as amended) (ECHR) Protocol 1.

125. Latin maxim referring to a significant loss of status or liberty. See Black's Law Dictionary, <http://thelawdictionary.org/capitis-diminutio/> accessed 22 July 2016.

Chapter Three

Can Human Rights Be Grounded by Ethical Responsibility to Suffering?

INTRODUCTION

So far, the argument I have presented to support the search for a paradigm shift to an ethical justice that includes other animals cites veganism as a response to suffering and the legal claims of vegans as expressing ethical responsibility to nonhuman animals. I have explained that the human rights claims of vegans for suffering others are considered under the individual right to autonomous freedom of conscience but have suggested that this is not appropriate because the claims of vegans are motivated in the context of witnessing suffering. Explained this way, we can articulate the claims of vegans as representing an element of the natural justice that motivated the UDHR: claims that defend the right to extend compassionate justice in the face of suffering.

The suffering of nonhuman animals that is presented by vegans to law cannot be dealt with in the current formulation of human rights due to three factors. Firstly, exclusive human rights manifest prejudice towards nonhuman animals. Secondly, protection for the rights of vegans to practice duty to suffering relegates concern for animals as a matter of individual human conscience. Thirdly, the orthodoxy of autonomy, the application of legitimate aim and proportionality in that context, and the false assumption of neutrality in the application of law, will function to dissolve the centrality of (animal) suffering presented in the rights claims of vegans. On the basis of these obstacles, the previous chapter proposed a new way to think about the foundation of human rights in order to better accommodate the claims of vegans and register, in human rights, the moral imperative to attend to suffering nonhuman animals.

This chapter examines critical human rights theory and Emmanuel Levinas's ethics of alterity and the argument that ethical responsibility in the face of vulnerability and suffering is an inescapable, innate characteristic of humanity. It explains the essential elements of Levinas's thesis, his thoughts on the existence of human rights, and how his philosophical theory inspires a branch of critical human rights theory that promotes the amelioration of suffering as the mission of a protective rights enterprise.

Critical human rights theory, categorised as 'protest scholarship,'[1] develops an ethics of alterity for human rights. It argues that the essence of humanity is a desire for, and to consider others in, community, and that this idea of human nature should orient the ethics of human rights. The chapter explains that Levinas's philosophy grounds a reorientation of the ethics of human rights because it promotes a human identity of duty, innate responsibility, compassion and kindness to others, in opposition to the orthodoxy of autonomy and its primary focus on rights for individual subjects.

The purposes of assessing this philosophy and the critical human rights literature are to: ascertain the principles upon which human identity is argued to be inherently compassionate to suffering others, identify how this philosophy is utilised to explain the ethics of human rights, and to discover the extent to which it includes or considers the suffering of nonhuman animals (thus determining its utility to register the moral imperative to attend to suffering in the presentation of the claims of vegans).

The chapter explains that critical human rights scholars identify, in Levinas's thesis, a non-abstract, relational ethical event that grounds the concept of human rights in duty. It illustrates how this is applied in current scholarship to reorient the idea of human rights away from the rights of individuals and towards a system which honours an a priori natural right of the vulnerable other.

The chapter finds that Levinas's ethics of alterity do ground responsibility and duty to others and can undergird a system of protective rights, but that current discourse excludes consideration of whether nonhuman others can feature in such a framework. Before addressing this limitation in chapter 4, this chapter firstly explains protest scholarship, Levinas's ethics of alterity, his justification for natural rights, and the way his theory has been utilised and developed by critical human rights scholars.

CRITICAL HUMAN RIGHTS LITERATURE

The body of critical human rights scholarship that centres on duty and the suffering of others has been categorised and defined by Marie-Bénédicte Dembour as the 'protest school' of human rights.[2] Dembour observes that in this school of thought, human rights are 'first and foremost a language of protest.'[3] She notes that protest scholars are motivated by Emmanuel Levinas because they identify with feeling 'summoned by the suffering of the other.'[4]

Protest scholars believe that humans desire to live in community and that there is a social bond that is created by an acknowledgment of universal mutual suffering. On this basis, they firmly believe that 'human rights (a) are moral, (b) must be raised when they are not socially recognised, and (c) should concern every human being, especially those who are "forgotten."'[5] The importance of the work of Levinas to critical human rights scholars is that the ethics of alterity is not an abstract theory. Levinas claims that since ethics arise in encounters with others, they arise in concrete situations. As such, critical human rights scholars believe in the utility of otherness as a practical principle for enhanced social justice.[6]

Dembour cites Upendra Baxi and Costas Douzinas as two human rights activists whose work can be described as protest scholarship. In addition, I also cite the later work of William Paul Simmons to be situated within the protest school of human rights on the basis that it emphasises that human rights should pertain to the amelioration of suffering.[7] His work also looks to Levinas's ethics of alterity to ground fundamental rights for the specific purpose of giving a voice to those most forgotten.

The critique of existing human rights presented by these authors is based on the observation that human rights abuses are prevalent across the globe, and that despite many decades of the existence of the UDHR, suffering is widespread and immense. Their analytical approach is holistic, involving an assessment of human rights which encompasses practical utility, ontological assumptions, and congruence with emancipation. They conclude that the idea of human rights is a powerful and necessary concept to alleviate suffering, but that current thinking and practice are misguided because they focus on autonomy and individuality, rather than duty to others.

Protest scholarship demands that the suffering of others be addressed as a paramount concern of human rights, that otherness becomes implemented as a transcendental ethical principle for justice, and that human rights education should be reformed in line with Levinas's ethics of alterity and his notion of ethical humanity.

Before examining the work of these authors, it is first necessary to understand Levinas's philosophy on the ethics of otherness.

LEVINAS'S PHILOSOPHY ON THE ETHICS OF ALTERITY

The branch of philosophy known as the ethics of alterity is principally associated with Lithuanian philosopher and theologian Emmanuel Levinas.[8]

Levinas's thesis on the ethics of alterity is a philosophy that rejects immanent, autonomous reason as the essence of ethical human identity.[9] Levinas's contribution to philosophical enquiry can be considered Continental or modern European, in that it considers ethical responsibility and socio-political issues.[10] The work of Levinas was developed following his thoughts on and analysis of the works of Husserl and Heidegger.[11] Levinas's work has been categorised as phenomenology, a branch of philosophical enquiry that predominantly concerns the way in which a subject experiences and makes sense of their surrounding world.[12] Levinas is said to be one of 'the most profound, exacting and original thinkers of twentieth-century Europe,'[13] who has 'changed the course of contemporary philosophy,'[14] with a philosophy that 'enjoys unprecedented popularity.'[15]

Levinas considers the essence of human identity and humanity, and the extent to which individuals are free, autonomous, atomistic subjects. Advocating the possibility of human identity being constructed by external events of relationality, Levinas departs from mainstream phenomenological theory that explains human identity in terms of the autonomous, self-made meaning of individuals who exist in constant conflict with each other. Levinas argues that rather than interpreting events and making meaning for oneself, meaning is made through relational encounters with 'the other.'[16] For Levinas, it is relational encounters with others that produce ethics. He argues that the other dissolves the autonomous spontaneity of the subject. Levinas explains that '[w]e name this calling into question of my spontaneity by the presence of the Other ethics.'[17]

As a philosophy of the 'humanism of the other,'[18] Levinas explains how the moral priority of the other takes precedence over an individual ego being-for-itself. This is the foundation of Levinas's theory on the ethics of alterity: ethics arise through relational encounters with different others who disrupt the will of the subject's ego. This is Levinas's entire philosophy.[19]

Levinas blames the history of Western philosophy for the creation of an oppressive totality of reason. He believes that the assumed supremacy of human reason has denied individuals their uniqueness and suppressed the innate human desire for dutiful relationships. He argues that this philosophical tradition and its focus on human reason have constructed an unethical totality of oppressive sameness rather than giving expression to innate otherness.[20] What Levinas means is that, in the orthodoxy of autonomy, others are assumed to be the same as the observer and assumed to experience the world in the same way. In this totality of reason, Levinas also highlights that the uniqueness and individuality of others are also reduced by oppressive themes and categories created by reason. For Levinas, this system of social relations, as organised on the basis of the primacy of reason, only encourages disharmonious relations.[21]

The theory of an ethics of alterity challenges the dominant Western philosophical tradition of the primacy of human reason. It replaces the idea of reason being the basis for a homogeneous human identity with a vision of a heterogeneous community of unique individuals who experience, first and foremost, responsibility to others. In this theory, reason is important, but a posteriori to a naturally occurring event that creates humans as ethical. Thus, human Becoming, as explained by the principle of autonomous reason, is challenged by an alternative idea that explains Becoming in the context of relational responsibility. This idea can be described as a theory about an external phenomenological[22] process of ethical subjectivity that is facilitated by interconnected, social beings.

A BRIEF NOTE ABOUT READING LEVINAS

Reading Levinas presents certain difficulties for understanding. For example, in translation from French to English, word substitutions justified by translators may not represent the true and accurate meaning of the writer.[23] In addition, Levinas uses a profoundly complex style of writing. There are also problems associated with a reader's unfamiliarity with Levinas's use of concepts and with his ideas, which originate from intense, deep and creative philosophical thinking and from his fusion of philosophy with theology.[24] Levinas aims to develop an eschatological[25] philosophy of human 'being' or human identity. His aim is to explain the positive destiny of humankind in order to find a way to give hope following the atrocities of two world wars and the barbaric and pessimistic acts of humankind.

A significant difficulty is grasping Levinas's notion of responsibility. Though the subject is responsible to the other, responsibility is infinite because it is a responsibility owed to all others. As such, it cannot be fulfilled because there are many others. Richard Kearny observes that '[w]e are all responsible for everyone else—but I am more responsible than all the others.'[26] He notes that 'not only am I more responsible than the other but I am even more responsible for everyone else's responsibility!'[27] Colin Davis suggests that although readers may think they understand the written text, there may still be a problem with getting the point, that Levinas leaves too many questions unanswered and that his ideas are unclear.[28] Baxi has suggested that reading Levinas 'requires enormous exegetical labours; the dense intertexuality of his corpus remains forbidding, even for the *cognoscenti*.'[29] This reputation for complexity is largely responsible for scholarly avoidance, but Levinas's philosophy is as thought-provoking as it is demanding. Though it has a limited presence in critical human rights discourse, it certainly deserves much more consideration, especially in an attempt to disrupt the autonomy orthodoxy of human rights to support the emancipation of other animals.

THE ESSENCE OF THE ETHICS OF ALTERITY

For Levinas, the ethics of alterity are the first philosophy; the unique other is always and already present and acknowledged before being assessed and articulated through the reason of the subject. The other emits a non-semantic 'saying' that signifies and expresses their presence.[30] The other metaphorically speaks to the subject with questions that demand a response. The other says 'you have entered my world. Here I am. It is me in my world. I am subject to the forces of mortality. I am vulnerable and precarious' and asks 'how will you respond?'[31] As such, apprehension of the unique other precedes reason. In the totality of reason, this 'saying' is reduced by 'said' (verbalised) oppressive themes and categories that create subservience, imperialism, domination, hierarchy, and discrimination. In this system, the unique other is acknowledged but reduced by the oppressive categorisation of the self on its own terms through reason. To address this problem, Levinas promotes the ethics of alterity as requiring '[a]n openness of the self to the other, which is not a conditioning or a foundation of oneself in some principle.'[32] This openness creates a more dutiful, compassionate, and ethical humanity that honours innate responsibility.

Levinas explains that innate responsibility is experienced in encounters with others, who demand a response from the subject. The subject is, thus, made responsible and is forced to respond to this responsibility. Responsibility to the other precedes all else. It is ethics itself because it is the force and the experience that creates ethical humanity and defines an essential characteristic of human identity. Levinas explains: 'The fact that in existing for another I exist otherwise than in existing for me is morality itself.'[33] What Levinas means by this is that the self is primarily constructed by the existence of others who always require a response prior to the subject's reasoning. This idea is in stark contrast to one that explains that the essence of human identity is the ability to reason and that immanence is the source of ethics.

Levinas's thesis is grounded by the idea that human ethics are produced in the context of relational encounters within a community, rather than in the self-legislating individual. To understand this idea, the following section will explain in some detail the essential elements of Levinas's ethics of alterity. These elements are Levinas's views on the essence of humanity and the innate characteristics of human identity.

THE ETHICS OF ALTERITY AND THE ESSENCE OF HUMANITY

For Levinas, humanity manifests an important pre-social condition of human existence. This is the natural human tendency to live in community. Levinas observes that humans have an innate sociability and need to exist with each other cooperatively. He observes that humanity is composed of intertwined, interacting others who have a strong sense of duty towards each other.[34] In addition, each individual is 'absolutely dissimilar,' possessing an identity that is 'non-interchangeable, incomparable and unique.'[35]

Levinas argues that humanity is the result of a break with the bare, biological being of nonhuman animals in the natural world. The evidence is the social system of humanity that can only stem from subjects apprehending and responding ethically to multiple others. For Levinas, the fact of the social community is evidence that humanity is not grounded in autonomous existence. Only nonhuman animals of the natural world need autonomy to fight in a world of struggle and fear, where the self exists for the self.[36] Humanity, on the other hand, is grounded in a compassionate a priori responsibility to others. The break with the natural order is caused by the subject recognising and acknowledging the existence, suffering, and needs of different others, to whom they are obligated and have no choice but to respond. This encounter constitutes the moment of ethical transformation from what is considered basic, instinctive animality into humanity. It is in the 'breaking with this biological order of being that ethics and "the human" arise. Thus, the human and ethics are something like miracles.'[37] These conditions of humanity arise from Levinas's notion of individual human identity.

THE ETHICS OF ALTERITY AND HUMAN IDENTITY

Levinas argues that individuals are unique. In his view, the 'inner world' of others cannot be known by the subject. Being composed of absolutely dissimilar beings that are incomparable and non-interchangeable, humanity represents much more than a 'common species.'[38]

Human beings are mortal subjects at the mercy of the life process and are, essentially, vulnerable and weak. This universally shared characteristic is recognised and is the reason for innate kindness and compassion offered for suffering others. The subject recognises suffering in others and, at the same time, cannot know how that suffering is experienced. Identifying shared mortality, but not understanding or knowing how the other experiences their world, the subject instinctively shows compassion and kind regard.

In Levinas's theory, then, human beings have four essential characteristics that are denied in the totality of reason. Firstly, they are unique individuals. Secondly, they are conjoined by a pre-social sociability. This means that they are born with a predisposition to desire community. Thirdly, they have an innate ability to create responsibility and generate compassionate responses from others. Finally, they possess an innate capacity to respond compassionately.

In Levinas's ethics of alterity, the pre-social interconnection of individuals is ipso facto ethical association. It manifests what Levinas calls 'responsibility,'[39] as evidenced by the way a subject responds to the other, eliciting compassion, sentiment, and duty. This phenomenon is the essence of ethics. Though the encounter in which ethics is produced concerns a subject and another, the ethical event is an asymmetrical responsibility to the other. Levinas describes this event as an event of transcendence in '*[l]e visage d'autrui'*: transcendence in 'the face of the other.'[40]

That ethics emerge in the face of the other is a paramount element of Levinas's ethics of alterity. Levinas explains that '*le visage*'—'the face'—is the expressive presence of the other that elicits a response from the subject. The face, as the facilitating mechanism in the production of ethics, is explored in more detail below.

THE FACE AND THE PRODUCTION OF ETHICS

Levinas describes the concrete experience that is the basis for ethical humanity. It is an event in which the subject becomes ethically engaged in an encounter with the face of the other. The face is encountered in a transcendence of the self. It halts the spontaneous, autonomous ego of the subject's self. Levinas explains that '[t]he way in which the other presents himself, exceeding *the idea of the other in me,* we here name face.'[41] It is in the face-to-face encounter that an individual becomes aware of the infinite nature of the other, their mutual vulnerability, and the obligation to respond to infinite responsibility.

Levinas refers to the face not merely as a physical object, but as the most significant representation of the other's presence and expression. The other is infinite, but the face represents the first encounter with the living presence. It is an epiphany: '[t]here is a commandment in the appearance of the face, as if a master spoke to me.'[42] 'The face is a living presence; it is expression.' It 'speaks' and 'is already discourse.'[43] The other, however, is not reducible to the physical face, its features or expressions. The face does not represent the other in its entirety because one can never grasp the other through exposure to the face. The other is individual and cannot be absolutely conceptualised.

The encounter with the face is, thus, much more than a vision of the physical features of another.[44] In reality, the 'face' does not appear to the subject and cannot be seen. The face—that is, the Levinasian face—is not to be confused with the observation of the object that is a physical face. Levinas instructs: '[t]he best way of encountering the Other is not even to notice the colour of his eyes! When one observes the colour of the eyes one is not in social relationship with the Other.'[45] He explains that 'the whole body—a hand or a curve of the shoulder—can express as the face.'[46]

Through the face, the other signifies 'exceptional presence'[47] that transcends autonomy, themes, categories and all ontology. It is this presence that 'speaks to me.'[48] '[I]n its mortality . . . the face before me summons me, calls me, begs for me . . . and calls me into question.'[49] The face signifies the presence of the other, commands responsibility and expresses the first word and the commandment 'thou shalt not kill.'[50]

The face-to-face encounter is, thus, an event in which the subject experiences an infinite, unknowable presence; the signification of a mortal, vulnerable other; and a profound responsibility for the other, a command to take care and do no harm, that 'pre-exists any self-consciousness.'[51]

Levinas defines the other as a mortal subject at the mercy of the life process, capable of metaphorically 'speaking' of vulnerability and weakness. He presents the other's 'extreme precariousness':[52] an expression that communicates the vulnerability and mortality of another, who automatically, without effort or intention, takes a subject hostage and asks for a response. In reply (recognising universally shared mortality, shared suffering, and vulnerability), the subject (being naturally predisposed to care and compassion) welcomes the unique other. This welcome is ethics itself. The presence of the mortal, vulnerable other overrides the ego of the subject with what Judith Butler refers to as 'the wordless vocalization of suffering.'[53] The encounter is, and induces, ethics because it disrupts the autonomous selfish ego, creating 'responsibility,' a dutiful subject in the presence of another.

In the face of the other, the individual, thus, undergoes a transformation from animal to ethical and from autonomous to heteronomous. Experiencing the face of the other is a concrete ethical experience and constitutes an ethical relation which dissolves the ego and from which one cannot be released. 'The other concerns me in all his material misery,' Levinas wrote.[54] '[I]t is impossible for me to free myself by saying, "It's not my concern." There is no choice, for it is always and inescapably my concern. This is a unique "no choice," one that is not slavery.'[55] Levinas makes it clear that sentiment and compassion for others are paramount in ethics and evident in the original encounter. On this basis, Levinas regards suffering, vulnerability, caring, and compassion as essential human characteristics, intrinsic to ethics. Human identity is that which is predisposed to welcome the vulnerable other in all their difference. To be human, on this view, is to be responsible; and to be responsible is to be ethical.

The production of ethics, thus, depends on a face-to-face relationship between the subject and the vulnerable infinite other, who cannot be known. This encounter of close proximity creates in the subject an awareness of additional dimensions of responsibility involving third parties, which Levinas describes as the infinity of ethical responsibility, which I will now explain.

THE INFINITY OF ETHICAL RESPONSIBILITY

Ethics are a result of the original demand for a response made by others in close proximity. In this proximity, Levinas argues that individuals become aware of the potential demands of multiple others. He states that '[t]he third party looks at me in the eyes of the Other.' The other in immediate proximity, thus, indicates and serves all the others and alerts the subject to infinity of responsibility. Levinas remarks that '[t]he face in its nakedness as a face presents to me the destitution of the poor one and the stranger,' and '[t]he presence of the face, the infinity of the other, is a destituteness, a presence of the third party (that is, of the whole of humanity which looks at us).'[56] Thus, an event of facing in close proximity is an event of facing not only the infinity of the unknowable other, but the infinity of responsibility for all others and the infinity of the ethical demand. Levinas, thus, believes that responsible and dutiful people not only act ethically in relational encounters, but simultaneously think ethically, knowing that there are always others to whom they owe the same ethical duty of responsibility.

LEVINAS'S THOUGHTS ON HUMAN RIGHTS

Levinas maintains that the natural right of man is the original, a priori fact of the uniqueness or the absolute of the person.[57] Human rights express the uniqueness and incomparable nature of each individual human being and the other's right to this status. For Levinas, human rights are the measure of all law and its ethics. Levinas believes his philosophy is inclusive because it aims to accommodate profound difference.

Levinas believes that the right to life, identity, and equality are natural rights. They are a priori: 'independent of any power' or of individual merit. As such, human rights cannot be conferred. The very fact that human rights exist already acknowledges a pre-social interconnection in which the subject is aware of and responsive to the other.

Regarding the development and implementation of a universalised system of legal justice, Levinas raises an important question which is answered by his ethics of alterity:

> Legal justice is required . . . But it is very important to know whether the state, society, law and power are required because man is a beast to his neighbour or because I am responsible for my fellow. It is important to know whether the political order defines man's responsibility or merely restricts his bestiality.[58]

In terms of legal justice, Levinas suggests that the origin of the rule of law is not to permit individual egos to fight for individualised rights against one another. Rather, a 'different 'authority' from that established in the totality of reason is required.[59] This is the higher authority that recognises compassionate goodness as a normative social principle. It is 'the first language,' and it will reflect the pre-social a priori concern for the unique, absolutely different other, who is acknowledged in the face-to-face relation where, in the face of suffering, one is for the other.[60]

The required conditions for practical rights are those that will emerge when humanity has assumed the first right of absolute difference.[61] This first right requires the 'I' to be freed from returning to the self. It requires the subject to regard the other; not simply to be aware of the other, but to Become in connection with the other. It is a relationship in which being concerned for the other—welcoming and caring for the other—is to facilitate one's own ethical being. These conditions represent the prior peace of a higher authority in which goodness is the first language of freedom.[62] Levinas insists that these conditions ground natural law and practical human rights. In a human rights based on the non-metaphysical face-to-face relation, one and the other are responsible, endowed with duty, and absolved in a peaceful unity with infinity.

In Levinas's system of human rights, one regards the other from the position of unity. It is a unity with infinite responsibility, as experienced through encounters with the face. In this system, the 'I' frees itself from the ego, 'answers for the other,' and does not return to self.[63] It is a process of natural justice that, for Levinas, also recognises responsibility as the 'original goodness in which freedom is embedded.'[64] It is a way of relating in which non-indifference to the other represents a paramount aspect of human identity. It inspires and facilitates infinite responsibility. This is a liberating 'freedom in fraternity, in which the responsibility of one-for-the-other is affirmed, and through which the rights of man manifest themselves *concretely* to consciousness as the right of the other, for which I am answerable.'[65] On this view, each-for-all, rather than one-for-self, is the ethical Becoming of humanity, the foundation of basic moral rights and the principle to be established in the operation of practical human rights.

RESPONSIBILITY IN THE FACE OF DIFFERENCE

Levinas's ethics of alterity is a complex and provocative theory that opposes the established orthodoxy of autonomy and the primacy of human reason. It offers an explanation for the essence of compassionate humanity and human identity. At the heart of this philosophy is the notion that human beings become ethical in encounters with others because being in the presence of another invokes the infinite question of 'what to do next.' It configures human identity as heterogeneous[66] and heteronomous,[67] and explains relational and infinite ethical responsibility.

Despite developing an ethical theory of otherness, in which duties to others are paramount and infinite, Levinas did not develop a comprehensive thesis or attempt a diligent application of his ethics of alterity to human rights. His notion of the legitimacy of fundamental rights is, though, very clear. There exists an original right. It is an original right that is pre-social, grounds the very notion of rights, and has grounded this notion since the inception of time. It is the right to be recognised as different and the subject of a precarious mortality.

Levinas's thoughts on justice and human rights are, thus, not comprehensive. Though he does explain how they should be grounded by the principle of otherness, they do not indicate a set of normative principles that can be used to configure current human rights. What he does say is that human rights represent the fact of a priori sociability and original responsibility. He also maintains that this notion of human rights espouses a liberating principle, in which the subject can be released from the constraints of the totality of reason to live according to a true, innate characteristic of ethical responsibility for others.

On the principles of Levinas's philosophy, critical human rights scholars propose the ethics of alterity as a model for the existence and operation of human rights. Of particular significance is that Levinas's theory promotes the a priori nature of human sociality and responsibility as indicative of an innate desire to respond to and accommodate difference, live in community, and extend compassion to others. This critical human rights discourse is important to understand how Levinas's philosophy is interpreted and applied as the foundation of justice, to identify the scope for the inclusion of nonhumans and to ascertain its value in the presentation of human right claims of vegans.

THE APPLICATION OF THE ETHICS OF ALTERITY IN PROTEST SCHOLARSHIP

The critical human rights scholarship that highlights the utility of Levinas's theory has been loosely categorised by Marie-Bénédicte Dembour as 'protest scholarship.' In the application of Levinas's ethics of alterity to human rights, protest scholarship develops an ethics of alterity for human rights, arguing that the existence of human rights recognises pre-social responsibility but entrenches a Western philosophical focus on individuality and the primacy of reason. As such, it is argued that it has become a system that falsely represents the individual and humanity.

The value of the ethics of alterity to protest scholarship is that they facilitate the practical opportunity to entrench and act out the primary condition of ethical responsibility. This primary condition of responsibility in the presence of others is also observed as human liberation because it facilitates human freedom. It facilitates intertwined Becoming in a community of others who embrace and deploy the innate characteristic of compassion for others.

To transform the unethical totality of reason and reclaim humanity, protest scholarship aims to locate the encounter with the 'face' of another as the non-abstract, concrete ethical principle capable of rupturing the assumed immanence of ethics. Scholars want the primacy of reason to be replaced with the ethics of alterity and for relational encounters to be acknowledged as transcendent. In this paradigm for social relations, the absolute, inescapable, infinite duty to the other breaches the imposed order of unethical totality, and humanity realises its ethical destiny: to be primarily welcoming, caring, and responsible for others, with the support of social institutions.[68]

The following sections examine the utility of Levinas's theory for realist Upendra Baxi, postmodernist Costas Douzinas, and deconstructionist William Paul Simmons. These scholars are motivated by the work of Emmanuel Levinas in their search for guiding ethical principles for the existence and operation of human rights. Of particular interest is how these authors interpret Levinas's philosophy and whether they develop specific normative principles for the practice of a suffering narrative of human rights that may offer assistance to vegans in their claims that re-present the precarious mortality and suffering of nonhuman others.

UPENDRA BAXI

Suffering is central to Upendra Baxi's understanding of human rights. He agrees with Klaus Gunther that 'human rights are best understood as the result of the process of the loss and recovery of voice with regard to negative experiences like pain, fear, and suffering.'[69] For Baxi, this should be the context for discourse.

Baxi makes a distinction between 'modern' and 'contemporary' human rights. He rejects the legitimacy of modern human rights that emerged from the Enlightenment. He claims that the definition of man, as possessing reason and autonomous will, was a powerful 'peculiar ontological construction' that excluded vast numbers of human beings.[70] He argues that the emphasis on rationality was the 'justification of the unjustifiable: namely colonialism and imperialism.'[71] For Baxi, the primacy of individual reason produced an ideology in which hierarchy could be used by the superior as an evil weapon to dominate the inferior: modern human rights encouraged oppression and suffering.

Baxi puts forward the view that contemporary human rights emerged from a context of violence and that it is 'axiomatic that the historic mission of contemporary human rights is to give voice to human suffering, to make it visible, and to ameliorate it.'[72] He points out that human rights cannot function effectively and efficiently without sentiment or proper, compassionate consideration for others. For this reason, compassionate listening and hearing the voice of the other—to the extent that one is able to imagine with genuine concern the other's lived reality in empathetic role reversal—is a crucial and basic requirement. Baxi urges humanity to adopt this process and listen patiently to suffering others: '[t]o give language to pain, to experience the pain of the Other inside you, remains the task, always, of the human rights narratology.'[73] On this view, otherness is a core value in the ethics of human rights that 'seems to command consensus.'[74]

For Baxi, contemporary human rights are the mechanism through which humanity has formalised the fundamental, universal moral value of empathy and compassion for the other in its endeavour to alleviate suffering. Regarding the meaning of otherness, Baxi concurs with Levinas: otherness is recognizing the absolutely different.[75]

Baxi also draws on a point made by Levinas when he reiterates the importance of acknowledging that difference is the fundamental ethic of a project to furnish those who suffer with protective rights.[76] When Levinas's ethics of alterity is introduced into human rights, the point must be made that Levinas believed that rights are required to protect each individual in their difference as 'absolutely dissimilar' and possessing an identity that is 'non-interchangeable, incomparable and unique.'[77] Baxi applies this sentiment to human rights, upholding them as representing recognition, respect and protection of difference—not as entitlements for homogenising sameness.

Baxi does not move beyond general terms about the importance of the ethics of alterity for human rights. Whilst grounding his ethics generally in Levinas's philosophy, there is no attempt to translate Levinasian ethics of alterity into a workable political principle for social justice. He notes that scholarly work on legal theory and practice suffers a paucity of analysis from a Levinasian perspective, [78] but that the philosophy of Levinas is complex and that there is potential for 'vulgar Levinasian' theorising.[79] Baxi himself, perhaps on this basis, does not develop his theory of human rights in the context of a deep analytical approach to Levinas, but does ground his thesis on the moral obligation to respond to human suffering.

Baxi has faith in the human rights project. He believes it to be a culture of cultures. By embracing plurality, human rights are dynamic and able to constitute new contexts as they evolve to eradicate all oppression. Further, he emphasises that what human rights can be—in the context of its dynamic nature and its ability to exist in new and unimagined paradigms—remains to be seen.

Baxi urges a reform of human rights education as a 'first step' in implementing otherness in human rights.[80] This reinvigorated human rights education would promote uniqueness, rather than reduce human diversity to a 'common essence.' As such, it would advocate entrenching the ethics of alterity in a human 'right to be different.'[81]

In *The Future of Human Rights*, Baxi states a belief that the mission of human rights is threatened by a discourse that creates hierarchy and excludes marginalised voices. He observes the 'ever new bases for reconceptualising human rights as ethical imperatives'[82] but is similarly critical of some human rights discourse and activism. Baxi observes that animal rights activism expands human rights activism, but he also identifies an evangelicalism and romanticism in human rights that may verge on fanaticism and over-optimism. Nevertheless, noting the reality of pain and suffering, Baxi believes that the language of human rights should not disguise suffering and oppression, and that human rights activism should target structural oppressive forces. This point is clearly relevant to discussing the human rights claims of vegans for other animals in the context of the language of human rights, its standards, principles, and orthodoxy.

Baxi identifies the endlessly inclusive potential of what he refers to as the contemporary human rights paradigm, and, in later work, seriously reflects on the challenge of posthuman theory,[83] noting the 'immense significance' for re-thinking human rights in terms of what Donna Haraway refers to as our 'constitutive partners.'[84] Baxi expresses support for a discourse that includes nonhuman others and understands that it 'invites re-thinking human agency and responsibility (as well as human rights languages and logics) in a new key.'[85]

Baxi remains a realist. Whilst he accepts the value of a variety of posthuman contributions for the invigoration of human rights discourse, suffering, and emancipation remain central to his thinking. He believes in the possibility of structural forces of oppression[86] and 'above all' in the right to interpret human rights.[87] These sentiments express otherness and a commitment to emancipation from suffering, and it is within this context that Baxi can be regarded as being supportive of a discourse that identifies nonhuman suffering to be within the scope of a politics *of* and *for* human rights.[88]

COSTAS DOUZINAS

Douzinas is very negative about current human rights, but believes that Levinas's philosophy may offer a postmodern principle of justice to save them from complete failure.[89] Applying directly, and in more detail, the philosophy of Emmanuel Levinas, Douzinas emphasises that the existence of human rights both recognises and represents the a priori nature of obligation to the other. Stating that human rights concretise duty and the rights of the other person, Douzinas claims that human rights are 'the instruments of ethics.'[90] Rights, he asserts, 'are a formal recognition of the fact that before my (legal) subjectivity always and already has come another.'[91]

Douzinas, thus, concurs with Levinas and believes that human rights are pre-social. They 'exist *a priori*, independently of any legislative conferred or state authorisation because the other is a priority.'[92] As such, Douzinas regards the ethics of alterity to be the foundational principle of natural human rights. He believes that '[a]ll humanity and every right proceed from this primacy of ethics of being and of obligation over need or interest.'[93] Douzinas believes that Levinas's philosophy has 'changed the ontological, epistemological and moral assumptions of modernity,' and that human rights would benefit enormously from incorporating and promoting, specifically, Levinasian ethics of alterity.[94]

For Douzinas, the obligation of human rights is to attend to suffering, empower oppressed victims, and generally recognise and give priority consideration to unique, singular others. Douzinas identifies human rights, as did Levinas, as serving egoistic, same-for-self ideology, rather than providing a means to eliminate suffering. For Douzinas, current human rights function as a mechanism of personal and social delusion because they encourage same-for-self claim rights and have resulted in atomistic human egos that are antithetical to the creation of a community of humanity. Douzinas argues that human rights have been derailed from their original purpose of entrenching responsibility and duty as primary principles upon which others would be protected from domination and oppression. He claims that rights (unfortunately) now only give legitimacy to same-for-self morality, rather than facilitate or promote compassionate duty to others.[95]

Douzinas argues that human rights ought to transcend the subject and reclaim their purpose as functional in a community of 'unique others.'[96]

In consideration of one's absolute duty to the other, Douzinas asserts that 'before my right and before my identity as organised by rights, comes my obligation, my radical turn towards the claim to respect the dignity of the other.' Since rights have meaning only in relation to others whose rights are established a priori to mine, then 'the right of the other always and already precedes mine.'[97]

Douzinas agrees that the other generates an 'ethical imperative'[98] that motivates the self to action. The self becomes the agent of the other. Rather than autonomy forming the categorical imperative, the moral will is instead constituted, made available and made responsive only in the context of the ethical demand of the other. Thus, Douzinas concurs that the ego—the self—becomes ethically and morally empowered to access freedom through responsi-bility in the presence of the face of the other. This freedom espouses interconnection, community and compassionate relations.

For Douzinas, a system of non-metaphysical human rights, imbued with the ethics of alterity, would entail a concept of humanity where the social bond is changed 'to the public recognition and protection of the becoming human with others.'[99] Douzinas explains that this would be a process of 'righting' which would 'open human identity to the new and unknown as a condition of its humanity.'[100]

For Douzinas, 'otherness is not just a moment in the dialectic of the same and the different, but the transcendence of the system.'[101] In the absence of an ethics of alterity in human rights, they fail and perpetuate suffering because they contribute to a totalising system in which everyone is caught up in a totality that perpetuates self-delusion. Individuals are constructed to be isolated, autonomous beings with self-fulfilling endeavours to pursue. In this system, there is little scope for the development of a value for duties to others. Law assimilates each and the other into an objective totality[102] by promoting an individualism that denies that we come 'into existence in common with others, that we are all in community.'[103]

Douzinas argues for a new non-metaphysical legal relation that does not depend on 'the past or obedience to tradition'[104] but on acceptance that selves flourish through relationships with others and that the essence of humanity is to be 'near Being and care for the human as well as the other entities in which Being discloses itself.'[105] Such a new relation will utilise the benefits of relational ethics. He, thus, calls for an attack on the current defining concept of humanity to protect human beings and to facilitate a compassionate humanity which is yet to come.

In Douzinas' application of Levinas's ethics of alterity, he argues that human rights will no longer function in the interests of the powerful at the expense of the disempowered. In the radical, natural law of the ethics of alterity, the recognition of difference is paramount, and human rights will facilitate a 'loving turn to the suffering and unique other that bestows on the individual her own singularity.'[106]

Levinas's ethics of alterity offers Douzinas a promising concept for a postmodern principle of justice.[107] In this regard, he raises questions concerning who are legitimate others, owed duties and entitled to protective rights. Though Douzinas predominantly focuses his thesis on human others, he, nonetheless, advances the possibility for nonhuman otherness to feature in a suffering narrative of human rights by pointing out that:

> [t]he animal rights movement, from deep ecology and anti-vivisection militancy to its gentler green versions, has placed the legal differentiation between human and animal firmly on the political agenda and has drafted a number of Bills of animal entitlements. Important philosophical and ontological questions are involved here.[108]

Douzinas identifies that in this postmodern principle of justice, the other can be 'most strange and foreign,' 'most alien,' and 'incomparably unique.' It also entails a goodness that 'does not exclude any other and does not try to impose the preference of the self upon the stranger.'[109] It is a postmodern principle of justice, espousing a 'radical sensitivity' that can adapt to the 'shifting boundaries of the social' in relation to suffering.[110] In Douzinas' postmodern theory, the other is dynamic over time and space, but is, ultimately, always an entity that generates responsibility.

Douzinas has illustrated how human rights can be grounded in suffering. In his thesis, a straightforward application of Levinas's ethics of alterity offers a generalised principle of otherness upon which human rights could function. Douzinas does not attempt to develop a critical analysis of the limitations of the ethics of alterity, but he accepts the theory at face value as having a beneficial, emancipatory function for human rights.

Douzinas applies the ethics of alterity to human rights according to his postmodern theoretical tendencies. He does not develop a discussion on the exclusion of nonhuman animals, which is surprising, given the opportunity within the postmodern tradition to deconstruct oppressive binaries. His application of Levinas's ethics of alterity, and the development of otherness as a postmodern principle of justice, implicitly and explicitly provoke debate about the exclusion of nonhuman others.

In his explanation of how suffering and the ethics of alterity could underpin human rights, Douzinas observes that they would reorient same-for-self claim rights. This is particularly relevant because the claims of vegans are not same-for-self. Unlike claims made by women, disabled people or same-sex couples, for example, the claims of vegans present a moral imperative to attend to the suffering of nonhuman others. In this regard, the legal recognition of veganism as representing the claims of those who seek to present the moral standing of nonhuman others points to the transcendental principle of justice he seeks.

In explaining that human rights should serve a humanity whose essence is compassion, Douzinas identifies that the totality explained in Levinas's philosophy includes an unjust administration of human rights that is entirely focused on individualism. In his application of the ethics of alterity, he envisages a process of 'righting' that would construct a culture of becoming ethical in the context of co-existing others. In the context of the observed problematic tradition of individualism that affects the claims of vegans, such a righting would pertain to a break of what he refers to as problematic past traditions. Clearly, this could include the traditional legal methods on which the claims of those who represent animal suffering are assessed.

Douzinas grounds human rights in suffering and applies the ethics of alterity to explain how human rights can function better. He explains that otherness will function as a positive postmodern principle of justice. In his vision, a protective rights enterprise would also care for an entity in which Being discloses itself. On this basis, protective rights built upon the ethics of alterity can include nonhuman animals, promote vegan values and offer protection to vegans because it would honestly acknowledge duty to other animals.

WILLIAM PAUL SIMMONS

Simmons believes—as do Baxi and Douzinas—that the purpose of human rights is the alleviation of suffering and that human rights must prioritise the suffering other. He concurs with Baxi and Douzinas regarding the problems created by homogenising Western philosophy and its institutions. He singles out this specific characteristic of human rights as the most important to dismantle. What Simmons wants is for human rights to 'create an anti-hegemonic discourse that will overturn those invisible ideologies that undergird the system.'[111]

Simmons is partly influenced by Derrida's philosophy of human rights and the idea that they are founded on 'an invisible ideology that conceals an original violence.'[112] Simmons' target is to highlight the ways in which homogeneity is entrenched in legal theory, process, and practice, to apply the methods of postmodern deconstruction to identify oppressive relationships, and to develop a transformative, functional principle for a paradigm shift from entrenched homogeneity to a new system of law that is based on heteronomy. That principle is the Saturated Marginalised Other.

Simmons cites Baxi as the authority for the importance of otherness in human rights. He agrees that appropriate human rights education is required and that a human rights of the other requires compassionate and patient listening to the voice of the suffering other. He does not discuss Douzinas' view of human rights or Douzinas' perspective on Levinas's ethics of alterity. Adopting a more positive and optimistic view of human rights law than Douzinas, he agrees that human rights must be constantly deconstructed in the tradition of postmodernism, but notes that, thus far, despite being exposed to Levinas's ethics of alterity, postmodern thought has been unable to provide a concrete, universal principle for the just and ethical operation of human rights. Simmons develops the idea of the Saturated Marginalised Other as an exit route to current human rights limitations and conceptual difficulties in postmodern reasoning.

In his endeavour to develop human rights, Simmons is attracted to Levinas's ethics of alterity because it provides a non-abstract ethical theory from which a political principle for heteronomy (and the subsequent inclusion of Marginalised Others) can be developed. Simmons retains the basis of Levinas's ethics of alterity but explores the limitations of the original ethical theory in the context of a specific application of additional philosophy, political theory and literature in phenomenology. He firstly explains how human rights law, theory, and practice marginalise and silence voiceless others before applying his principle to real human rights situations. In so doing, he illustrates the power of the concept of the Saturated Marginalised Other as a concrete universal principle to reinvigorate human rights and a transformational postmodern principle of justice.

Simmons believes that homogeneity, as the original violence in human rights, 'cauterises' the Marginalised Other.[113] By this, he means that human rights are an institution that firstly, declares the other to be rightless; secondly, dismisses the voice of the other; and finally, powerfully portrays the voice of the other as unimportant, facilitating a functional dumbing-down of feelings associated with compassion for the other's suffering.

Whilst Simmons accepts that the transcendental experience of the face-to-face relation is capable of grounding the call to question human rights and all typologies, he points out that Levinas's original ethics are limited and constrained by a number of issues. Firstly, Simmons is critical of Levinas's theological dimension.[114] He points out that where deconstruction of human rights and all typologies relies on an ethics of alterity that is created and sustained by God,[115] God cannot be removed from ethics and, as such, cannot form the basis of either human rights or ethics, nor have any positive impact on the development of ethical politics. Secondly, Simmons draws attention to the equality of faces in Levinas's theory. For Levinas, all faces generate an ethical response regardless of whose they are: the face of a cold-blooded executioner and that of a homeless, abused child equally call the observer to their duty to welcome and to protect. This is particularly limiting for Simmons because his objective is to secure an ethical principle to enhance the potential for emancipation of Marginalised Others. Simmons, therefore, adopts a phenomenological approach that allows him to establish a hierarchy of responses, enabled by the face-to-face relation.

Through the application of Dussel's philosophy of otherness and the individualising phenomenology of Marion, Simmons is able to create a hierarchy of ethical responses by resituating the point at which the ethical transformation takes place. The phenomenology that appeals to Simmons locates and explains the ethical transformation more precisely in the observer, rather than as an inevitable, inescapable duty resulting from becoming a passive hostage through the Levinasian encounter with the face of the other. Whilst the face of the other still grounds the ethical transformation, the power producing the ethical response is subsequent to the overwhelmed ego of the observer:

> The Saturated Other bedazzles the ego and overwhelms the ontological categories that support it. . . . The Other cannot be comprehended by the ego's gaze, and when he or she draws near from outside the system, the ego's entire frame of reference is shaken because such epiphanies 'shake the very pillars of the system that exploits them.'[116]

The experience of the face of the other remains solid, as in Levinas's theory, and requires a positive response from the ego—but rather than being a result of an unknown hyper-presence related to theology, it is caused by 'provocation from the person behind the ontological categories.' 'The approach of the marginalised Other incessantly calls the *ego and* its system into question and thus calls the ego to a deeper or more saturated responsibility.'[117] For Simmons, the Saturated Other presents the ego with information, more information and potentially a super-abundance of information, and calls for an affirmative duty to distinguish between faces. It is upon this principle that he believes the injustice of current hegemonic human rights discourse can be shattered, giving way to a focus on bringing the marginalised to the centre.

The deeply Saturated Other is the Marginalised Other who emerges from outside the hegemonic system, and it is this other to whom human rights owes the highest duty. This other—who transcends the system, its ontology, and all typologies—must be given priority, because welcoming the other means not imposing existing, oppressive categories. Oppressed others ought not be 'cauterised': branded, dismissed, ignored, silenced, or required either to speak the language of the system—a system that by its nature excludes those who speak differently or, by extension, those who cannot speak the language of the system at all. Rather, a reversal of such cauterisation is the acknowledgement that the highest responsibility is owed to the Saturated Marginalised Other, because there is clear transcendence of all categories and clear questions about the system.

What Simmons wants is transcendence by those who suffer the most in the totality of the current exploitative system. He wants the other, who saturates the ego of the subject with expressive presence, to shake the foundations of human rights. Simmons recognises that the phenomenology of the Saturated Other must be universalised for it to be applicable to human rights. He firmly believes that it is the catalyst for the development of a new system of law based on a concrete universal principle that begins from the voice of the other.

Simmons considers neither the exclusion of nonhuman animals in human rights nor the situation of vegans. Despite a thought-provoking consideration of the existence and operation of human rights, conducted in the tradition of deconstruction, nonhuman animals are typically ignored. As such, his thesis raises additional questions about the notion of saturation, the idea of the original violence of human rights, and who, in the foundational idea and original violence of human rights, is cauterised, ignored, and dismissed. Nonetheless, Simmons explains how human rights can be more responsive to suffering by explaining how otherness, as a workable principle of justice, can be implemented.

ANALYSIS OF PROTEST SCHOLARSHIP

Protest scholarship rejects autonomous reason and focuses on the ethics of alterity as a compelling alternative philosophy for the ethical orientation of human rights. What is clear in the literature surveyed is the consensus that the ethical basis of human rights ought to emphasise the natural human predisposition to desire community, and it should recognise the significance of a cognitive and emotional interconnection with suffering others. Protest scholars believe that such a reorientation in the groundwork of human rights has significant potential. Baxi, particularly, notes the dynamic and evolving nature of human rights and the real possibility of such a transformation. Douzinas believes that a human rights of otherness is particularly important as a principle of justice for a critical postmodern era, and Simmons shows how the principle of otherness can work in practice to give a voice to seriously marginalised others.

Building on the idea of an innate desire for community underpinned by an appreciation of universal, unique suffering, protest scholars have, thus, explained how suffering and the ethics of alterity can justify protective rights. This discourse is not, however, one that includes nonhuman animals or considers the intertwined community of human and nonhuman others. Despite this, Douzinas explicitly remarks that the animal rights movement has a legitimate and valid contribution to make to debates about the ontological foundations of exclusive human rights.

What the protest school of human rights takes from Levinas is that suffering (and the human response to it) is a truism and that this is the non-abstract foundation of the ethics of alterity. A human rights which fails to accommodate this, as Douzinas argues, is denying humanity the opportunity to reach its full potential, because it creates the conditions in which egos become self-satisfying, atomistic and ever more separated from their natural predisposition to live in community and extend compassion to others.

The philosophy of ethics that protest scholarship advances is, thus, a theory of ethical subjectivity in which humanity is predisposed to a motivational force in the face of suffering. That force is responsibility, and it is generated by innate compassion. In other words, to be human is to be responsible and compassionate. On this view, responsibility and compassion are synonymous with humanity. This is true, whichever phenomenological theory one accepts. If the motivational force that moves one towards responsibility for the other—to welcome, to care, to empathise with the other—resides in the phenomenological, external realm (as in Levinas's original ethics), one becomes compassionately engaged at the moment of the face-to-face relation. If, as preferred by Simmons, the motivational force resides within the ego but is facilitated subsequent to the overwhelming category-denying, typology-denying phenomenological experience, then one is also moved to compassionate action at the same relational moment. On the basis of this notion of ethical subjectivity for a system of fundamental rights of the other, the question of responsibility in the face of nonhuman animal suffering is relevant and important.

For the purposes of recognising the utility of protest scholarship for nonhuman others and veganism, it is not necessary to surmise the origin of the ethical force in metaphysical terms. As Simon Critchley notes, for the purposes of advancing a theory of ethical subjectivity, if the experience of a radical ethical demand is acknowledged and accepted, then it is not necessary to engage with the unknowability of that force.[118]

What is advanced in protest scholarship is that the radical demand of the other causes conscious awareness of, firstly, a perception of a concrete self (which can be named the ego), and an awareness of the concrete other (defined as that which cannot be known, but which brings an infinite ethical demand that one is compelled to welcome). In this light, protest scholarship advances a theory of ethical subjectivity, in which human beings are what

Critchley regards as 'hetero-affectively'[119] constituted. The ethical subject exists as a split subject whose autonomy is always appropriated by the infinite demands of infinite others but who 'is defined by commitment or fidelity to an unfulfillable demand, a demand that is internalized subjectively and which divides subjectivity.'[120] For Critchley, this is the 'experience of conscience.'[121] In this context, protest scholarship, in its acknowledgement of hetero-affective demand and the overwhelming desire to meet this demand with care and responsibility, locates human conscience as central to the development of its ethics. Central to this consciousness are interconnected and intertwined individuals in community exercising an extension of compassionate responsibility for the suffering other. Though this discourse does not consider compassion and responsibility in the face of nonhuman suffering, it holds promise for their inclusion.

The Significance of Compassionate Responsibility

A consciousness of compassion and responsibility in the face of the suffering is under-developed in protest scholarship. For Baxi, Douzinas and Simmons, it is both implicit and explicit that compassionate responsibility in the face of suffering is related in important ways to the existence, origin and ethics of human rights.[122] Compassion, in relation to suffering, is a long-established principle of consideration in discourse on ethics, recognised in the early writings of Jean-Jacques Rousseau[123] as the 'pure emotion of nature,' and in various other works as characteristic of moral sense theory. In contemporary theory on human rights and justice, the concept of compassion has secured its own discursive niche as the politics of compassion,[124] which 'links the universal and the particular in that it assumes a shared humanity of interconnected, vulnerable people and requires emotions and practical, particular responses to different expressions of vulnerability.'[125]

Whilst the concept of compassionate responsibility has for a long time been related to notions of justice,[126] it also appears to suffer from an ambiguity which revolves around its related terms—sentiment, sympathy, pity, and empathy—and their use by various authors to suit their purposes.[127] Porter explains that the popular perception of compassion is a combination of feelings, empathy and co-suffering that espouses the capacity to feel and share suffering.[128] Lynn Hunt uses 'empathy' to represent pro-active identification with others, preferring to avoid 'sympathy,' which she feels often indicates pity, may imply condescension and may misrepresent true feelings of equality.[129] For Sylvester, '[E]mpathy taps the ability and willingness to enter into the feeling or spirit of something and appreciate it fully in a subjectivity-moving way.'[130]

By anchoring compassionate responsibility as an innate feature of consciousness, protest scholarship advances a view in which suffering is acknowledged by the subject, who is then able to imagine suffering, what is being suffered, and is motivated to action. This is particularly the intention of Simmons in the creation of a phenomenological hierarchy of human rights for the Saturated Marginalised Other. In this context, compassion 'helps us recognise our justice obligations to those most distant from us.'[131] The limitation of Simmons for vegans is, of course, that nonhuman animals do not currently feature as beings in the category of those most distant from us. When considering compassion and those most distant, a significant point to be made from the position of Levinas's ethics of alterity is that the influence of the other over the subject is a priori and must not be dismissed or reduced by categories and themes created by human reason. Nonetheless, the ideas of Simmons are a strong example of the way in which protest scholarship has potential for the claims of vegans with regard to nonhuman suffering and marginalisation.

Levinas's ethics of alterity have, thus, not yet been extensively developed and applied in a critical human rights discourse of compassion in the face of suffering. As Richard A Cohen remarks, however, on the basis that Levinas's philosophy is a theory of human emancipation from an unethical totality of reason, his work 'demands nothing less than a fundamental reorientation of Western spirit—philosophy, logic, rhetoric, praxis, ontology, science, art, politics, religion—in the light of morality and justice.'[132] Levinas's morality and justice involve a system of ethics in which one is for the other and in which others are defined as 'incomparable ones.'[133] In this regard, the utility of Levinas's thesis for an emancipatory rights enterprise can be considered further in terms of whether it can be developed to accommodate compassionate responsibility for suffering nonhumans.

The idea of responsibility in the face of difference has significant potential for a system of fundamental rights that can support the claims of vegans, because it offers the potential to extend the scope of responsibility to other-than-human vulnerability. Of significant appeal is, firstly, that Levinas's ethics of alterity is a philosophy of ethical becoming in community. This is explained in terms of a pre-social, innate desire to compassionately welcome the unique other. Secondly, in Levinas's ethics of alterity, there must be no reduction of the other. What Levinas means is that the subject must not impose the products of their reason upon the other. They must not develop, through rational activity, any oppressive themes and categories that would reduce the other. This principle has the potential to construct a positive approach to other-than-human life. A final point is that Levinas's ethics of alterity do not begin from a point of suffering, sentience, vulnerability or precariousness. These are concepts that facilitate understanding of the demand created in the original ethical encounter. They are terms created subsequently through reason. The ethical obligation to the other is, thus, not dependent on whether we grant sentiency or vulnerability, but is grounded by the voiceless saying of the being that expresses its presence and demands to be included in calculations of justice. It is an event and a responsibility that makes sense in the context of an innate universal human desire to live in non-violent community with others who also experience life in the world.

Taking into account the intertwined relationship of human and nonhuman beings, these principles have the potential to transcend the species boundary of human rights. They confirm that, in the context of a pre-social responsibility for the other, a constant and universal characteristic of humanity is the primacy of a compassionate welcome for others who are both vulnerable to mortality and who may be impacted further by the entry into and presence of the subject in their worlds—whether their suffering, sentience, or precariousness is understood by the subject. This principle has the potential to ground broad rights for other animals in a system of protective rights that would, thus, serve vegan values.

CONCLUSION

This chapter set out to ascertain whether human rights could be grounded in suffering. It has explained that Levinas's ethics of alterity ground the origin of human rights in the original right of the vulnerable other to exist as a unique entity. This idea is then supported by a concept of innate, compassionate responsibility that is extended by the subject to the other.

The chapter has observed that the value of Levinas's thesis is that it challenges entrenched Western philosophy on the centrality of individual human autonomy and the ontological assumptions at work in current human rights,[134] and that the origin of basic rights is the observation that there are already others with whom I co-exist.

The chapter has explained that critical human rights scholars argue that the mission and target of human rights are to acknowledge community and respond to the human desire to care about the suffering of others. It has identified that this discourse does not develop a discussion of nonhuman animal suffering and that the exclusion of other animals from the debate is unexplained. As such, the development of an ethics of human rights that recognises compassionate responsibility in the face of the other, the human desire to live in community, and the human desire to respond to the unique other's suffering require further examination.

In his introduction to *Totality and Infinity*, John Wild notes that Levinas's ideas about an alternative way of being were 'not yet fully explored'; an observation that encourages debate and developmental scholarship.[135] In this context, the ethics of alterity—as a philosophy that grounds moral standing on a non-abstract, concrete principle of intertwined, relational experiences—underpin an important debate regarding to whom we owe ethical duties.[136] This is a particularly pertinent point given the exclusion of nonhumans from a critical rights discourse that intends to honour the weak, marginalised, suffering other. As Deborah Bird Rose notes, '[t]o ask to whom, or to what, does one come face-to-face is to ask to whom or to what am I responsible? This is the question of our time.'[137]

Given that the ethics of alterity recognise the primacy of the unique suffering other, and that critical human rights discourse utilises this philosophy to consider the ethics of human rights, the next chapter asks whether the ethics of alterity concern nonhuman animals. The objective is to assess whether Levinas's ethics of alterity, as an explanation for the creation of human rights, validate the inclusion of nonhuman animals in a suffering narrative of human rights. If so, the fundamental rights of nonhuman animals can then provide the grounds for the moral imperative to respond to suffering to feature in litigation of cases presenting ethical responsibility to nonhuman animals, vulnerability and suffering.

NOTES

1. Marie-Bénédicte Dembour, *Who Believes in Human Rights*? (Cambridge University Press 2006).
2. Dembour (2006).
3. Dembour (2006) 11.
4. Dembour (2006) 11.
5. Dembour (2006) 245.
6. The potential limits of developing principles for justice are discussed in Desmond Manderson (ed), *Essays on Levinas and Law* (Palgrave Macmillan 2009).
7. Simmons (2014).
8. Peter Atterton, 'The Emanuel Levinas Web Page' <www.levinas.sdsu.edu/> accessed 10 June 2016.
9. Levinas, (1969/2000)
10. Matthew Calarco, *Zoographies: The Question of the Animal from Heidegger to Derrida* (Columbia University Press 2008).
11. Literature discussing the work of Levinas often highlights Husserl and Heidegger as influential thinkers. See, for example, John Lechte, *Fifty Contemporary Thinkers: from Structuralism to Post Modernity* (Routledge 1994) 115–119.

12. Strictly speaking, this is not an accurate representation of Levinas's philosophy because the force that produces ethics does not appear to the subject while 'phenomenology describes what appears.' (Levinas 1985, 85). There is some doubt about Levinas's priority being phenomenology, ethics or theology. Levinas remarks: 'You know they often speak of ethics to describe what I do, but what interests me when all is said and done is not only ethics, it's the holy, the holiness of the holy.' Quoted in Simon Critchley, 'Introduction' in Simon Critchley and Robert Bernasconi (eds), *The Cambridge Companion to Levinas* (5th printing, Cambridge University Press 2002/2008) 27.

13. Sean Hand (ed), *The Levinas Reader: Emmanuel Levinas* (Blackwell 1989/1996) v.

14. Hand (1989/1996) v.

15. Peter Atterton and Matthew Calarco, 'Editors Introduction: The Third Wave of Levinas Scholarship' in Peter Atterton and Matthew Calarco (eds), *Radicalizing Levinas* (State University of New York Press 2010) ix.

16. The word 'other' is capitalised in Levinas's work.

17. Levinas (1969/2000) 43.

18. 'From beginning to end Levinas's thought is a humanism of the other.' Richard A Cohen, 'Introduction' in Emmanuel Levinas, *Humanism of the Other* (Nidra Poller tr, University of Illinois Press 2006) xxvi. This source is a collection of three essays, in which Levinas describes how the other person creates another's being through the ethical response. The original French title of Levinas's (1972) book was 'Humanism of the other man.' This was changed to 'Humanism of the other' in the English translation (n8 xli).

19. Tamra Wright, Peter Hughes and Alison Ainley, 'The Paradox of Morality: An Interview with Emmanuel Levinas's (Andrew Benjamin and Tamra Wright trs) in Robert Bernasconi and David Wood (eds), *The Provocation of Levinas: Rethinking the Other* (Routledge 2014/1988) 172.

20. Robert Bernasconi and Simon Critchley, *Re-Reading Levinas* (The Athlone Press 1991) xi.

21. See Chapter 10, 'The Rights of the Other Man' in Emmanuel Levinas, *Alterity and Transcendence* (Michael B Smith tr, Columbia University Press 1999).

22. This simplified way of explaining the ethics of alterity would not be Levinas's description of the ethical event.

23. Translators frequently explain the difficulties associated with translating and their choice of substituted vocabulary.

24. Sean Hand refers to 'this complex and challenging philosophy': Hand (1989/1996) 75.

25. Eschatology is the theological interest in the destiny of mankind.

26. Quote from the nineteenth century Russian novel on the subject of ethics, free will and morality, entitled *The Brothers Karamazov* by Fyodor Dostoyevsky, cited by Richard Kearney, *Dialogues with Contemporary Continental Thinkers: The Phenomenological Heritage* (Manchester University Press 1984) 67.

27. Cited in Kearney (1984) 67.

28. Colin Davis, *Levinas: An Introduction* (University of Notre Dame Press 1997) 132 and 144.

29. Upendra Baxi, 'Judging Emmanuel Levinas? Some reflections on reading *Levinas, Law, Politics*' (Book review of Marinos Diamantides (ed), *Levinas, Law, Politics* (Routledge-Cavendish 2007)) (2009a) 72 (1) *The Modern Law Review* 116. Desmond Manderson also notes the paucity of literature on Levinas and law. He relates this, to some extent, to the difficulty and time needed to engage with the complexities presented: Desmond Manderson, 'Introduction' in Desmond Manderson (ed), *Essays on Levinas and Law* (Palgrave Macmillan 2009) 4.

30. For a full discussion of 'the saying' and 'the said,' see Emmanuel Levinas, *Otherwise Than Being or Beyond Essence* (Alphonso Lingis tr, Duquesne University Press 1998/2011).

31. Discussed in Emmanuel Levinas *Of God Who Comes to Mind* (Bertina Bergo tr, Stanford University Press 1986/1998).

32. Levinas (1998) 181.

33. Levinas (1969/2000) 261.

34. Levinas (1969/2000).

35. Emmanuel Levinas, *Outside the subject* (Michael B Smith tr, Continuum International Publishing Group 1987/2008) 92.

36. Levinas (1961/2000) 116.

37. Calarco (2008) 56.

38. Levinas (1987/2008) 92.

39. The other enables the ethical conscience of the subject. Levinas (1969/2000) 101.

40. Translated by Alphonso Lingis in Levinas (1961/2000) 24. The translation of 'le visage' as 'face' is well established.

41. Levinas (1969/2000) 50.

42. Levinas (1985) 89.

43. Levinas (1969/2000) 66.

44. The 'face' has been used to represent a community of others, a cultural group and even a nation. It has been used to describe many things, from a simple value of 'being nice' to others to the idea that one can read anything into Levinas (see Fred C Alford in Baxi (2009a) below). The priority given by Levinas is that the face concerns the affective experience of an entity that is perceived as vulnerable.

45. Levinas (1985) 85.

46. Levinas (1969/2000) and Levinas (1984) refer again to the body expressing face.

47. Levinas (1969/2000) 87.

48. Levinas (1969/2000) 198.

49. Emmanuel Levinas 'Ethics as first philosophy' in Sean Hand (ed), *The Levinas Reader* (Blackwell 1989b) 83.

50. Levinas (1985) 89.

51. Hand (1989/1996) 75.

52. Levinas (1984) and Levinas (1984) 167.

53. Judith Butler *Precarious Life* (Verso 2004a) 134.

54. Jill Robbins (ed), *Is it Righteous to Be?: Interviews with Emmanuel Levinas* (Stanford University Press 2001) 15.

55. Emmanuel Levinas, 'Ideology and Idealism' in Sean Hand (ed), *The Levinas Reader* (Blackwell 1989a) 247.

56. Levinas (1969/2000) 213.

57. Levinas (1987/2008) 92.

58. Levinas (1989a) 247–248.

59. Levinas (1987/2008) 97.

60. Levinas (1987/2008) 98.

61. Levinas (1987/2008) 93.

62. Levinas (1987/2008) 97/98.

63. Levinas (1987/2008) 98.

64. Levinas (1987/2008) 98.

65. Levinas (1987/2008) 98

66. Unique/dissimilar.

67. Subject to external influences that explain human Becoming and define identity.

68. Sean Hand explains how the face-to-face 'commandment breaks open immanence' and opens the 'closed order of totality.' Hand (1989/1996) 190. The preface to Levinas, (1969/2000) puts it like this: 'The first 'vision' of eschatology (hereby distinguished from the revealed opinions of positive religions) reveals the very possibility of eschatology, that is, the breach of the totality.' Levinas (1969/2000) 23.

69. Baxi (2009b) 199.

70. Baxi (2009b) 44.

71. Baxi (2009b) 44–45.

72. Baxi (2009b) 6.

73. Baxi (2009b) 159.

74. Baxi (2009b) 15.

75. Baxi (2009b) 15.

76. Baxi (2009b) 15.

77. Levinas (1987/2008) 92.

78. Baxi (2009a).

79. Fred C Alford claims that Levinas's work can say anything the reader wants to hear. Quoted in Baxi (2009a) 116.

80. Upendra Baxi, 'Random Reflections on the [Im]possibility of Human Rights Education' (*PDHRE*, no date, para 21) <www.pdhre.org/dialogue/reflections.html> accessed 11 June 2016.

81. Upendra Baxi, 'Concepts of Human Rights' in Upendra Baxi and Kenny Mann (eds), *Human Rights Learning. A People's Report* (*PDHRE*, 2006, 22) <www.pdhre.org/pdhre-report-2006.pdf> accessed 11 June 2016.

82. Baxi (2009b) 14.

83. See Upendra Baxi, *Human Rights in a Posthuman World* (Oxford University Press 2007).

84. Baxi (2007) 221.

85. Baxi (2007) 228.

86. Baxi draws on Michel Foucault: see Baxi (2009b) 66.

87. Baxi (2009b) 77.

88. A politics of human rights examines elements of power and the perpetuation of suffering. A politics for human rights looks at activism and the narratives of particular struggles. See Baxi, most notably 2009b.

89. Douzinas (2000). For a critique of Douzinas' view of human rights, see John Morss, 'Saving Human Rights from Its Friends: A Critique of the Imaginary Justice of Costas Douzinas' (2003) 27 (3) Melbourne University Law Review 889 <http://www.law.unimelb.edu.au/mulr/issues/previous-issues/2003-volume-27/2003-volume-27–3> accessed 13 March 2014.

90. Douzinas (2000) 353.

91. Douzinas (2000) 343.

92. Douzinas (2000) 352.

93. Douzinas (2000) 352.

94. Douzinas (2000) 348.

95. For a background discussion on the idea of human rights emerging from moral rights in human community, see Norberto Bobbio, *The Age of Rights* (Allan Cameron tr, Polity Press 1996).

96. Costas Douzinas, 'Seven Theses on Human Rights: (6) Desire' (*Critical Legal Thinking: Law and the Political*, 3 June 2013, para 17) <criticallegalthinking.com/2013/06/03/seven-theses-on-human-rights-6-desire/> accessed 11 June 2016.

97. Costas Douzinas, 'The End(s) of Human Rights' (2002) 26 (2) 445, 465 Melbourne University Law Review <www5.austlii.edu.au/au/journals/MelbULawRw/2002/23.html> accessed 11 June 2016.

98. Douzinas (2000) 349.

99. Douzinas (2000) 215.

100. Douzinas (2000) 216.

101. Douzinas (2002) 464.

102. Douzinas (2000) 465.

103. Douzinas (2002) 458.

104. Douzinas (2000) 215.

105. Douzinas (2000) 215.

106. Costas Douzinas and Ronnie Warrington, 'Antigone's Law: A Genealogy of Jurisprudence' in Costas Douzinas, Peter Goodrich and Yifat Hachamovitch (eds), *Politics, Postmodernity and Critical Legal Studies: The Legality of the Contingent* (Routledge 1994) 221.

107. Douzinas (2002).

108. Douzinas (2000) 185.

109. Douzinas (2000) 355.

110. Douzinas (2000) 355.

111. Simmons (2014) 226.

112. Simmons (2014) 5–6.

113. Simmons (2014) 10–11.

114. Simmons notes that other authors acknowledge this problem too, citing Badiou and Fraser. Simon Critchley can also be added to the list of scholars who discuss 'the ethical subject,' but who do so preferring to remove a theological dimension.

115. Levinas was very clear about the need to avoid locating divinity in the ethical relation: '[T]he passage from the other to divinity is a second step, and one must be careful to avoid stumbling by taking too large a step.' See Emmanuel Levinas, 'Ideology and Idealism' in Hand (1989a) 246.

116. Simmons (2014) 115.

117. Simmons (2014) 115.

118. Simon Critchley, *Infinitely Demanding: Ethics of Commitment, Politics of Resistance* (Verso 2012) 55.

119. Critchley (2012) 11.

120. Critchley (2012) 11.

121. Critchley (2012) 11.

122. Costas Douzinas identifies historical compassion in the humanitarian movement. See Costas Douzinas, 'The Many Faces of Humanitarianism' (2007) 2, 1 Parrheisa <parrhesiajournal.org/parrhesia02/parrhesia02_douzinas.pdf> accessed 11 June 2014.

123. Jean-Jacques Rousseau, *Discourse on Inequality* (1754) (G D H Cole tr) <https://www.aub.edu.lb/fas/cvsp/Documents/DiscourseonInequality.pdf879500092.pdf> accessed 11 June 2016.

124. Elisabeth Porter, 'Can Politics Practice Compassion' (2006) 21 (4) Hypatia, 97–123. See also Elisabeth Porter, *Peacebuilding: Women in International Perspective* (Oxon 2007) and Didier Fassin *Humanitarian Reason: A Moral History of the Present* (Rachel Gomme tr, University of California Press 2012).

125. Porter (2006) 99. For a theory of vulnerability as the grounds on which to explain and justify universal human rights, see Brian S Turner, *Vulnerability and Human Rights* (The Pennsylvania University Press 2006).

126. See, for example, Richard H Bell, *Simone Weil: The Way of Justice as Compassion* (Rowman & Littlefield Publishers 1998).

127. There is a body of human rights literature that examines ethics in human rights theory and promotes a sentimental education in human rights. The works of pragmatist Richard Rorty and Jose-Manuel Barreto may be of interest to some readers.

128. Porter (Oxon 2007) 101.

129. Lynn Hunt, *Inventing Human Rights* (Norton & Company 2007) 65.

130. Christine Sylvester, *Feminist International Relations: An Unfinished Journey* (Cambridge University Press 2002) 256.

131. Grace Clement, *Care Autonomy and Justice: Feminism and the Ethic of Care* (Westview Press 1996) 85.

132. Richard A Cohen, 'Foreword' in Emmanuel Levinas, *Otherwise than Being or Beyond Essence* (Alphonso Lingis tr, Duquesne University Press 1998/2011) xi.

133. Emmanuel Levinas, *Otherwise Than Being or Beyond Essence* (Alphonso Lingis tr, Duquesne University Press 1998/2011) 16.

134. For a well-regarded explanation of the dominant opposing narrative that centres on human reason and autonomous agency, see earlier, Griffin (2008/2013).

135. John Wild, 'Introduction' in Levinas, (1969/2000) 15.

136. David Clark, 'On Being the Last Kantian in Nazi Germany: Dwelling with Animals After Levinas's in Jennifer Ham and Matthew Senior (eds), *Animal Acts: Configuring the Human in Western History* (Routledge 1997) 168. Levinas's work insistently raises this fundamental question.

137. Deborah Bird Rose, *Wild Dog Dreaming: Love and Extinction* (University of Virginia Press 2011) 13.

Chapter Four

The Ethics of Alterity and Responsibility to Other Animals

INTRODUCTION

Despite Levinas's claims that the other is 'absolutely foreign,' 'refractory to every typology, to every genus, to every characterology, to every classification,' the face of the other is portrayed explicitly as that of man. Levinas confirms that 'it is only man who could be absolutely foreign to me.'[1] This suggests that nonhuman others are not in possession of the expressive face and that their exclusion from a system of protective rights grounded by the ethics of alterity could be justified.

This chapter examines how Levinas explains being in possession of face. It also explores other literature that analyses and comments on Levinas's philosophy, to explain how nonhuman animals are said to be in possession of Levinasian face, how they present their authenticity to human beings, elicit responsibility, and are, therefore, owed equal ethical duties.

The following section will give some background to existing literature in this area before examining in some detail Levinas's thoughts about nonhuman animals. The chapter will then discuss the work of other authors who have engaged with the debate on who, or what, can possess a face and, thus, elicit ethical duty.

BACKGROUND

A review of the literature on ethics of alterity and nonhuman animals shows that there is a fair amount of academic interest in the utility of Levinas's philosophy. Over the last few decades, academics working in the fields of philosophy, animal rights and environmental ethics have contributed to the development of discourse that revolves around different strands of Levinas's thinking. Questions raised include the nature of ethics; the moral status of anything other than human; who, or what, generates ethical responsibility; how Levinas's account of responsibility might influence environmental thought and politics; the importance of human language to his ethics; and his general notions of 'man' and 'nature.'

Scholars discuss the value of Levinas's work in an attempt to explain the conditions under which nonhuman animals can be declared moral subjects.[2] Within this specific body of literature, there is no critique of current human rights in terms of the vegan presentation of ethical duty to nonhuman others.

An apparent consensus among early scholars of Levinas is that, though the compulsion to welcome the unique, singular, vulnerable other in Levinas's ethics of alterity represents infinite responsibility, frees the subject from the domination of unethical totality, and provides the rupture necessary for humanity to move to its ethical destiny, it does not apply to nonhuman, unique, singular others. Though the 'face' is a living presence, it speaks and is already discourse, nonhuman others appear to be denied the expressive, ego-suspending presence that is the face of the other.[3] No infinite presence is seen to be expressed through an encounter with their being, and they cannot, thus, generate the ethical demand.

For Levinas, the face of the nonhuman animal is not a face 'whose exceptional presence is inscribed in the ethical impossibility of killing him. . . .'[4] Early scholars of Levinas, thus, concluded that he ascribed to nonhumans a status of 'things' that are brought into presence only by human beings.

A consequence of this early interpretation is that the application of Levinas's ethics of alterity is not relevant or helpful in the search for a paradigm shift to an ethical justice that necessarily needs to disrupt humanism and avoid dogmatic anthropocentrism.[5] Nevertheless, Peter Atterton believes that Levinas's philosophy is also considered 'one of the best equipped'[6] to oppose the entrenched, dismissed status of nonhuman animals. As such, it is possible that Levinas's philosophy can ground the case for moral inclusion and to articulate the undeniable, compassionate event that takes place in the presence of a suffering nonhuman other.[7]

In addition to literature assessing Levinas's original philosophy on ethical responsibility, there are two publications that stand out to scholars interested in the moral standing of nonhuman animals. One is a short essay which Levinas wrote in 1975, titled *The Name of a Dog, or Natural Rights*.[8] This essay concerns Levinas's reflections on his encounter with a war camp dog during his incarceration as a prisoner of war in Nazi Germany. The second, *The Paradox of Morality*, is a publicised transcript of an interview with Levinas that took place in 1986 at Warwick University in the UK.[9] In this interview,

Levinas is asked specifically whether nonhuman others are in possession of the obligatory face. It was a question to which Levinas could not respond with a categorical answer. These two publications reveal a tension in Levinas's original thesis on ethics that requires analysis and evaluation.

The next section will begin by outlining Levinas's explanation of the difference between unknowable human beings and knowable things, before moving on to examine these two significant publications.

THINGS DO NOT HAVE FACES

Levinas explains his rationale for the separation of man and things in *Totality and Infinity*.[10] Things can be known because they do not present the idea of infinity. What Levinas appears to suggest is that knowledge of things can be held in the conscience as absolute and finite. Things are given meaning to humanity only in the context of their construction and function. They are constructed as meaningful, but they do not produce an ethical demand. Things do not possess the required transformative power that ruptures the spontaneous will or autonomy of the individual. Levinas explains these relationships as ontological.[11]

The difference between being in a relationship with the other and being in a relationship with a thing is that the other cannot be reduced to understanding; the relationship with the other cannot be understood and is a pre-ontological relationship—one which Levinas refers to as the ethical event.[12] Levinas suggests that humans have transferred the meaning of suffering onto animals through the creation and event of human ethics but that they do not possess the power to create the ethical demand by suspending the autonomy of the subject.

This categorisation of other animals as things excludes nonhuman others from being in possession of face. Nonhuman animals are things which are brought into meaning in the current totality, but which essentially have no value in themselves. Prompted to discuss these circumstances in the interview of 1986, Levinas explains that the being of other animals is to struggle for survival in a Darwinian world without ethics. Levinas believes that animals function with total autonomy in the natural world because they have to survive: '[i]t is a question of might.'[13] In this negative world, '[a]n animal's need are inseparable from struggle and fear.'[14] There can, therefore, be no asymmetrical duty to others. The natural world is the enemy against which the self must exercise autonomous might for its own protection. The possession of face in their world could only disadvantage animals as they would be obliged to consider others before themselves. In the natural order, the self exists for itself, not for the other.

It is on this understanding of the natural world of animals and of the world of humans that Levinas explains the emergence of ethics and ethical human beings. Humans have created ethics in their break from animality through an encounter with the face of the other (human being). This elevates the subject beyond the simple being of species in nature. It is an event through which the human animal is released from the wild; it becomes ethical and capable of developing a dutiful, ethical humanity.

The acknowledgment of the face as 'exceptional presence,'[15] already discourse, the expression of the first word and the commandment 'thou shalt not kill'[16] is, thus, thought to be absent and, therefore, unable to generate ethical responsibility to nonhuman animals. Though discourse is the 'experience of something absolutely foreign,' Levinas insists that 'it is only man who could be absolutely foreign to me.'[17] In their fight for survival as mere biological beings, nonhuman animals are things because things 'exist for themselves.'[18]

The expressive power of the face (i.e., the subject's awareness of suffering or the potential to suffer) in Levinas's thesis is, thus, not apparent in relationships with other animals. Levinas maintains a strict, but inadequately explained, boundary between the autonomy of animals and the heteronomy of humans. This stance remains constant in Levinas's original and later writing but comes under intense scrutiny following his recollection of a personal encounter with a dog. In this encounter, Levinas appears to acknowledge responsibility through the affective presence of a nonhuman animal.

LEVINAS RESPONDS TO THE FACE OF THE NONHUMAN OTHER

Levinas's commitment to distinguishing between ethical responsibility to humans and to things in his original philosophy becomes intriguing in light of his later essay *The Name of a Dog, or Natural Rights.*[19] In this essay, Levinas recounts his experiences with a dog named Bobby, which occurred while he was interned by the Germans in a World War Two prisoner of war camp. This essay has generated significant interest and is widely discussed in available literature. Though it appears an ambiguous, unclear account of Levinas's intentions, it is claimed that the 'chief dividing line between the human and the animal threatens to vanish' in Levinas's own ethical discourse as a result.[20]

In this essay, Levinas is thinking about his experiences as a Jew in a Nazi-controlled war camp. His thinking combines the ideas of strong and weak species, the horrors of nature and the horrors of war. He sees 'devouring within species' as a sight which represents the 'horrors of war.' He comments that such barbarism of nature is represented by the 'plunge of your fork into your roast' to the extent that one may wish to limit 'the butchery that every day claims our mouths' and become vegetarian.[21] Levinas states that the purpose of this essay is to reflect on the dog, Bobby. For David L Clark[22] and John Llewelyn,[23] the combinations of Levinas's reflections may represent an 'analogy between the unspeakable human Holocaust and the unspoken animal one.'[24]

Clark argues that Levinas comes close to realising mutual oppression. He raises the possibility that Levinas brings into close proximity the suggestion of two forms of prejudice—one against the Jews and one against animals—and that Levinas may even identify that they 'are in some way comparable.'[25] At the same moment that Levinas considers prejudice, he reflects on his fond memories of Bobby, the stray war camp dog.

Levinas explains that he was a soldier in the French army, captured by the Germans in World War Two and working in a forest as a prisoner of war. He expresses his feelings when passers-by 'stripped us of our human skin. We were subhuman, a gang of apes.'[26] Levinas explains that the prisoners were 'thinking creatures,' but that they 'were no longer part of the world.' They were 'beings entrapped in their species; despite all their vocabulary, beings without language.' They wondered: '[h]ow can we deliver a message about our humanity which, from behind the bars of quotation marks, will come across as anything other than monkey talk?'[27] He then goes on to describe his encounter with Bobby. His description and choice of vocabulary give the reader the impression that he acknowledges the signification of the dog prior to the application of his autonomous reason:

> And then, about halfway through our long captivity, for a few short weeks, before the sentinels chased him away, a wandering dog entered our lives. One day he came to meet this rabble as we returned under guard from work. He survived in some wild patch in the region of the camp. But we called him Bobby, an exotic name, as one does with a cherished dog. He would appear at morning assembly and was waiting for us as we returned, jumping up and down and barking in delight. For him, there was no doubt that we were men.[28]

In this passage, Levinas remarks that the dog 'entered' the lives of the prisoners. That he 'survived,' wanted to 'meet' them, that they gave him a name and that he waited to greet them, expressing his joy. These elements of Levinas's reflections are held to be inconsistent with the idea that animals could be things that do not ask for (demand) a response.

Much attention has been given to Levinas's essay about Bobby. It is said to express the way Levinas felt about being degraded as less-than-human by the Nazis. Of relevance to critics is the way Levinas's thought is influenced by unacknowledged, traditional assumptions about the status of nonhuman life, and the lack of logic in his later thinking.

LEVINAS'S DENIAL OF A NONHUMAN FACE

Levinas's essay arguably represents anthropocentric dominance. The essay was a reflection written thirty years after the recalled event, and many years after Levinas's development of the ethics of alterity. Yet, Levinas insists on drawing an arbitrary distinction between himself and Bobby, despite acknowledging the unconditional, voluntary welcome of the nonhuman other and his personal extension of warmth, whereby he proceeds to respond to name 'a cherished dog.'[29]

Rather than consider his notion of survival, the possibility of mutual, intertwined oppression, or consider the ways in which Bobby may be expressing the presence that says 'it is me,'[30] Levinas, without further thought, displays a conventional, anthropocentric attitude in his dismissal of Bobby's welcome.

The dog's response to the prisoners was, for Levinas, evidence that the Jews were animalised and trapped as a 'species' in a particularly abhorrent ideology. Reduced to a perceived condition of animality by the German soldiers, Levinas looked to the dog for affirmation that he was a subject (a man) of the human community. The dog, through his greeting, did not distinguish between soldiers and prisoners; which, for Levinas, affirmed his status as a man. It was a greeting that reminded him that he was a member of the human race. Bobby displayed indifference in his welcome to indistinguishable human beings, despite the Nazi hierarchy of valid and invalid others.

What Levinas does not do is analyse the way in which the question 'to whom am I responsible' is raised in mutual oppressions. As Clark points out, '[t]he unstated analogy between the murder of Jews and the killing of animals in effect creates a rhetorical neighbourhood in which animals and humans dwell and summon each other into responsibility.'[31] Though Levinas denies Bobby a status of legitimate otherness, he, nonetheless, clearly responded to the expressive presence of the nonhuman other who communicated his authentic Being.

Clark provides a thorough, in-depth discussion and analysis of Levinas's short essay. He claims that 'Levinas's experience of Bobby is informed by conventional assumptions about animality that make it impossible for him straightforwardly to attribute dutifulness to a creature that is not human.' He urges that the dog is an 'enigma' for Levinas that presents an indeterminacy of ontological and moral status. As such, Bobby 'triggers Levinas's most dogmatic claims about nonhuman life and tests the limits of their coherence.'[32]

LEVINAS'S INCOMPLETE PHILOSOPHY

Clark, thus, maintains that Levinas's essay about Bobby essentially animalises animals: the essay is profoundly '[l]aden with animalistic rhetoric.'[33] In—perhaps inadvertent—traditional, anthropocentric, exceptionalist style, Levinas reconfigures the animal to configure the human. Clark also believes that if Bobby spoke for the other who is not in possession of face, then it would, in fact, also mean that Levinas regards other species as having transcendental power.[34] If metaphorical 'speaking' is possible, and Bobby, without face, expresses presence, then Levinas's ethics of alterity are incomplete and open to further development.[35]

In the interview at Warwick University in 1986, the integrity of Levinas's philosophy is directly challenged. When prompted to consider the possibility that nonhuman (as well as human) beings may express the ethics-inducing presence, Levinas himself alludes to the possibility that his philosophy is essentially incomplete. The question posed was: 'But is there something distinctive about the human face which, for example, sets it apart from that of an animal?' Levinas replies:

> One cannot entirely refuse the face of an animal. It is via the face that one understands, for example, a dog. Yet the priority here is not found in the animal, but in the human face. We understand the animal, the face of an animal, in accordance with *Dasein*. The phenomenon of the face is not in its purest form in the dog. In the dog, in the animal, there are other phenomena. For example, the force of nature is pure vitality. It is more this which characterizes the dog. But it also has a face.[36]

In response to another question about whether a nonhuman animal is the other who will be welcomed, Levinas replies:

> I cannot say at what moment you have the right to be called face. The human face is completely different and only afterwards do we discover the face of an animal. I don't know if a snake has a face. I can't answer that question. A more specific analysis is needed.[37]

Levinas's concept of face is, thus, regarded as ambiguous, unclear and confused. Despite representing a deeply committed approach to developing a philosophy of ethics for community that deals with suffering and vulnerability, scholars have identified inconsistencies in Levinas's logic. In this confusion, conclusions cannot be drawn on whether Levinas recognised that vulnerable, mortal, suffering, nonhuman others experienced an 'inner life'[38] that 'expresses itself'[39] in a demand for an ethical response.

Scholars, thus, conclude that Levinas's thesis is unfinished and incomplete because it did not adequately address whether the ethics inducing other can be nonhuman animal.

Levinas's restrictive ethics are, thus, controversial because it is clear, on an everyday common sense level, that people (generally) care for and limit, as far as possible, any potential harm to nonhuman others and (to some extent) the natural environment by deploying a pro-active, conscious effort to limit the spontaneous, unrestricted ego: as already noted in earlier chapters, the human community has legislated to protect other animals. As such, and accepting an element of Levinasian phenomenology,[40] the snake does indeed possess the obligatory face because it can be argued to generate the ethical responsibility required that limits the pursuits of the ego.

INCONSISTENCIES IN LEVINAS'S LOGIC

On a very general level, it can safely be assumed that a consensus view would be that the snake asks for a response and ought not to be harmed.[41] Further, the idea that a dog has some sort of 'secondary' face but that a more specific analysis is required to determine whether the snake has face would seem to indicate a, perhaps, inadvertent and unaddressed hierarchy of life forms and Being within Levinas's thought,[42] betraying the idea of a universal expressive 'presentation which consists in saying "It's me."'[43]

Peter Atterton emphasises the strength of evidence found in Levinas's work for the conclusion that the mere presence of the unique other is revealed through the silent representation of the face. In his view, Levinas's response to Bobby was thought and language that 'presupposes the originality of the face.'[44] This, precisely, he argues, is the instrumental foundation of Levinasian ethics. Responsibility for the other is at the level of revealed presence.[45] Atterton argues that:

> Levinas's own arguments concerning the otherness of the Other militates against interpreting ethics exclusively in terms of human interests and values, and, furthermore, that Levinas's phenomenology of the face applies to all beings that can suffer and are capable of expressing that suffering to me.

Consequently, where a nonhuman being's expression is affective, 'there is no justification for refusing to extend it moral consideration.'[46]

Given that Levinas's philosophy is written from a theological perspective and presents (what he believes to be) the destiny of humanity, it is perhaps unsurprising that he establishes human supremacy and hierarchy of Being through a fusion of ethics with his theological values. His notion of otherness, from this perspective, is very restrictive. It is not certain, however, that a theological account of ethics must necessarily adhere to an anthropocentric hierarchy or exclude nonhuman others. This is highlighted by Lucy Larkin's thinking on theology and otherness.

For Larkin, otherness is the context of relationships in a world where 'God, humanity and nature are inextricably intertwined and interconnected.'[47] Larkin argues that in the interconnected natural world, the face of the singular, unique other is a face representing God, and that such facing is not limited by human supremacy and hierarchy of being. When one faces nature, one faces God compassionately in a web of interconnected being. For Larkin, this theologically based facing requires nothing less than an acknowledgment that in God's world, nonhuman animals possess face.

Larkin, thus, rejects supremacy and hierarchy. In so doing, she develops the ethics of alterity in favour of a compassionate, ecotheological perspective that incudes other animals.

Levinas's partly theological humanism of the other, which explains the 'disruption of egoism, of a life that centres on the self,'[48] is frustrating in its inadequate explanation of why it is that nonhumans are not in possession of face. Peter Atterton remarks that Levinas fails to confirm the precise basis of whose face has priority, what constitutes a pure face and the characteristics of being in possession of face and that, consequently, Levinas's remarks do not constitute the last word on whether nonhuman beings are owed the same moral consideration as human beings.

Atterton goes on to argue that Levinas's theory is an insufficient basis upon which to withhold moral consideration from other beings, because compassion and consideration are secondary to the original encounter in which a subject acknowledges the presence of the others who seek a response. To apprehend, observe, encounter, to consider at all, or to extend a thought to a nonhuman surely means that the subject-hostage ethical encounter has already taken place. On this view, Atterton notes the limits of an ethics of alterity that is grounded by theological influences.

For Atterton, Levinas's hierarchy of Being and apparent difficulty in assigning a universal moral duty to all expressive life are a denial of the presence of face: it dilutes the ethical response the encounter requires. Thus, Levinas is accused of a form of anthropocentric, verbal violence against those (nonhumans) who reveal their living presence. On this point, Atterton insists that Levinas's ethics would be better developed in isolation from dogmatic, theological, anthropocentric theorising.[49] In the absence of this, Levinas's perspective can only result in the construction and maintenance of powerful, unethical, essentialist views, which Levinas already acknowledges as existing in the unethical totality of which he is critical. Derrida takes a similar view, claiming that in denying nonhuman others face, Levinas puts the animal 'outside the ethical circuit,'[50] which is surprising:

> coming from a thinking that is so 'obsessed' (I am purposefully using Levinas's word), so preoccupied by an obsession with the other and with his infinite alterity. If I am responsible for the other, and before the other, and in place of the other, on behalf of the other, isn't the animal more other still, more radically other, if I might put it that way, than the other in whom I recognize my brother, than the other in whom I identify my fellow or my neighbour? If I have a duty [*devoir*]—something owed before any debt, before any right—toward the other, wouldn't it then also be toward the animal, which is still more other than the other human, my brother or my neighbour?[51]

Perhaps in the context of Levinas's dire circumstances, it is unsurprising that, upon his encounter with Bobby, he may have wished to avoid theorising about the possibility of including ethical duty to nonhuman animals in his theory of (infinite) ethical responsibility.[52] To have done this, and potentially acknowledge the limitations of his own thesis, might have revealed an unwelcome and uncomfortable comparison with Nazi ideology: tying a knot in the Möbius strip[53] of life is the 'greatest force of history and the inspiration for systematic violence.'[54] Nevertheless, the commandment 'thou shalt not kill' can be interpreted as 'thou shall not put to death or thou shalt not take the life from one who lives and breathes.' If Levinas's ethics take their impetus from such a commandment, then, surely, as Donna Haraway remarks, '[t]hou shalt not make killable'[55] is a reinterpretation fundamental to the debate of who possesses face and ethical responsibility. As such, responsibility must be considered in a much broader appreciation of the way a living being expresses its presence than Levinas allows. An important critic of Levinas, in this regard, is deconstructionist, Jacques Derrida.

DERRIDA'S RESPONSE TO THE STATUS OF ANIMALS IN LEVINAS'S ETHICS OF ALTERITY

Jacques Derrida's deconstruction of Levinas's early works drew scholarly interest in Levinas's ethics of alterity and inspired much interdisciplinary scholarship on 'the question of the animal.'[56] Derrida is responsible for a comprehensive interrogation of Levinas's work, including assessing the implications of his philosophy for nonhuman others. In his critique, Derrida insists that Levinas's philosophy of the other is fundamentally flawed because it does not take into account the concrete suffering of a vulnerable, nonhuman other. Following an analysis of Levinas's famous essay about Bobby, Derrida responds with a scathing attack on Levinas for retaining a Cartesian[57] tradition and incorporating this into his ethics of alterity, in which difference is paramount and signified.[58] He is dumbfounded by Levinas's attempt to ascribe to the dog a status as nothing more than *a something,* capable of imitating a signifier but with nothing to signify. For Derrida, the dog clearly expressed the required presence, in order for it to address a respondent, by saying: 'Here I am, it is me, a precarious being in my world.' Derrida asks:

> If I am responsible for the other, and before the other, and in place of the other, on behalf of the other, isn't the animal other more other still, more radically other, if I might put it that way, than the other in whom I recognize my brother, than the other in whom I identify my fellow or my neighbour?[59]

Derrida concludes that Levinas's philosophy is insufficient for an ethics of the wholly different, unique other because it is not a philosophy that advocates 'thou shalt not kill' in general, but a philosophy that retains the value for not killing specifically human beings only. Derrida accuses Levinas of failing to observe the overwhelming evidence that nonhuman animals have an affective, disruptive force on human autonomy. Derrida sees the disruptive force as clear and obvious: the animal presents an enigma[60] that motivates humans to question what it means 'to be.'

For Derrida, the fact of the enduring concern with other animals is evidence of the call of the expressive authentic nonhuman other and there is violence in an ethics of alterity that fails to observe this. Violence is, of course, in the very idea and naming of the heterogeneous group known as 'animal,' and Derrida's thoughts point to the oppressive themes and categories of a dysfunctional ideology, such as the totality of reason.

Derrida, thus, raises questions about the construction of 'the animal' in Levinas's philosophy. He comments on the false homogenisation of groups and the disservice done to those excluded. He maintains that throughout history, nonhuman animals have been subjected to various negative, violent narratives. He takes it for granted that this is clear: 'no one can today deny this event—that is, the *unprecedented* proportions of this subjection of the animal.'[61] This subjugation of nonhuman animals, he argues, is representative of other false ontologies, which function as negative, exclusionary narratives in the history of humanism. Arguing that the humanist tradition relies and depends on multiple sacrifices, he thus observes that Levinas continues a tradition of profound humanism by failing to 'sacrifice sacrifice.'[62] Derrida describes the society of humanism as logocentric, phallocentric, and, importantly, carno-phallogocentric:[63] an ideology in which carnivorous virility is falsely assumed to be intrinsic to human identity,[64] the violence of which is dissimulated and made invisible by strategic mechanisms of humanity's disavowal. Regarding the construction of the subject, he argues:

> Authority and autonomy . . . are, through this schema, attributed to the man (*homo and vir*) rather than the woman, and to the woman rather than to the animal. And of course to the adult rather than to the child. The virile strength of the adult male, the father husband, or brother . . . belongs to the schema that dominates the concept of subject. The subject does not want just to master and possess nature actively. In our cultures, he accepts sacrifice and eats flesh. I ask you who would stand any chance of becoming a *chef d'Etat* (a head of State) . . . declaring him- or herself to be a vegetarian?[65]

DERRIDA: THE FACE AND SUFFERING

Derrida's perspective highlights and addresses a limitation in Levinas's thinking, which lead to his apparent uncertainty about whether a snake has face.[66] Derrida fervently believes that the suffering of nonhuman animals is a disruptive, ego-limiting and compassion-generating event that is currently denied but cannot be contested:

> Everybody knows what terrifying and intolerable pictures a realist painting could give to the industrial, mechanical, chemical, hormonal, and genetic violence to which man has been submitting animal life for the past two centuries. Everybody knows what the production, breeding, transport, and slaughter of these animals has become. Instead of thrusting these images in your faces or awakening them in your memory, something that would be both too easy and endless, let me simply say a word about this 'pathos.' If these images are "pathetic," if they evoke sympathy, it is also because they "pathetically" open the immense question of pathos and the pathological, precisely, that is, of suffering, pity, and compassion; and the place that has to be accorded to the interpretation of this compassion, to the sharing of this suffering among the living, to the law, ethics, and politics that must be brought to bear upon this experience of compassion.[67]

It is at the level of compassion in the face of innate and universal suffering that Derrida believes nonhuman animals should be considered in any discourse which claims to advocate for the unique, wholly different other. In this regard, Derrida refers to the words of Jeremy Bentham to propose a protocol.[68] Bentham had objected to the way a developing ontology of rights discourse excluded nonhuman animals in its emphasis on subjects being in possession of language and reason: archaic ideas, Derrida notes, 'from Aristotle to Heidegger, from Descartes to Kant, Levinas, and Lacan.'[69] For Derrida, '[t]he *first* and *decisive* question would rather be to know whether animals *can suffer*.'[70] This question concerns the real elements of, firstly, identity; secondly, powerlessness; and thirdly, mortality: identity, as in being constituted by precarious vulnerability; powerlessness to avoid such vulnerability; and suffering and mortality as that which 'belongs to the very finitude of life, to the experience of compassion, to the possibility of sharing the possibility of the nonpower . . . the anguish of this vulnerability, and the vulnerability of this anguish.' In this question, we put our trust not in Levinas's face, but in 'what is undeniable.'[71] Derrida explains:

> No one can deny suffering, fear, or panic, the terror or fright that can seize certain animals and that we humans can witness. . . . Some will try . . . to contest the right to call that *suffering* or *anguish*, words or concepts that would still have to be reserved for man. . . . 'Can they suffer?' leaves no room for doubt. In fact, it has never left any room for doubt; that is why the experience that we have of it is not even indubitable; it precedes the indubitable, it is older that it. No doubt either then, of there being within us the possibility of giving vent to a surge of compassion.[72]

For Derrida, the response is undeniable: 'yes they suffer, like us who suffer for them and with them,' and this response precedes all other questions.[73] It is a question of sentiment and compassion, not pity. It is a question concerning human responsibility, obligation, necessity, and constraint, from which there is no escape. Nonhuman animals express their Being and reveal their unique otherness and, with it, their inner world: 'The animal looks at us, and we are naked before it. Thinking perhaps begins there.'[74]

NONHUMAN SIGNIFICATION AND VALUE

Derrida observes that 'animals' have inner worlds: they look at us. They are present and significant to us on account of their presence, they signify their authenticity and we are sensitive to their suffering. In Derrida's deconstruction, the legitimate, authentic other in possession of face certainly includes nonhuman animals but would ultimately be ahuman[75] following a process of comprehensive, anti-anthropocentric deconstruction of the influences leading to categorical distinctions between beings of the world.[76] Implicitly supportive to this extent, but also very critical of Levinas's thesis, Derrida grounds the affective, disruptive force of nonhuman others in their undisputed ability to signify their authenticity. If ethics emerge in a human to human 'compassionate response to the vulnerable suffering other,'[77] awareness of the authenticity and signification of nonhuman others has equal transcendental power. As such, Derrida observes and argues for the universality of cross-species vulnerability to which human beings are sensitive. Derrida, thus, concurs with other pro-animal scholars: nonhuman animals should not be denied the 'face' that generates ethical responsibility. If the other expresses their authenticity and presence through a signifying saying that requires a response before the said product of reason, then ethical encounters also concern nonhuman others.

Levinas clearly explains the 'saying' and the 'said.'[78] The 'saying' is the primary expression of the other revealed through an encounter. It is through '[t]he face, pre-eminently expression'[79] that presence is passed to the recipient. Spoken language in that moment is subsequent to and in the service of ethical responsibility. Levinas states: 'Saying opens me to the other, before saying something said, before the said that is spoken in this sincerity forms a screen between me and the other. It is a saying without words . . . silence speaks.'[80] This does not mean that the ethics of alterity begin in an event of apparent suffering. They begin when the unique other signifies their authentic presence to the subject. In this encounter, the subject is aware of precarious mortality and is created ethically responsible to the welfare of the other. Whether the other is actually suffering at that moment is irrelevant to obligatory, ethical responsibility.

The early consensus view, that Levinas's original ethics of alterity cannot accommodate nonhuman animals, has, thus, both inspired and provoked a range of responses.[81] For some scholars, nonhuman others are authentic, based on a literal, analytical, or deductive interpretation of Levinas. For others, such as Derrida, nonhuman animals are authentic others but on different, but similar grounds—in Derrida's case, because it is undeniable that nonhumans signify themselves in the context of universally shared understanding of vulnerability and mortality.

The presentation of the 'face' in the ethics of alterity is, thus, problematic. The responses to Levinas, outlined above, offer support for the face of the nonhuman animal to feature in the ethics of alterity to prevent them from being denied ethical duties. Diane Perpich comments on the problem of ascribing 'face,' noting that in Levinas's frustrating and difficult texts there seems to be 'neither an assurance that animals have a face nor the conviction that they do not.'[82] Perpich suggests a new way to think about responsibility to animals by moving away from thinking about the face itself as representing value. She puts forward the idea that 'the ethical mode in which the other faces me opens the possibility of valuing without itself existing as a value. Whatever does this work, I will suggest, can be or have a face.'[83] Perpich seems to be saying that whatever is individually valued can be said to possess the face.

RESPONSIBILITY TO SUFFERING: AN ALTERNATIVE VIEW

By removing intrinsic ethical value from the problematic face, Diane Perpich appears to see ethics generated from ethical openings in the social realm. She argues that 'it is simply not the case that without an animal face we will have no responsibility to or for animals.'[84] Suggesting that both consensus and positive Levinas scholars share a common misconception regarding Levinas's thinking, Perpich proposes that questions about animals, in Levinas's philosophy, are essentially questions about what humans value and how such valuing is socially negotiated.[85]

What Perpich means is that in prioritising the human face, Levinas is not suggesting that the ethical does not extend to anything else. In fact, she observes that in the interview with the Warwick University students, Levinas states that 'the ethical extends to all living beings,'[86] and that not wanting to make animals suffer is the 'prototype'[87] of human ethics. She also suggests that in stating that '[v]egetarianism, for example, arises from the transference to animals of the idea of suffering,'[88] Levinas does not intend to subjugate nonhuman others. Rather, Levinas is merely indicating that since it is humans who are subject to the miraculous break with animality, it is they who create the conditions in which ethics exist and they who subsequently create the categories. In the face-to-face encounter that ruptures pure Being (Perpich indicates that this can be anything that opens the subject to valuing), ethics then flow through the discursive negotiations intrinsic to the social and political community of humanity.[89]

This open discourse does seem important to the evolution of ethical humanity in Levinas's philosophy. Levinas speaks of the importance of accommodating difference, the individuality intrinsic to human Being, and the need to confront subjective certainty by listening to the views of the other. It seems to be this democratic, socially negotiated valuing aspect of Levinas's philosophy that appeals to Perpich. Levinas states:

> The dawn of truth comes up, and the first gesture of universalization is made, when I become aware of the coherent discourses that are different from mine and stand alongside my own, and when I search for a common language. . . . To respect the other is, before all else, to refer to the other's opinions.[90]

What Levinas is suggesting is that from one-to-one communication to the multitude and plurality of social communications, a careful listening is required to negotiate and accommodate individual valuing that leads to consensus. Though each individual may have singular valuing, universal values will evolve. On this view, what is subjectively valued will be registered through democratic discourse and socially negotiated in community.

On this understanding of Perpich's reading of Levinas, outlined previously, ethics arise in the social world because it is individuals who make value. An entity may be intrinsically valueless apart from in the way they are constructed by human beings. Entities are, nonetheless, valued and this value is presented to the social order of society. The valued entity is, thus, registered and becomes a negotiated, ethical principle of humanity. In this way, the human appears as a priority because it is the only way through which humanity can justify and argue respective ethical positions. In Perpich's reading of Levinas, though the human face necessarily takes priority as a vehicle for ethical discourse, it is certainly not the *form* of the ethical address. The form of the affective address is categorically the affective address that halts the spontaneous drive and brings the ego into question through its capacity to open valuing in the subject.

Levinas's argument is that humanity is essentially compassionate and responds to frailty, vulnerability, and suffering. This, he points out, is evident in the face-to-face encounter and is the source of ethics. On Perpich's thesis, ethics are a result of human communication but remain subsequent to an influencing, a priori affective moment with what can be described as possessing the face.

Levinas maintains that careful listening to ethical openings is the 'dawn of truth . . . and the first gesture of universalization.' In this regard, the human response to nonhuman others has long been an ethical matter of collective conscience in community and is a social truth that is not (or is no longer) a matter of personal subjectivity or private conscience.

From the above accounts of how ethics emerge, whether in the face-to-face encounter or from social negotiation, it is clear that nonhuman animals express their authentic being and have long been incorporated into the socio-political system of humankind. As such, they have constituted the affective ethical address and have subsequently been submitted to social negotiation as ethically valued entities. This is arguably a relevant point to consider in the rights claims being made by vegans because, as I have suggested, the legal claims of vegans re-present the vulnerable, acknowledged, and valued other.

CONCLUSION

This chapter set out to establish whether the ethics of alterity concern nonhuman animals to ascertain whether a philosophy of otherness could ground a system of inclusive reoriented protective rights. Judith Butler aptly expresses the form of responsibility that would ground the proposed inclusive suffering narrative of rights: '[t]o respond to the face, to understand its meaning, means to be awake to what is precarious in another life or, rather, the precariousness of life itself.'[91]

Through his own recollections of his encounter with the dog, 'Bobby,' it is clear that Levinas found himself responding to animals in a way that did not denigrate them as mere 'things.' This is observed by David Clark, who argues that the dog Levinas named Bobby signified his authentic presence, and that Levinas responded to this. Peter Atterton also argues that Levinas's response to Bobby was thought and language that presuppose the originality of the face.

In addition, Levinas himself stated that further analysis around the presence of face was required. Philosophers working in the domain of animal ethics have engaged with the need for further analysis, recognised the value of Levinas's philosophy for the moral standing of nonhuman animals and highlighted certain limitations in Levinas's philosophy. Peter Atterton notes that Levinas's ideas are limited by religious and anthropocentric dogma, and others argue for the authentic signification of nonhumans, emphasising that they are also unique, singular others who express the required precarious mortality that Levinas maintains is universally shared and understood.

If, as Levinas maintains, ethical responsibility arises in the non-abstract ethical encounter, then, based on an examination of existing literature in animal ethics, it cannot be concluded that only precariously mortal humans are capable of demanding an ethical response. Derrida argues, quite strongly, that the indisputable nature of the human concern with nonhumans is precisely because humans conceive of their real Being and suffering. Noting the historical concern with animal suffering, this fact, he observes, is indisputable evidence of the authentic signification of animals, to which humans respond.

Diane Perpich suggests that philosophy does not need to establish whether nonhuman others are in possession of the obligatory face as a precondition to the production of ethics. On her reading of Levinas, Perpich puts forward the view that the obligation to the face itself does not have to be proven to be the source of ethics. Ethics, she suggests, may be a human construct resulting from the function of the face, which is to create multiple ethical openings that are then negotiated in a democracy. If the face cannot be categorically identified in the signification of nonhuman animals, it does not mean that humans have no obligation to treat animals ethically. Referring to the face as functioning to open the possibility of valuing, Perpich suggests that what is ethical is socially negotiated following a priori ethical openings that create value in the other entity.

On this account, the ethical duty owed to animals does not depend on a categorical affirmation that ethics emerge in the presence of the face, or that nonhuman others are in possession of a specifically Levinasian face. It merely depends on whether ethical opening to the predicament of nonhumans has achieved a widespread accepted value in democracy. Clearly, the idea that animals matter has normative value: there is undisputed acknowledgment that other sentient beings are intertwined with human society, it is empirically evident that humans recognise the authenticity and signification of nonhuman animals and have come to value and express the social good of extending ethical duty, care and compassion to them.

Existing literature on the ethics of alterity is inconclusive on the matter of whether nonhuman animals are in possession of a specifically Levinasian face, but establishing this fact, as Perpich suggests, is unnecessary to evidence the affectivity of nonhuman others. It is clear that nonhuman others express their presence, have elicited a response, and are, therefore, entitled to be included in a suffering narrative of protective rights and an extended system of justice, in which they are protected on account that their precarious lives and suffering matter in the extended community of legitimate others. This chapter, therefore, concludes that the logic of otherness, formative to Levinas's philosophy, can be applied equally to humans and nonhuman animals as the basis for establishing an extended inclusive community, in which ethical duty to others is the foundation of justice.

If, as argued, nonhuman animals are entitled to benefit in a suffering narrative of rights, an inclusive rights framework will acknowledge the primary duty of 'otherness' and abandon the concept of primacy of the self-legislating, autonomous individual in favour of duty based obligations. This clearly has implications for human exploitation of other animals as natural resources. In such a framework, ethical duties owed to nonhuman animals entitle them to specific rights that support the wider mission of bringing about a paradigm shift in anti-oppressive social relations.

The ramifications of establishing an inclusive suffering narrative of rights for animal others in community are enormous. Levinas argued that the entity that signifies its authenticity transcends the totality that is the orthodoxy of autonomy and *all* its categories. This necessarily requires us to honestly examine all aspects of animal oppression and explain how they function to create the social conditions in which prejudice against them flourishes. From there, it is possible to suggest measures for their protection that honour the ethical duty. These measures necessarily need to abolish the oppressive conditions currently at work in the orthodoxy of autonomy and give expression to the moral and legal standing of animal others.

This conclusion has profound implications for the idea and practice of exclusive human rights—and for litigation in claims that present ethical responsibility to nonhuman others. The following chapter considers the ramifications of the conclusion that the ethics of alterity, as utilised in the suffering narrative of protective rights, accommodates both human and nonhuman others. It assesses the implications of including the moral standing of nonhuman animals in a protective rights enterprise and explains the positive impact it has on claims presented by vegans.

NOTES

1. Levinas (1969/2000) 73. As stated previously, historical references to the male gender represent unconscious bias and are an issue for the totality referenced in the ethics of alterity but are out of scope in the present discussion.

2. David Wood argues that Levinas's philosophy is a powerful and refreshing development in ethical subjectivity. It comes to the 'scene as rain to the cracked earth of a parched landscape.' David Wood, 'Introduction' in R Bernasconi and D Wood (eds), *The Provocation of Levinas: Rethinking the Other* (Routledge 2014/1988).
3. David Wood questions Levinas's retention of anthropocentric tendencies in posthuman philosophy: David Wood, 'Comment ne pas manger—Deconstruction and Humanism' in H Peter Steeves (ed), *Animal Others: On Ethics, Ontology and Animal Life* (State University of New York Press 1999). Derrida questions Levinas's retention of humanism by excluding animals: Jacques Derrida, '"Eating well," or the calculation of the subject: An interview with Jacques Derrida' in E Cadava, P Connor and J-L Nancy (eds), *Who Comes After the Subject* (Routledge 1991). Llewelyn examines the significance of human language for ethical subjectivity: John Llewelyn, 'Am I Obsessed By Bobby? (Humanism of the Other Animal)' in Robert Bernasconi and Simon Critchley (eds), *Re-reading Levinas* (Indiana University Press 1991). Edward Casey and Alphonso Lingis examine the face in relation to the environment in the context of moral imperative and 'practical necessity': Edward Casey, 'Taking a Glance at the Environing World' in D J Martino (ed), *Confluences: Phenomenology and Postmodernity, Environment, Race, Gender* (Duquesne University Silverman Phenomenology Centre 2000) and Alphonso Lingis, 'Practical Necessity' (1998) 20/21(2/1) Graduate Faculty Philosophy Journal 3.

3. Levinas (1969/2000) 66.

4. Levinas (1969/2000) 87.

5. Calarco (2008) insists that philosophy today is faced by the animal and that non-anthropocentric philosophy is the way forward.

6. Peter Atterton, 'Levinas and our Moral Responsibility to Other Animals' (2011) 54(6) Inquiry 633.

7. Jacques Derrida claims that it is undeniable that a suffering nonhuman generates an ethical demand: Jacques Derrida, *The Animal That Therefore I Am* (David Wills tr, Marie Louise Mallet ed, Fordham University Press 2008) 28.

8. Levinas (1963/1990) 151.

9. Wright, Hughes and Ainley (1988).

10. Levinas (1969/2000) 74.

11. Emmanuel Levinas, 'Is ontology fundamental?' in Adriaan Theodoor Peperzak, Simon Critchley and Robert Bernasconi (eds), *Emmanuel Levinas: Basic Philosophical Writings* (Peter Atterton tr, Indiana University Press 1951/1996) 10.

12. Levinas defines this relationship in theological terms: 'A relationship of prayer which can be termed religion.' Levinas (1951) 8.

13. Wright, Hughes and Ainley (1988) 172.

14. Levinas (1969/2000) 116.

15. Levinas (1969/2000) 87.

16. Emmanuel Levinas, *Ethics and Infinity: Conversations with Philippe Nemo* (Richard A Cohen tr, Duquesne University Press (1985) 89.

17. Levinas (1969/2000) 73.

18. Levinas (1969/2000) 74.

19. Emmanuel Levinas, *Difficult Freedom: Essays on Judaism* (The John Hopkins University Press 1990).

20. Calarco (2008) 57.

21. Levinas (1990) 151.

22. David Clark, 'On Being the Last Kantian in Nazi Germany: Dwelling with Animals After Levinas's (1999) in Ham J and Senior M (eds), *Animal Acts: Configuring the Human in Western History* (Routledge 1997).

23. John Llewelyn, 'Am I Obsessed By Bobby? (Humanism of the Other Animal)' in Robert Bernasconi and Simon Critchley (eds), *Re-reading Levinas* (Indiana University Press 1991).

24. Llewelyn (1991) 235.

25. Clark (1997) 45.

26. Levinas (1990) 153.

27. Levinas (1990) 153.

28. Levinas (1990) 153.

29. Levinas (1990) 153.

30. For an extended discussion about the meaning of 'the saying' 'here I am' or 'it is me,' see Emmanuel Levinas, *Otherwise Than Being or Beyond Essence* (Alphonso Lingis trs, Duquesne University Press 1998/2011). For a specific analysis of language and the question of whether the ethics of alterity concern animals, see Atterton (2011).

31. Clark (1997) 54.

32. Clark (1997) 1.

33. Clark (1997) 42.

34. Bobby can be observed to suspend the autonomy of Levinas.

35. Ralph Acampora is in agreement with Clark's assessment that Levinas's ambivalent anthropocentrism requires the development of ethics that goes 'past Levinas to pursue the neighbourly status of nonhuman animals to broaden our corporal attention (beyond the face as such)—so as to become aware of *whole-body* encounters and their ethical significance.' Ralph R Acampora, *Corporal Compassion: Animal Ethics and Philosophy of Body* (University of Pittsburgh Press 2006) 88.

36. Wright, Hughes and Ainley (1988) 169. In this response, Levinas uses Heidegger's term *Daesin* to mean simply Being. Levinas's ethics of alterity are a recognition of a break with this natural Being.

37. Wright, Hughes and Ainley (1988) 172.

38. Levinas (1969/2000): the inner life is indispensable to Being (240) in the separation of the Same (54).

39. Levinas (1969/2000) 51.

40. I use the term loosely, recognising that the welcome of the face cannot be understood in the traditional sense of phenomenology as a philosophical method: John Wild (2000).

41. Animal rights activist and philosopher Brian Luke believes that it is innate to human Being to care for nonhuman animals. It is 'the normal state of humans generally.' See Brian Luke, 'Justice, Caring, and Animal Liberation' in Josephine Donovan and Carol Adams (eds), *The Feminist Care Tradition in Animal Ethics* (Continuum Press 1996) Chapter 5, 86. Similarly, Gary Francione argues that no one thinks of animals as things: Gary Francione, 'Animal Welfare and the Moral Value of Nonhuman Animals' in E Anderson, A Bjork, K Jennbert and A-S Lonngren (eds), *Exploring the Animal Turn: Human-Animal Relations in Science, Society and Culture* (Pufendorf Institute: Lund 2014).

42. Calarco also discusses this briefly: Matthew Calarco 'Deconstruction is Not Vegetarianism: Humanism, Subjectivity, and Animal Ethics' (2004) 37 Continental Philosophy Review 175.

43. Levinas (1969/2000) 296. David Wood is also critical of Levinas for developing a philosophy of absolute singularity, yet judging nonhumans by human standards when it comes to representing Being. See David Wood, 'Comment ne pas manger—Deconstruction and Humanism' in H Peter Steeves (ed), *Animal Others: On Ethics, Ontology and Animal Life* (State University of New York Press 1999) 19.

44. Peter Atterton, 'The Talking Cure: The Ethics of Psychoanalysis' in Peter Atterton and Matthew Calarco (eds), *Radicalizing Levinas* (State University of New York Press 2010) 188, (quoting Levinas [1969/2000] 202).

45. For a similar discussion on this issue, see also B Plant, Welcoming Dogs: Levinas and the Animal Question (2011) 27(1) Philosophy and Social Criticism 49.

46. Atterton (2011) 633.

47. Lucy Larkin, 'Turning face-to-face with Limobius Mixtus' (2002) 7(1) Journal for the Study of Religion Nature and Culture, Ecotheology 30, 31.

48. William Edelglass, James Hatley and Christian Diehm (eds), *Facing Nature: Levinas and Environmental Thought* (Duquesne University Press 2012) 5.

49. Atterton (2011).

50. Derrida (2008) 106.

51. Derrida (2008) 107.

52. Levinas was a prisoner of war because he was a Jew. Members of his family were killed by the Nazis.

53. The Möbius strip was discovered by German mathematicians and is an infinite, non-orientable surface.

54. Historian and friend of Costas Douzinas, Joanna Bourke discusses this in the context of what it means to be human. She is in favour of nonhuman animals being 'persons,' of the singularity of Being, and of the unknowability of another's Being. Joanna Bourke, *What It Means to Be Human: Reflections From 1791 to the Present* (Virago Press 2011) 378.

55. Donna Haraway explores 'knowing' and 'Being.' She believes it to be wrong to separate the 'world's beings into those who may be killed and those who may not': Donna Haraway, *When Species Meet* (University of Minnesota Press 2008) 80.

56. Calarco, Atterton, Bernasconi and Wood all credit Derrida as the first influential figure in drawing attention to the work of Levinas. See Peter Atterton and Matthew Calarco, 'Editors Introduction: The Third Wave of Levinas Scholarship' in Peter Atterton and Matthew Calarco (eds), *Radicalizing Levinas* (State University of New York Press 2010); and David Wood, 'Introduction' in Robert Bernasconi and David Wood (2014/1998).

57. Descartes is famous for insisting that nonhumans felt no pain. He famously used thousands of dogs in live dissections to prove they had no nervous system but then used a similar number to disprove his theory. That animals have awareness of pain and suffering is commonly accepted and, in addition to other cognitive experiences, is declared highly significant to their Being by the 2012 Cambridge Declaration on consciousness <http://fcmconference.org/img/CambridgeDeclarationOnConsciousness.pdf> accessed 27 July 2016.

58. Derrida (2008) 117.

59. Derrida (2008) 107.

60. Derrida (2008) discusses the effect of being subject to the glare of a cat. He asks: 'What is the living character of Being?' (155).

61. Derrida (2008) 25.

62. Jacques Derrida, 'Eating well,' or the calculation of the subject: An interview with Jacques Derrida' in E Cadava, P Connor, J-L Nancy (eds), *Who Comes After the Subject* (Routledge 1991) 113.

63. Derrida (1991) 113.

64. Much scholarly work is available on veg*ism in relation the domain of sociology of food and eating.

65. Derrida (1991) 114.

66. Derrida (2008) 109.

67. Derrida (2008) 26.

68. Llewelyn (1991) also favours Bentham's proposal.

69. Derrida (2008) 27.

70. Derrida (2008) 27.

71. Derrida (2008) 28.

72. Derrida (2008) 28.

73. Derrida (2008) 28.

74. Derrida (2008) 29.

75. Derrida (2008) 132. Ahuman theory takes an abolitionist stance against using the word 'animal' or promoting the idea of 'nonhumans.' An overview of research in this area can be found at Suzanne Becker, 'Patricia MacCormack Talks About Ahuman Theory, Importance of Non-Speciecist Ways' (*Daily Nexus*, 6 November 2013) <http://dailynexus.com/2013–11–06/patricia-maccormack-talks-about-ahuman-theory-importance-of-non-speciecist-ways/> accessed 24 October 2019.

76. Agamben advocates a jamming of the anthropological machine to reorient humanity on a more ethical path. Gorgio Agamben, *The Open Man and Animal* (Kevin Attell tr, Stanford University Press 2004).

77. William Edelglass, 'Levinas on Suffering and Compassion' (2006) 45(2) Sophia 43.

78. This clarity was given by Levinas in *Otherwise than Being,* after his seminal ideas of the other were developed in *Totality and Infinity*: 'my exposure without reserve to the other, which is saying' 168.

79. Levinas (1969/2000) 178.

80. Emmanuel Levinas, *Of God Who Comes to Mind* (Bertina Bergo tr, Stanford University Press 1986/1998) 74.

81. All of these examine Levinas in terms of the face producing ethics where there is 'cause and effect.' See Casey (2000) and Alphonso Lingis, 'Practical necessity' (1998) 20/21(2/1) Graduate Faculty Philosophy Journal 3.

82. Diane Perpich, *The Ethics of Emmanuel Levinas* (Stanford University Press 2008) 151.

83. Perpich (2008) 152.

84. Perpich (2008) 160.

85. Perpich makes a distinction between ethics and politics in Levinas's work. I am using the idea of politics as 'social' in this instance, because Perpich distinguishes between ethics and politics insomuch as humans are social political animals that have ethical ideas. Distinguishing ethics and politics in this specific way leaves aside developments in politics as a discipline. For example, Bunch discusses the characteristics of Levinas's political realm in the context of Foucauldian ideas about biopolitics and developments made by Agamben. Both scholars argue that human subjectivity is violated by powerful biopolitics. Mary Bunch takes this idea and applies it to the posthuman call for an ethics to challenge biopolitics and to Levinas's ethics of alterity. She does this through a discussion of Bobby and of Levinas's statement about Bobby being 'Kantian.' She argues that if Bobby was the only ethical being in Levinas's world, then bare being is related to the ethics of alterity and subsequently to a posthumanist ethics that can challenge biopolitical power. The area of biopolitics is important in studies concerning the animal question, but it is broad in scope and would detract from the present discussion. See Mary Bunch, 'Posthuman Ethics and the Becoming Animal of Emmanuel Levinas's (2014) 55(1) Culture, Theory and Critique 34.

86. Wright, Hughes and Ainley (1988) 172.

87. Wright, Hughes and Ainley (1988) 172.

88. Wright, Hughes and Ainley (1988) 172.

89. As discussed previously, Levinas is aware that the infinity of responsibility via the entry of the third person requires adjudication. Justice is born from the necessary political sphere. See Levinas (1998).

90. Levinas, 'Exclusive Rights' (1990) in *Difficult Freedom* 239: Following the initial ethical moment, communication is used to advance helpful relationships.

91. Judith Butler. Butler is well aware of the problem of transference: 'It has to be an understanding of the precariousness of the other.' She takes up the notion of affective presence as an 'undoing' of the subject. Judith Butler (2004a) 134 and Judith Butler, *Undoing Gender* (Routledge 2004b).

Chapter Five

The Implications of Including Nonhuman Animals in an Ethics of Alterity for Protective Rights

Animal Rights, 'Remorseful Justice,' and Vegan Litigation

INTRODUCTION

If, as concluded in the previous chapter, the ethics of alterity can be applied to nonhuman animals, then we must acknowledge the inclusive reach of the suffering narrative of human rights and the issues presented by the protest scholars in their call for a rejection of the orthodoxy of autonomy of human rights. If rights seek to ameliorate suffering, then the first right, which is the right of the other to be free from arbitrary power and exploitation, applies to human and nonhuman animals equally, and human society should legislate to entrench compassionate duty to all living beings who are subject to the forces of mortality and vulnerable to oppression, and protect those who seek to live with respect for other animals.

In this a reorientation of human rights, it is imperative to acknowledge the vulnerability in precarious mortality and that additional, imposed suffering is unethical and unjust. Anything less would be to deny the significance of the original, autonomy-suspending, ethical encounter with the unique other,[1] and betray authentic, non-abstract witnessing, or, in other terms, betray the empirical valuing already evident. Such a denial would serve only to protect and perpetuate an anthropocentric totality of reason that reduces and subjugates the unique other and their duty invoking expression of presence. This assertion does not offend humanity. Rather, it reaffirms Becoming in community, the idea that humanity is fundamentally moral[2] and that a declaration of protective rights articulates the grounding principle of justice that we, first and foremost, wish to do no harm to suffering others in community.[3]

We must also understand the critiques put forward by existing critical human rights scholars as applicable to both human and nonhuman animals, revisiting the vulnerability and suffering of the nonhuman other in our appreciation that rights concern loss and recovery of the voice of all suffering others. Questions to be raised concern who is not recognised, who is most forgotten, who is profoundly different, and who suffers from 'the evil weapon to dominate' (the orthodoxy of autonomy) and the injustice of allocating rights to only those with complex characteristics.

It is also imperative to entrench the idea that we are duty bound to accept that the original right is the right of the human and nonhuman other, that it already exists and cannot be conferred, and, importantly, that the restorative value of the ethics of alterity facilitate human freedom to live with human and other animals in community as inescapable to becoming human. These implications of including other animals in an ethics of alterity that ground human rights, give effect to animal rights and vegan values and defend those who seek to live with respect for other animals.

Including other animals in an ethics of alterity for human rights also brings vegan activism and the rights claims of vegans in the fold of the human rights narrative of protest and its recognition of the struggle for ethical justice. In this narrative of suffering and struggle, the rights claims of vegans, brought under the human right to freedom of conscience, must be understood as representing the inescapable duty, inseparable from the human conscience, to vulnerability and suffering. The rights claims of vegans, whether they are heard in or dealt with out of court, must be regarded to be grounded by the non-negotiable, fundamental duty to extend moral consideration in the face of vulnerability and suffering, and as an essential matter of and for justice. If the protest scholars look to otherness as the postmodern principle of justice to rescue human rights, and other animals matter, then, as I have argued, it is this principle, not autonomy, that must be recognised as the motivation for claims of conscience for other animals, as observed and defended in the rights claims of vegans.

In the context of the call for a paradigm shift necessary for animal liberation and intersectional justice, this chapter assesses the implications for human rights of the conclusion that the suffering narrative of rights, grounded by the ethics of alterity, also concerns nonhuman animals and, thus, undergird the rights claims of vegans. It explains that nonhuman animals should be granted basic rights and that the principles of the suffering narrative of human rights can feature in the presentation of the rights claims of vegans: claims that should be regarded as re-presenting ethical imperatives, rather than as qualified, inessential, optional, secondary, unnecessary, or voluntary modes of regard, associated with the primacy of individual, personal, and private reason. This argument is grounded by the basic, normative principle that is explained in the ethics of alterity and represented in the groundwork of the protective rights enterprise: that human beings are born into community, observe alterity, deploy otherness, and recognise moral standing and duty through a priori responsibility acknowledged in the presence of the transcendent other, or that such a process underpins community values around duty to suffering.

I will, firstly, outline how the principles of a system of protective rights built upon the ethics of alterity, can be envisaged in abstract and explain and give examples of how the principles of the ethics of alterity can inform a rights enterprise that accommodates nonhuman animals. My explanation of how a reorientation of human rights accommodates other animals and validates the claims of vegans, does not, however, lead to the conclusion that the rights claims of vegans will always be successful. As Levinas points out, justice necessarily entails sacrifice, it is remorseful; it is the way the community of others balances competing demands and establishes priority. In justice, there are always winners and losers. In a legal system built upon the ethics of alterity, justice remains remorseful, but what I propose in this chapter is that adjudication in a system built upon the ethics of alterity engages in ethical facing. The deep remorse of justice is frustrating and disappointing but overtly embedded, in a system of protective rights that acknowledges and builds on ethical otherness.

The chapter concludes with three points. Firstly, that in a system of protective rights informed by a suffering narrative, and built upon the ethics of alterity, vegan values are paramount. Secondly, nonhuman animals have a strong level of protection because an important feature of the ethics of alterity, the transcendence of the (nonhuman) other, necessarily requires that oppressive themes and categories, endemic in the unethical totality of reason, must be prohibited. Thirdly, that the suffering narrative of human rights has value for the claims of vegans.

The Abstract Development of a Rights Enterprise That Includes Nonhuman Animals

In a suffering narrative of rights that commits to the a priori knowledge of others, nonhuman animals are included on the basis that they are universally recognised as vulnerable beings, subject to the forces of mortality. They appeal through an affective address, require a response and create responsibility. For a concept of universal suffering to ground rights, a shift in the telos of the rights enterprise is required. This involves replacing the supremacy of human individuality and the orthodoxy of autonomy, acknowledging the 'otherness' inherent in the human community and conceding that the moral community always and already, but inadequately, considers and accommodates nonhuman others.

Such a paradigm shift speaks to a human identity that is already aware and appreciates that unique, singular others have lives that are already precarious and will inevitably suffer from the pursuits of unrestrained egos. In this regard, the rejection of the primacy of a rational self restores the a priori value of community and duty to alterity and facilitates acceptance of heterogeneity. This notion of human identity promotes the foundational principle: that it is encounters with unique others that create an ethically responsible, social, and political humanity and legal justice.[4]

In this reconstructed notion of human identity, responsibility to nonhuman otherness is, therefore, a paramount characteristic. It is born in the 'compassion of being.'[5] As a philosophy that indicates the essence of human beings, the ethics of alterity credits humanity universally with unlimited compassion for others, on the basis that the life force presented reveals uniqueness and the presence of a subjective experience of being at the mercy of mortality. Alterity provokes a response that is, for Levinas, a response indicating Being-for-the-other before Being-for-the-self. The other transcends the self of the subject, and such transcendence is, for Levinas, 'conscience.'[6] Being for-the-other before being for-the-self is a consciousness brought about in witnessing or, as Levinas explains, the 'event of ethics.'[7]

In a rights enterprise that recognises the importance of others, there is a moral requirement to 'do good,'[8] but not a 'doing good' in which the 'I' assumes a positive[9] value in recognition of others.[10] Rather, as Levinas urges, it is a requirement to recognise that otherness is 'morality itself.'[11] On this basis, the 'I' does not have a right, but it has moral duties for which limits may be sought through adjudication.

Grounding rights on this idea of ethics requires an understanding of the 'naturalness' of extending compassion to others. Rather than identifying compassion as indulging in egotistical acts of personal charity, individuals are aware of the value to society of the formative, transcendental nature of an encounter with another.[12] In this regard, the subject is responsible to individual human and nonhuman others equally.

Through the development of the ethics of alterity as a model for a reoriented system of protective rights that concerns nonhuman others, human identity is reformed. Instead of being defined in terms of the ability to reason, human identity acknowledges the significance of being born into existing community, the significance of others, and a desire to do no harm. The paramount features of a reshaped humanity are: firstly, an emphasis on alterity; secondly, otherness; thirdly, a priori responsibility in community; and, finally, the infinity of responsibility. Each of these four principles will be discussed in turn, in relation to an abstract reorientation of a rights enterprise that concerns nonhuman animals. Alterity, as a characteristic of human identity, will be discussed first.

Protective Rights and the Recognition of the Unique Nonhuman Other

One of the first principles of a reoriented system of protective rights is the acknowledgement of singular heterogeneity. It is paramount that homogeneity is deposed in an understanding that there are unique others whose experience of living and suffering may be entirely different from that of the subject. Unique others have always been present in the world of the subject and will continue to make their presence known. The singularity of the unique other is apprehended in the face-to-face relationship and is the origin of the ethical demand made in immediate proximity.[13] It is in encounters with uniquely different others that humanity emerges as essentially sociable, compassionate, caring, and welcoming.

The extent of heterogeneity is unlimited and requires an appreciation of the alterity of the other. This is not limited by observable differences between the subject and the other,[14] but through an appreciation of the uniqueness and singularity of the experience of being in the world. This means acknowledging and accepting other-than-human subjective experience of being in the world. In the application of the ethics of alterity, ways of being and different elements or degrees of suffering must not be dismissed in a process of reducing the other through oppressive categories or themes, which would dismiss their subjective reality.[15] It is through an acceptance of unique and different accounts of life experiences that the ethics of alterity aim to expand justice by observing difference. Since protective rights always and already recognise the other and their right to be unique, precarious, and vulnerable in the presence of the subject who enters their world, then nonhumans also possess basic rights.

A remodelled system of rights—based on the ethics of alterity and including nonhuman animals—upholds in its foundational philosophy a reference to the uniqueness of all life. This inclusive model of justice dissolves the false human-nonhuman boundary and promotes radical difference in recognition of the continuum of life and moral standing across species boundaries.

A universal system of protective rights that acknowledges alterity would also depose the current themes and categories of reason that subjugate others in the current totality of the established orthodoxy. This requires establishing non-oppressive and non-reductionist themes and categories that aim to emancipate, rather than appropriate. This principle would, for example, prohibit the use of categories and terms, such as 'vermin,' 'pets,' 'laboratory animals,' 'circus animals,' and 'farm animals,' and emphasise respect and duty to individual others.

The principle of alterity, as outlined above, is fundamental to a reorientation of human rights because it gives expression to the breadth of heterogeneity. Otherness, as a characteristic of human identity, will be discussed next.

Protective Rights and Nonhuman Animal Otherness

Otherness, in the ethics of alterity, expresses the essence of humanity as being composed of co-existing individuals that desire sociality and community. Otherness is utilising and extending the innate characteristic of compassion in recognition that others, whose experience of the world cannot be known, are always and already present in the community into which we are born. Otherness is inherent in the a priori responsibility of the subject to others and generates valuing and ethics.

Otherness is, therefore, an innate characteristic of being human. Its practical manifestation is brought about by others, who signify their difference and mortal existence. While the alterity of the other is entirely different, in that they alone know the way in which they experience life, the subject, nevertheless, recognises the universality of precariousness and vulnerability to suffering. The subject becomes aware of the other's unique inner life and is opened to compassionate responsibility, and duty to the vulnerable other is enacted.

In a reformed rights enterprise, the principle of otherness means that basic rights are conferred in consideration of responsibility to others. This establishes, in the groundwork of rights, the significance of the experience of affectivity, which halts the spontaneous ego and directly or indirectly creates responsibility.

In a rights enterprise based on an ethics of alterity that concerns nonhuman others, otherness is demonstrated by the enactment of a positive response to responsibility, rather than by action based on (unethical) reasoning that defines nonhuman others as means to anthropocentric ends. Otherness is demonstrated through acts of responsibility that are grounded by the human desire to offer a compassionate welcome to human and nonhuman others alike, as legitimate beings of moral concern. Otherness concerns conduct that demonstrates that the subject involved in an encounter with a unique nonhuman other does not harm or intend to harm, but does not pursue such conduct in recognition of a requirement to offer a degree of personal charity. Rather, by extending compassion to the unique nonhuman other, the subject asymmetrically and unconditionally accepts the unique alterity and subjective existence of nonhuman others, who must not be reduced to oppressive categories of convenience that are utilised to justify their appropriation.

This idea of otherness, established in the groundwork of reoriented human rights, necessarily includes all other animals. The a priori responsibility, intrinsic to otherness, will now be explained.

Protective Rights and A Priori Responsibility to Nonhuman Animals

In a reorientation of human rights built upon the suffering narrative of rights and the ethics of alterity, responsibility to otherness is asymmetrical and paramount. The a priori fact, explained in the philosophy of otherness, is the pre-ontological, pre-social responsi-bility that is created by the other. A response is demanded in the face-to-face relationship with the other, and it is in response to the signification of being that the subject becomes cognitively compelled to be engaged with the other, with a desire to extend compassion.

A remodelling of the groundwork for rights would, therefore, recognise that in a community of unique others, a priori responsibility to the other is the foundation of ethical justice and grounds the duty to be compassionate. The value of basic rights in this context is, thus, directed away from the notion, as explained by Douzinas and Simmons, that rights are the means by which self-governing, autonomous beings establish claims. Instead, basic rights are, as Levinas urges, rights of the other. They recognise difference, innate duty, and responsibility.

In a reoriented rights enterprise that recognises a priori responsibility, nonhuman animals are recognised as authentic beings of ethical concern because they have signified their presence and been valued. As such, they have generated ethical responsi-bility, either as entities with ethical value or, as Perpich prefers, entities whose ethical value is secured in the social domain of humanity.

On this basis, the principle of a priori responsibility protects nonhuman animals in relationships of close proximity with humans. The human subject, who is commanded to respond to responsibility, recognises legitimate otherness, precariousness and vulnerability, and is ethically obliged to consider duty to nonhuman animals—as non-reduced, legitimate others with unqualified moral standing. Responsibility in close proximity does not limit the extent of general responsibility. Levinas maintains that responsibility is infinite, which will now be explained.

Protective Rights and the Infinity of Responsibility

In the proposed reorientation of human rights, infinite, ethical duties are owed by humans to nonhuman animals. The infinite nature of responsibility in the ethics of alterity is particularly important to analyse in the context of a proposal for the philosophy of the ethics of alterity to ground legal rights. As such, it requires a more in-depth discussion to explain the scope of duty to nonhuman animals.

The ethics of alterity promote absolute responsibility when a subject is engaged in an encounter with the face of another in close proximity. Levinas maintains that '[i]f I am alone with the Other, I owe him everything.'[16] Thus, any reduction of the other in close proximity dismisses and violates the principle of responsibility in the face of alterity.[17] Levinas was clear that the face encountered in close proximity was, simultaneously, an event of infinite facing:

> The third party looks at me in the eyes of the Other . . . the epiphany of the face qua face opens humanity . . . the *third party,* [is] thus present at the encounter. . . . The presence of the face, the infinity of the other, is a destituteness, a presence of the third party (that is, of the whole of humanity which looks at us).[18]

Levinas goes on:

> It [proximity/responsibility] is the summoning of myself by the other, it is a responsibility toward those whom we do not even know. The relationship of proximity does not amount to any modality of distance or geometrical contiguity, nor the simple 'representation' of the neighbour.[19]

On the basis of Levinas' explanation, Indaimo summarises proximity and its relationship to infinite responsibility to others as 'not limited to a relationship measured by space or time, or a collectivity of similarity.' Infinite responsibility, as in responsibility for unknown and un-encountered others, is, for Indaimo, essentially a '*first person* responsibility—the same responsibility as that which the self has toward the immediate other.'[20] Thus, ethical duty in a personal encounter involves a simultaneous ethical encounter with multiple others.

In his explanation of infinite responsibility, Levinas promotes the ethics of alterity as not merely essential to the social and political organisation of humanity, but as a philosophy of personal responsibility that is already inherently social and political.[21] It is inherently so because it is the 'fact of the multiplicity of men and the presence of someone else next to the Other, which conditions the laws and establishes justice.'[22] Levinas explains: '[t]he fact that the other, my neighbour, is also a third party with respect to another, who is also a neighbour, is the birth of thought, consciousness, justice and philosophy.'[23] As such, Levinas appears to express how infinite knowledge of others in community create and affect justice and its measures. This principle grounds the human motivation to create a framework for justice, including protective rights entrenching duty in community.

A system of rights built upon the principle of alterity would utilise the personal, one-to-one origin of ethics as a foundational feature of justice in social and political organisation. In so doing, it would recognise and explicate that the difference acknowledged in the face-to-face relationship, while commanding an immediate ethical response, also indicates a simultaneous ethical awareness of multiple others. The infinity of responsibility, suggested by the ethics of alterity, requires that at all times, the ethical conduct of the subject needs to orient towards limiting the impact of the subject on the other and all the others that are recognised in an event of single facing. The justice of rights would demonstrate a politics in the service of such ethics, as observed by Simmons, Douzinas, and Indaimo,[24] because '[j]ustice is the way I respond to the face that I am not alone in the world with the other' and 'ethics . . . is the foundation of justice.'[25] It is in this regard that Levinas, Douzinas, Indaimo, and Simmons concur that the current discourse of human rights can be invigorated through an approach that recognises infinite duty to the other, rather than retaining a rights-of-the-self tradition.[26]

In stating that the whole of humanity is represented in one single facing of the other, Levinas is presenting the infinite responsibility to allow, listen, and respond to the valuing being done by all beings in their singular experience of its world. [27] It is an open listening in acknowledgment of the infinity of responsibility to listen to all others, whether present or not.

Levinas insists that in calculating ethical responsibility, the multiplicity of others must not be ignored. He argues that 'multiplicity does not allow the—let us say does not allow me—to forget the third party who pulls me away from the proximity of the other.'[28] It is in this regard that a protective rights enterprise, born of the ethics of alterity, requires justice in the form of equal responsibility for infinite, incomparable individuals.

A system of rights of the other that espouses the principle of infinite responsibility clearly presents an obvious problem.[29] Levinas himself was aware of the difficulty of transposing the demand of the face in close proximity to the infinity of demands of unique others in community. He speaks of the difficulty in deciding who has the first face and of the possibility of the terrible task of being forced to compare.[30] He notes that:

> Primary obedience is upset by the third person emerging next to the other, the third person is himself also a neighbour, and also falls within the purview of the *I's* responsibility. Here, beginning with this third person, is the proximity of a human plurality. Who, in this plurality, comes first? This is the time and place of the birth of the question: of a demand for justice! This is the obligation to compare unique and incomparable others.[31]

The problem of infinite competing demands on the subject creates an insurmountable burden. Duties in community must be balanced in difficult calculations of justice. Justice is necessary but unfortunate. In the proposed reoriented system of protective rights, justice is deeply remorseful because sacrifice cannot be avoided. This problem will now be addressed in more detail.

Protective Rights for Other Animals and Remorseful Justice

In the face-to-face encounter, the other is owed everything,[32] but in the practical and pragmatic accountability for one's personal infinite responsibility, it is necessary 'to weigh, to think, to judge, in comparing the incomparable.'[33] Levinas contemplates that '[j]ustice is necessary, that is comparison, coexistence, contemporaneousness, assembling, order, thematization, the visibility of faces and thus intentionality and the intellect, and in intentionality and the intellect, the intelligibility of a system.'[34] Justice is a remorseful system in which it is necessary to 'moderate this privilege of the Other.' In this regard, Levinas asks '[w]ho is my neighbour?'[35]

Levinas describes the balancing required in ascertaining duty and responsibility as the 'deep remorse of justice,' because it necessarily requires sacrifice.[36] Levinasian justice is an apologetic justice in its recognition that an ethical response to one may dissolve an ethical response to others. Nevertheless, it is a justice derived from the first conscience-opening signification.[37] As such, it must be continually ethically engaged and never espouse dogma, because it is only a justice such as this that serves the uniquely different other.[38] For Levinas, the justice of legislation is in its unwavering endeavour to establish kindness in its foundations, remain always unfinished, aspire to ethical excellence, and evolve according to a progress of reason. Such a justice offers the gift of inventing new forms of dutiful coexistence.[39]

Where the ethics of alterity reorient and underpin a system of protective rights, the administration of justice must, therefore, 'always be held in check by the initial interpersonal relation.'[40] The reference to the initial relation indicates the importance, to Levinas, of justice being underpinned by the evolution of the ethics of law. He believes that this evolution will reveal an inclusive justice from emergent universal principles that are based on a compassionate response to vulnerable, mortal others, who are currently marginalised or silenced. In this regard, a justice that responds to an infinite ethical responsibility to nonhuman others is within the spirit of Levinas' endeavour. In an ethics of alterity, it is not permissible to choose to disregard the ethical demand, and it is imperative to speak with and for vulnerable others who are routinely, or may be, betrayed. Given that nonhuman animals are vulnerable and predominantly have limited power to defend themselves, it is critical to establish an inclusive system of deeply remorseful justice that is sensitive to these circumstances.

To address the difficulty infinite responsibility presents, Levinas explains the function of a remorseful system of justice as a practical solution. To be sensitive to the human conscience, the ethical approach of such a system of justice must also entrench the expression of deep remorse for any limitation of responsibility and duty. The proposed reorientation of human rights would entrench remorse for any limitation of responsibility and duty to human and nonhuman animals alike. The reality of remorseful justice is an uncomfortable but persistent truth that does not sit well in the human conscience. This problem will be revisited in later sections of this chapter.

On the basis of the above explanation of the principles of infinite responsibility, the abstract development of the argument from an ethics of alterity that concerns nonhuman others would regard infinity of responsibility as equally applicable to either human or nonhuman life. Although ethical responsibility and duty to others are bound to be limited by weighing, judging, comparing, and balancing, they must be practised in a process of application that is forever in constant revision and subject to non-dogmatic reason, with regard to the ethical standing of the other in the original encounter.[41] In a system of justice in which dogma cannot prevail, the current, exclusive, anthropocentric human rights system gives way to the inclusion of nonhuman animals to avoid diluting the original ethical demand. As Levinas explains, justice itself cannot make us forget the origin of the right or the uniqueness of the other.[42] Despite a process of necessary (but deeply remorseful) justice, multiplicity remains a context for 'not ignoring the suffering of the other, who falls to my responsibility.'[43] In this regard, the subject has a duty to advocate for the other, who is victim to violent acts of their other. Upholding the rights claims of vegans who advocate for the ethical treatment of the other, and the other's other, would be entirely within the spirit of this element of justice in the ethics of alterity.

In the creation of a practical and pragmatic justice of infinite responsibility that does not dilute the original ethical demand, intentional and willing violence toward nonhuman animals would not be promoted as acceptable in any circumstances. As instructed, in close proximity, the other is owed everything because the other creates the subject dutiful and responsible. Cruel acts of reduction and subjugation are to be prohibited. Any killings done in the name of categorisation pertain to an oppressive totality that ignores and dismisses ethics and the transcendental nature of the other. In the ethics of alterity, '[t]o be in relation with the other face-to-face—is to be unable to kill.'[44] As such, the principle of infinite responsibility for a reorientation of human rights has the potential to dissolve anthropocentric supremacy. The themes, categories, and practices currently utilised to subjugate nonhumans, become obsolete because they function to reduce the other and deny their moral standing as legitimate others.[45]

These principles grounding a reorientation of human rights offer specific basic rights for nonhuman others that will be discussed next.

PROTECTIVE RIGHTS FOR OTHER ANIMALS

The previous section outlined, in abstract, the grounding principles for basic rights in a reoriented system of rights built on the ethics of alterity. It explained that difference, otherness, and ethical responsibility cannot be reduced by oppressive themes of reason, such as those currently at work in the totality, and that the transcendental presence of nonhuman others is relevant for a protective rights enterprise that looks to otherness for its grounding principles.

For the ethics of alterity to undergird moral and legal rights for other animals on account of responsibility, there are four elements that must be entrenched. Firstly, the idea of heterogeneous life must be upheld. Secondly, there must be acknowledgment that the inner worlds of heterogeneous life cannot be treated as insignificant simply because they are not understood by human beings. Thirdly, there must be acceptance that nonhuman animals are present in community and metaphorically ask for an ethical response that must not be subsequently reduced through the unethical application of oppressive human reason. Finally, there must be acceptance that an encounter with another in close proximity indicates the infinity of ethical responsibility to all others.

Grounding the moral and legal standing of nonhuman animals in the application of an ethics of alterity for a reoriented system of rights relies on an explanation of human reason being secondary to affectivity and the implementation of subsequent ethical measures for universal, inclusive justice. This is the context for the system of protective, remorseful justice that limits infinite duty, rather than one that grounds and permits competitive, individualistic gains at the expense of marginalised and silenced others. It formalises otherness as the foundation of a requirement to be responsible and dutiful to others who are always and already present, a priori individual human reason.

It is empirically clear that nonhuman animals, in all their difference, have expressed their presence to human beings and that they exist and are extensively considered in the socio-political domain. In so doing, they have impeded the autonomy of human reason, created responsibility, and influenced thinking. Clearly, the demand for responsibility has already been made and partially accepted, but ethical responsibility has not been adequately acknowledged and entrenched in the form of granting basic rights to other animals: indeed, the orthodoxy of autonomy only subjugates nonhuman life. To give effect to an ethics of alterity informing a protective rights enterprise, the duty of humans not to harm other animals must be expressed in terms of the basic rights of other animals.

On the argument presented above, human beings are ethically responsible to nonhuman animals, who are brought into the realm of justice as legitimate others with at least five basic moral entitlements that can be viewed as falling into three groups of rights. In a system of justice grounded by otherness, nonhuman animals have a right to life and to liberty. On the basis of their alterity, they have the right to self-defined identity, and on the basis of the ethical duty in close proximity, they have the right to care and to assistance.[46] These three groups of basic rights will now be explained.

An Animal's Right to Life and Liberty in the System of Otherness

In an inclusive system of justice grounded by otherness, nonhuman animals, in all their difference, are acknowledged and they are protected from prejudice and its negative social manifestations. Responsibility requires that they be granted the right to life and living their lives according to their own mode of existence. Their inclusion in a reoriented system of rights requires respect far beyond the call for the abolition of ownership of other species. Nonhuman animals have the right to live out their natural lifespan, be supported by human intervention[47] and be unimpeded by (intentional or inadvertent) oppressive human conduct that would cause their premature death. This entitlement prohibits a broad range of current practices: there is no concept of 'ownership,' killing for food, using other animals for entertainment or sport, or for the production of products of their labour as commodities. These are non-anthropocentric requirements of responsibility to the material and corporeal existence of nonhuman others, whose expression of their one and only precious life says, 'it is me.'

In a reorientation of human rights, built upon the ethics of alterity that espouse an infinite responsibility to others, it is, thus, not for sure that human beings would take priority over nonhuman animals in all situations. In adjudication, the act of balancing, judging, and comparing would necessarily need to be accomplished according to responsible and universal compassionate community values. Legitimate, vulnerable, suffering, and precarious others cannot and must not be intentionally harmed or killed on the basis of oppressive categories, created in the totality of reason. Where a calculation of justice cannot avoid sacrifice, this must be honestly acknowledged and openly communicated as inherent to a deeply remorseful system of necessary justice.[48]

Unfortunately, the ethics of alterity do not explain the normative principles of a practical justice that follows their implementation.[49] The entitlements of nonhuman animals are, however, equal to those of human beings and impose negative and positive duties,[50] and the administration of a remorseful system of justice would adjudicate on a case-by-case basis. Unfortunately, sacrifice is inherent in justice and necessarily involves *thinking the unthinkable* and *comparing the incomparable* in a remorseful requirement to limit the infinite duty to both human and animal others.

For example, in a one-to-one encounter with a small insect that is attempting to find a way through a glass window pane, there is a negative duty not to cause harm to the vulnerable creature and a positive duty to open the window and assist in their endeavour to fly away.[51] In some circumstances, the duty to the small creature may be limited if there is a significant threat to the wider community, such as the alleged threat from the mosquito that causes the Zika virus.[52] Though there is a duty to recognise inherent value and that the mosquito has the right to exist as a different mortal other, free from entrenched prejudice, the duty owed to a multiplicity of others—including the other's others—may take precedence in a balancing of primary and infinite duty. In the context of the recognition of a general threat to a multiplicity of others, a remorseful system of justice can adjudicate that duty to the immediate other is limited, on the basis that the wider community of others requires protection. Though, in principle, killing remains prohibited,[53] it may, nevertheless, be remorsefully justified in special and specific circumstances and contexts. In this way, anti-oppressive, nonanthropocentric principles and respect for life and liberty, insofar as is ethically and practically possible, are acknowledged in the foundations of an anti-speciesist system of justice.

Animals' Right to Self-Defined Identity

The third basic right of nonhuman animals in a system of rights based on an ethics of alterity, is the right to self-defined identity. All nonhuman animals have the right to exist in the context of the sapient order of their species, free from the imposition of oppressive themes and categories.

The entitlement to self-defined identity would prohibit any reduction of nonhuman life to themes and categories that, either intentionally or inadvertently, cause oppression or permit arbitrary abuse. On this basis, current vocabulary that describes nonhuman animals in the reductive terms of oppressive categories would be redefined as vocabulary that reduces the other through themes of anthropocentric convenience. Categories, such as 'pets,' 'farm animals,' 'laboratory animals,' 'vermin,' 'race-horses,' and 'livestock,' would become obsolete because they pertain to the creation of an oppressive totality of reason. It would not be permissible to refer to nonhuman animals in derogatory terms, because it would function to reduce and subjugate their being. This entitlement does not preclude interaction with nonhuman animals. In fact, a reorientation of rights is likely to support a wide range of enhanced relationships, including cohabitation.

A Nonhuman Entitlement to Care and Assistance

Given that the ethics of alterity ground an absolute duty to the other in close proximity and an infinite duty of care, nonhuman animals have two further basic entitlements—to care and to assistance. This entitlement goes beyond the demands of total emancipation.

Entitlements to care and assistance require the extension of kind acts of compassion that would enable the other to pursue their life and to ensure no loss of life. For example, there is a positive duty to open a window to let out a fly that had accidentally entered an enclosed space, to stop and attend to nonhuman animals who have been involved in road traffic accidents, and to respond kindly to assist all nonhuman others encountered in close proximity. This entitlement implies both positive and negative duties, and under no circumstances must the other be reduced by oppressive themes and categories that would justify arbitrary appropriation, abuse, relegation, or dismissal.

This entitlement is in contrast to the suggestion, put forward by Gary Francione, that there is no requirement for human beings to intervene to protect other animals from other sources of harm. In a system of protective rights informed by the ethics of alterity, the scope of duty changes from no legal duty for individuals to aid others to the primacy of the ethical duty to assist, especially those in close proximity.

A PRACTICAL EXAMPLE: IMPLEMENTING ANIMAL RIGHTS

The five basic entitlements of nonhuman animals are the positive effects of including them in a system of justice that is built on the ethics of alterity. They clearly have broad ramifications that require tremendous shifts in thinking about the prejudice towards other animals, the operation of law as a mechanism of justice, the administration of protective rights, and the ways in which other animals are sometimes treated by human beings.[54] An example of the shift in thinking and practice required can be explained using a recent controversial incident involving a dog who was killed by police officers on a road in North Wales.[55]

In this incident, armed police officers intentionally killed a dog on the road in the interests of public safety. The officers reported that the dog could not be caught. To avoid danger to the public, who would be travelling in cars at speed on the road, the officers made the decision to instigate a fatal collision with the dog, using their vehicle at high speed. People for the Ethical Treatment of Animals (PETA) complained that 'Law enforcement officers are entrusted with protecting the innocent and the vulnerable, and that does not include deliberately running them over with the intent to kill.'[56] On the other hand, Chief Inspector Darren Wareing was reported as stating that:

> the 'potential for a serious collision was present throughout' and there was 'no alternative way' for them [the officers] to minimise risks to motorists. 'The only safe option was to run the dog over at sufficient speed to ensure that it was destroyed and would not suffer. Other methods of destruction were considered but were ruled out on the grounds of public safety.'[57]

The principles of the remorseful system of justice intrinsic to the ethics of alterity require that, at all times, the balancing and calculations involved in situations concerning facing others must be from the point of view of the ethical duty invoked in close proximity. This means observing that, in close proximity, the other is owed everything and that the prohibition on intentional harming and killing is the way in which the essence of human identity and duty to others are manifested and protected. On this requirement of reoriented rights, the conduct of the police officers comes under scrutiny.

The officers drove the police car at the dog at high speed to kill her/him following a 'review' of other options, which were ruled out on the grounds of public safety. This course of action could be deemed disproportionate on the grounds that the dog was intentionally killed because it was an animal and not a human being. In failing to respond ethically to otherness, reducing the value of the life of the dog and imposing inequality of ethical regard, it may be deemed that the officers failed in their duty of care and that the intervention was wholly unjustified and even criminal.

In determining a fair and reasonable application of remorseful justice, questions raised concern the possible options available to protect the public and the dog from harm. Other options not stated as considered in this case would be, for example, those used in other road traffic incidents and which are routinely implemented, such as stopping traffic, closing the road, or using barriers. Although in a remorseful system of justice, killing may be necessary, these events turned on the fact that it was a dog in the road rather than a person. The dog was reduced and denied ethical responsibility and—through a broad and widely used system of oppressive thematisation and dismissive categorisation—the action taken was not considered as a matter of ethical responsibility in close proximity, in which the presence of the 'dog' also demanded an ethical and dutiful response.

Protective rights for nonhuman animals are grounded by an inclusive ethics of alterity that explains entitlements in terms of foundational duties emerging from moral responsi-bility. Principles are general and, as already noted, it is not possible to extract a set of normative practices that determine specific action required in all eventualities. The ethics of alterity serve as a foundation for establishing and outlining the general mode of conduct owed to nonhuman animals and can function to underpin a dynamic and non-dogmatic approach to animal ethics in all contexts by transcending the oppressive totality that has secured their subjugation. In this regard, it is a platform on which existing, evolving, and new models of practical justice for nonhuman others can be evaluated and potentially supported.

Measures for practical justice that would support the philosophy of otherness will facilitate a remorseful system of justice honestly, and will not allow anthropocentric privilege to enter through the back door. Theories and models of inclusive justice—such as those advocating nonhuman inherent value,[58] sentiency,[59] consciousness and interests,[60] capability,[61] citizenship,[62] and 'vulnerability'[63]—may be useful to ascertain the way forward in an ethics-inspired, remorseful system of justice; but they must be scrutinised to ensure that no elements pertain to an anthropocentric-motivated totality of reason.

The shift in thinking required to initiate equality of legal consideration for nonhuman animals, as required for the proposed reorientation of human rights, is, unfortunately, unlikely to reform the socio-legal landscape in the near future. Though, theoretically, the case for such a reorientation can be made, a paradigm shift that can support anti-oppressive practice does not appear to be imminent. The general principles that ground the reorientation and establish the entitlements of nonhuman animals can, though, be applied to the human rights claims of vegans through the presentation of a reconceptualisation of the current justification for protective rights and the right to freedom of conscience: away from the orthodoxy of autonomy and towards the inclusive ethics of otherness. This entails registering the suffering narrative of protective rights, the affective significance of the vulnerable, suffering other to the human conscience, and the vegan re-presentation of the other in their rights claims.

A RECONCEPTUALIZATION OF THE IDEA OF RIGHTS AND THE HUMAN RIGHT TO FREEDOM OF CONSCIENCE

A reconceptualization of rights is based on the understanding that the groundwork of existing human rights observes otherness. Evidence for this has been given by the critical human rights scholars, who note that the protective (human) rights framework was devised following the observation of suffering and awareness of the human potential to cause harm and suffering in a universal community of vulnerable others. It was not, they argue, intended to generate and prioritise extensive claim rights for competing, self-legislating human individuals.

A protective rights enterprise exists, therefore, to express responsibility and duty, and is the means through which humanity aims to deal with its recognition of, and care for, the vulnerability and suffering of others. In the reconceptualisation of rights, otherness replaces the emphasis placed on autonomy in the groundwork of rights, and nonhuman animals, who are also legitimate suffering others to whom humanity is responsible, should be included in its protective reach.

This idea of protective rights is accessible and sensible. Protective rights primarily benefit others and the human rights protection of veganism—as ethics in practice or as indistinction in practice—makes sense if the first right is the right of the other not to be harmed. On this view, the exercise of conscience is, first and foremost, an expression of duty to the vulnerable other and the right to freedom of conscience necessarily recognises, acknowledges, and permits the fundamental expression of duty as the fundamental exercise of human conscience: to extend ethical regard to suffering others in community; to speak for and with suffering others; and to present others and third parties to justice for protection. In a reorientation of rights and the right to freedom of conscience, individuals would not have to defend a right of conscience for vulnerable suffering others, because the exercise of this notion of the free conscience is fundamental to justice.

As was seen in chapter 1, the right to freedom of conscience is the principle upon which ethical responsibility to the moral standing of nonhuman animals has been accepted as coming within the scope of protection in current human rights. The human rights claims of vegans arguably, therefore, bring human rights to a threshold where otherness is most visible:[64] if regarded as a culture in response to responsibility, veganism is the embodiment of an ethics of alterity that is animated by and enacted in current human rights. As such, the right to freedom of conscience, rather than existing primarily to accommodate the claims of self-seeking, atomised individuals can be seen as the vehicle that permits the otherness of human conscience to paradoxically serve to protect other animals in the current exclusive paradigm of protective rights:[65] as previously explained, the legal accommodation of vegans facilitates changes in public and private sector policies and practices.

This way of thinking about the exercise of the right to freedom of conscience in the legal claims of vegans, is transformational because the otherness intrinsic to their claims dissolves the autonomy orthodoxy. Through the claims of vegans, the enterprise that is exclusive human rights grounded by the assumption of autonomy, facilitates otherness, observes and accommodates nonhuman affectivity, and also, paradoxically, supports the moral standing of nonhuman animals and gives expression to their suffering, despite their exclusion from protective basic rights.

On the basis of the argument presented, vegans have, thus, raised ethical responsibility to nonhuman animals as an issue that bears heavily upon exclusive protective rights, and, I suggest, present a challenge to the assumption of autonomy and the concept of the self-legislating individual with a right to freedom of conscience. The legitimacy of veganism in law, when viewed as the presentation of the moral imperative to include the suffering of animals in measures of justice, disrupts the security of speciesist prejudice, intrinsic to exclusive human rights.

On the reconceptualisation of rights presented, the affirmative response from human rights to the ethical claims of vegans has transformative value, because it contributes to dissolving the human-animal boundary. This is because a positive response from human rights to veganism implies that legal reasoning is, arguably, able to look to and speak from a position of otherness, rather than immanence. On the basis of these observations, veganism in law presents a demanding interface of human and nonhuman moral standing that has a place in the discussion on creating a paradigm shift to bring about ethical socio-political relations. If law accepts that ethical veganism is a matter of and for justice, then the principles of the suffering narrative of rights, otherness and ethical responsibility should overtly feature in the litigation of cases in the current exclusive system of rights.

THE IMPLICATIONS FOR VEGANS OF INCLUDING NONHUMAN ANIMALS IN THE ETHICS OF ALTERITY FOR HUMAN RIGHTS

The individual right to freedom of conscience is a product of the autonomy orthodoxy and, thus, considered to be a primary human right in a protective rights framework that entrenches prejudice towards nonhuman animals. On the logical principles of the ethics of alterity, this prejudice manifests a profound dismissal of ethical responsibility, approves, and permits the appropriation and resource status of nonhuman animals, and perpetuates the use of oppressive categories and themes, through which their commodification is justified. The autonomy orthodoxy creates the conditions in which a vegan response to ethical duty is considered a matter for the personal a private human conscience, despite empirical evidence that the suffering of other animals matters.

The denial of innate compassion for nonhuman others in the groundwork of existing protective rights is, as explained, problematic because it manifests the view that, since living practically with moral indistinction towards other animals is a matter of personal and private conscience, it can be lawfully limited in the interests of the wider majority, without reference to animals themselves. In this paradigm, however, a vegan's legal subjectivity presents the suffering of animals, intertwined human-animal social relationships and the undisputed worthwhile value, to human society, of inclusive, ethical responsibility to nonhuman others: the ethical obligation to nonhuman others and their original rights are ipso facto re-presented in vegan complaints of interference with their ethical practice.

Where vegans have been positively received in law and granted a qualified right to practically manifest their ethical convictions, such as in the European system of human rights and in equality provisions in Great Britain, the applicant can be asked to show that they have suffered a personal disadvantage: or, as was seen in the case of *Vartic*, a significant disadvantage.[66] In other situations, vegans have been ordered to kill animals in the interests of public health, for example by exterminating rats near to property, or been required to accept vaccination. These cases typically revolve around the principle that there is underlying legitimate law that is required for a good reason, such as public order or public health, and that there is a lawful, legitimate aim to be met. In these cases, the concepts of disadvantage and proportional interference with the vegan manifestation of practice are determined in the context of human supremacy and the wider social need, compared to the severity of a limitation on the manifestation of a personal and private matter of conscience. The suffering of animals is not presented, and there is no honest and clear expression of remorse for the sacrifice of one in favour of another.

In the absence of a complete reorientation of protective rights that would give effect to otherness and duty, the claims of vegans, and cases that concern compassion for all living animals can challenge the marginalisation of other animals by profiling the right to free conscience as a provision that expresses a fundamental element of justice: duty to vulnerable others and the right to practice original conscience opening ethical duty to suffering as, and as a matter for, justice. If rights exist to express duty to suffering in community, as the critical human rights scholars argue, and animal ethicists show that we are also in ethical community with other animals, then, as I have already explained, the right to free vegan conscience is a most basic human right because it gives expression to the first right, that of the vulnerable other to not suffer harm.

For example, discussing the case of *H v the UK* from the context of reoriented rights produces a different outcome. Though it was confirmed that vegans can be protected under the Convention, this case was inadmissible because there was a law that was required for a very good reason (order in prison) and this grounded a requirement that the applicant contributes to work in the prison print facility. It was decided that the requirement to work in the prison print facility was proportional interference with personal and private convictions, because there was an overriding wider interest. In the ethics of alterity, this ruling is a human rights wrong.

What could be discussed in this type of case, is whether, given the vegan applicant's duty to commit to the original principle of justice, the appropriation of other animals as commodities to produce printing dye is a just element of a law being used against the applicant's manifestation of normal and natural ethical duty. If the principle of honest, remorseful justice was applied in such cases, the outcome would necessarily have to be that the law required for a very good reason was not useful to the respondents because, in this case, it relied on what would be unlawful commodification of, and thus, unlawful denial of the natural rights of other animals, and thus the expression of the free human conscience to respond to suffering as a matter of human rights. This way of dealing with the legal process around the claims of vegans confronts the (in)justice of the current method of calculation in existing human rights process and forces law to face nonhuman animal suffering as relevant in human rights claims. On the view presented, in this particular case, it is a human rights wrong to deny the applicant the right to exercise moral duty.

Other examples in which the principles of (current) justice and legal process can come under scrutiny are those in which vegans are required to compromise their ethical convictions to implement a programme of 'pest control.' In cases where there is a complaint about rats, and a vegan is ordered to exterminate the rats on the basis of a law required in the interests of public health, it is likely that the current law will be deemed legitimate, and interference with vegan convictions proportionate.

This type of case, however, questions the application of legitimate aim and proportionality in the requirement to exterminate as a measure of controlling the rats. For example, the question should be what, exactly, is the legitimate aim, and how is that represented in the regulation or legislation itself? In the context of presenting the suffering narrative of rights and the ethics of alterity, it could well be that a different intervention could be implemented, such as displacing the rats to a new location to adequately protect public health. In this case, law is required to go beyond a mere acceptance that there is a legitimate law that grounds interference with the natural and normal convictions of vegans, and the principle of legitimate aim and proportionality should face, rather than deface, other animals.

There is strong support in European law for vegan food to be provided to vegan prisoners. The ECtHR has declared that diet is a direct expression of an applicant's convictions, and therefore a manifestation of the (individual) right to freedom of conscience. However, in some jurisdictions, even within Europe, this principle is unlikely to be upheld without further legal challenge. In resistant legal systems around the world, the human right to freedom of conscience is an important ally that serves vegans in their mission to raise the moral standing of other animals as a matter of and for human rights. As Douzinas maintains, 'before my legal subjectivity, there is always and already another,' therefore, claims presented by vegans under the individual right to freedom of conscience serve to re-present the other, and this is their value. This right, however, may not be sufficient on its own, given the prejudicial social conditions and the lawfulness of underlying rules, regulations, and legal principles that serve traditional practices manifesting prejudice. In terms of a human rights that recognises otherness, failure to uphold these applicants' claims are, again, human rights wrongs.

Vegans, presenting cases in resistant legal systems, could strengthen their claims by grounding them in a reconceptualisation of rights and the original ethical duty to articulate the moral imperative to extend a compassionate response to other animals as a matter of and for justice. This approach may be helpful to explain veganism in the context of a requirement to satisfy elements of legal tests that seek to confirm that the applicant's non-religious belief is capable of making sense of, or articulating 'the meaning of life,' or answering the 'big questions' of existence. Even in cases that are likely to succeed, explaining the essence of ethical duty in term of moral obligation rather than individual personal and private conscience can profile other animals, and our duty to them, more prominently.

In these cases concerning the provision of vegan food, a transparent and honest justice would acknowledge that other animals must not be rationalised as food, and that there is overwhelming evidence that human beings, at all stages of life, can flourish on a plant-based diet. As Prisco, and everyone in the vegan law movement, argues, there is also undisputable, supporting scientific evidence.

While preparing this book for publication, the world is currently in the midst of the coronavirus pandemic and some vegans have started to raise questions about the possibility of mandatory vaccination. As in the other types of cases, this is also, clearly, an area in which legal subjectivity can profile the animal other, but if human rights are the 'instrument of ethics' and 'before my legal subjectivity there is always and already another,' the question is 'to whom am I obliged in this specific situation?'

In the proposed reoriented system of protective rights, other animals cannot be reduced to commodities or resources for human gain, and it would be unlawful to exploit them. This does not mean, however, that vaccines would not be developed or that they would be indisputably dangerous. It means that a new paradigm for the creation and testing of any medicinal interventions must be pursued in the context of an ethics of alterity that is applied universally. In such a system, vegans would not need to consider the current moral dilemma of vaccination or compulsory vaccination.

Since cases for adjudication must consider the duty to the other, and duty to an infinite number of others, vegan ethical duty in community necessarily points to the need to consider the multitude of human and nonhuman others, who are vulnerable and suffering. Some may argue that participating in compulsory vaccination compromises moral convictions, while for others, not participating in compulsory vaccination could compromise the ethical duty to the human others, who the subject may infect.

This problem is born of an autonomy orthodoxy that has established the resources status of other animals. The issue of compulsory vaccination in that specific context creates an unconscionable situation for vegan navigation in the application of the ethics of alterity to current human rights. If, as Levinas urges, the balancing required must be conducted on the original facing, then the infinity of responsibility and duty must not overlook those most distant, those marginalised, those silenced.

On this view, in principle and logically, a vegan applicant alleging interference with the freedom of conscience should be protected from a requirement to rescind what is intrinsic to the 'human conscience.' On the other hand, notwithstanding the unjust appropriation of other animals, the duty to protect the other also includes the infinite human population. In the current system of human rights, lawful interference with the conviction of vegans includes a measure to protect public health. Where otherness is the principle of justice in a legal system built upon the ethics of alterity, it may also serve to be the unjust principle that will inadvertently function to justify and perpetuate the denial of original justice in the existing system that deems the convictions of vegans as a matter of 'personal and private' conscience.

In the desired approach to litigating vegan claims of conscience, the suffering of other animals would be raised in the balancing calculation required. This process would concern a remorseful justice that, openly and honestly, acknowledges the precarious, mortal lives of others, ethical duty, and the problem of infinite, competing duties owed to the other by the subject. Such a calculation would be conducted in the context of the original value, intrinsic to ethical facing, which essentially means—in the context of ethical responsibility—a commitment to the principle of not killing and not doing harm, and to extending a compassionate welcome as far as is possible. Litigation would not overlook the suffering of nonhuman animals in calculating the fate of the applicant, and there would be no resort to oppressive themes of convenience or any prioritisation of unevaluated practices that pertain to the current, subjugated status of nonhuman others. In this new approach, cases would be judged as matters of ethical opening that re-present ethical responsibility as directing human identity and explaining the existing, widespread, compassionate regard for nonhuman animals.

Legal reasoning would not, therefore, seek developments that limit state duty to vegans—such as raising the standard for disadvantage, or creating law built upon the oppressive thematisation intrinsic to the orthodoxy of reason. Instead, legal reasoning in litigation would focus on the applicant's presentation of a priori ethical responsibility in the face of nonhuman suffering that shifts the emphasis from human rights claims for self to human rights claims for the other: as the original duty of human conscience to the suffering, but inadequately protected nonhuman other; or, to use Simmons' expression, the cauterised other.

Such a process would not, however, guarantee outcomes that would always be immediately acceptable to vegans, and some logical implications of such a system would require a brave new world ready to accept the prospect of both necessary human and nonhuman sacrifices. Justice is necessarily remorseful and has no choice but to sacrifice some in a community of others and there are a multitude of complex issues to consider. The production of food for all living beings, the way we travel, where we build homes, what we make and wear, and the resources we commodify are demanding challenges in a justice that aims to entrench an ethic of otherness.

The deep remorse of justice in the ethics of alterity is a warning that offers some consolation in that it will be transparent, honest in its acknowledgement that the human system of justice can harbour arbitrary harm, and open in its inclusive balancing calculations to ensure the veganism in human conscience can be 'as far as is possible.'

Despite the unlikely turn to a vegan form of legal justice for other animals, and the deep remorse of justice, the suffering narrative of rights can feature in the rights claims of vegans. In the totality of the established orthodoxy, Derrida points to the construction of the non-vegan subject and cites the 'animal' as a category of oppression. In this context, the suffering narrative of human rights offers a compassionate subject some useful tools to re-present the demand of precarious life that is intrinsic to intersubjective becoming, and for cross-species justice for the vulnerable, oppressed, nonhuman others, always and already present in the grounding idea of human rights.

CONCLUSION

A reconfiguration of the concept of human rights, based on the ethics of alterity, upholds vegan values, basic rights for other animals and the rights claims of vegans for suffering others as a matter of and for justice.

I have suggested that in a reoriented system of protective rights that draws its principles from the ethics of alterity, nonhuman animals have moral and legal standing, based on their alterity, the principle of otherness, and the a priori and infinite responsibility that the relational ethical encounter between a subject and another facilitates. I have explained that, on these principles, nonhuman animals have basic entitlements: to life, liberty, self-defined identity, and to care and assistance.

The chapter has identified, therefore, that the implications of including nonhuman animals in a rights enterprise built upon the ethics of alterity are positive and profound. Nonhuman animals are, in theory, offered a strong degree of protection, and law recognises vegan values and the human rights claims that re-present the vulnerability, suffering and oppression of other animals.

I have argued that the re-presentation of other animals in human rights cases should not be judged as claims of personal and private conscience, in which personal disadvantage must be proven. Instead, I advocate for a reconceptualization of the right to freedom of conscience to contextualise claims for compassion to all living beings as expressing original duty in community that is, itself, formative to the idea of justice in the human rights project. It orients to the naturalness of compassion and duty to vulnerability and suffering as an inescapable, essential feature of the free human conscience, challenges the current concept of autonomy and the primacy of the individual in current human rights.

I have shown in this chapter how other animals feature in a suffering narrative of protective rights and that the human rights claims of vegans are relevant to the development of an anti-oppressive discourse for a paradigm of socio-political-legal relations, in which other animals are no longer betrayed by the orthodoxy of autonomy and its manifestations. I have also highlighted, however, that the deep remorse of justice necessarily requires uncomfortable thinking and balancing in calculations of justice. Even an open, honest, and transparent remorseful system of justice in a community of others, is unlikely to always be able to produce the kind of outcomes some ethical vegans would wish to see, and, in some instances, may require ethical vegans to think carefully about their wider duties in community.

Issues in remorseful justice involve intensely complex discussions, which are fraught with frustration and disappointment. For example, it is not for sure that the ethics of alterity, as applicable to both human and nonhuman animals equally, would ensure fewer construction projects on the basis that they will have negative impacts on the natural environment, and that the communities and homes of other animals would subsequently be annihilated. Equally though, it is not for certain that human beings will take priority in all situations.

Since the ethics of alterity promote infinity of ethical responsibility to a community of unique others, and a system of justice necessarily requires sacrifice, I explained that it may be necessary to thematise and categorise, but that this must not be pursued in the interests of the totality of reason that confers unjust privilege to the human subject. In this regard, I explained a requirement to refrain from the creation of oppressive themes and categories that reduce and subjugate different classes of other animals in the interests of anthropocentric privilege.

NOTES

1. In the case of nonhuman animals, this is true whether we perceive them to have ethical value themselves or their ethical value has been socially negotiated. They are already of profound significance to human beings.

2. 'The central fact is that man is fundamentally a moral being, that the light we have is imperfect does not matter so long as we are always trying to improve it.' Eleanor Roosevelt, 'On the Adoption of the Universal Declaration of Human Rights' (video clip of speech, 9 December 1948) https://www.youtube.com/watch?v=g5qcgYNFrkE accessed 26 July 2016.

3. 'Human rights can be seen as primarily ethical demands. They are not principally 'legal,' 'proto-legal' or 'ideal-legal' commands. Even though human rights can, and often do, inspire legislation, this is a further fact, rather than a constitutive characteristic of human rights.' Amartya Sen, 'Elements of a Theory of Human Rights' (2004) 32(4) Philosophy & Public Affairs <http://www.jstor.org/stable/pdf/3557992.pdf> accessed 26 July 2016.

4. The presence of others is already presumed in the creation of human rights. It is in the context of an awareness of others that such an enterprise could emerge. What is explicated by the present system is individualism on the basis of assumed a priori reason. The dignity of humanity resides in a notion of a priori reason, rather than an a priori encounter with others in a shared world. For Levinas, this represents 'Intersubjective Reduction' because it represents the ego of basic Being: Levinas (1998/2006) 86.

5. Levinas (1985) 10.

6. Levinas (1969/2000) 261.

7. Levinas (1985) 12.

8. Levinas (1969/2000) 261.

9. Or, indeed, a superiority.

10. Levinas' ethics are not concerned with mere acts of individual kindness, although daily doing good is evidence of the innate capacity to offer generosity to the other. Levinas' ethics directly concern the social and political ordering of humanity by the state, because in promoting peace and non-violence, the state is obliged to 'affirm the infinite responsibility of everyone, for everyone, and to everyone' Roger Burggraeve, *The Wisdom of Love in the Service of Love: Emmanuel Levinas on Justice, Peace, and Human Rights* (Marquette University Press 2002) 177. The ethical event that reveals responsibility of each to the other is intrinsic to the nature of social humanity and the foundation of harmonious relations.

11. Levinas (1969/2000) 261.

12. I use the word 'natural' here to refer to an earlier explanation of the 'compassion of Being,' i.e., it is natural to be compassionate.

13. Ethical responsibility and proximity are discussed in more depth below.

14. Observing physical characteristics is not exposure to the face of another.

15. In the ethics of alterity, an appeal to reason to sustain oppressive categories for other life speaks only to the perpetuation of an unethical totality that has been created by an emphasis on the primacy of human reason.

16. Levinas (1985) 90.

17. In this regard, Soren Stig Andersen advocates proximity as a possible way of achieving justice for animals. Anderson argues that the current discourse of animal rights has limitations, which can be addressed through an ethico-legal conception of proximity and direct duty. Soren Stig Andersen, 'Proximity: A Levinasian Approach to Justice for Animals' (2015) 1 Global Journal of Animal Law (GJAL) <https://ojs.abo.fi/index.php/gjal/article/view/1381/1686> 13 June 2016.

18. Levinas (1969/2000) 213. The face in close proximity is an event of ethical opening, not a limitation of responsibility that would absolve infinite duty.

19. Emmanuel Levinas, 'Substitution' in Adriaan Theodoor Peperzak, Simon Critchley and Robert Bernasconi (eds), *Emmanuel Levinas: Basic Philosophical Writings* (Peter Atterton tr, Indiana University Press 1968/1996) 81. Also quoted in Indaimo (2015) 204.

20. Indaimo (2015) 204.

21. This point is also made by Douzinas and Indaimo.

22. Levinas (1985) 89.

23. Levinas (1998) 140.

24. This point is made by Simmons (2014) 100, by Douzinas in the context of human rights failings (2000) 343–369 and by Indaimo (2015) 203–204.

25. Wright, Hughes and Ainley (1988/2014) 174–175.

26. For Simmons, the ethical is enacted in a phenomenological appreciation of severe marginalisation. Levinas' ethics of alterity exceed phenomenology, but, nonetheless, can be applied normatively in this way to include nonhuman animals.

27. Levinas (1969/2000) 213.

28. Levinas (1998/2006) 195.

29. Simmons develops the principle of saturation to assist inclusion in this regard.

30. Wright, Hughes and Ainley (1988/2014) 174.

31. Levinas (1998/2006) 166–167.
32. Levinas (1985) 90.
33. Levinas (1985) 90.
34. Levinas (1998/2011) 157.
35. Levinas (1985) 90.
36. Levinas (1998/2006) 229.
37. Levinas (1998/2011).
38. Cohen (1998/2011) xiii.
39. Levinas (1998/2006) 230.
40. Levinas (1985) 90.
41. Levinas and Indaimo make this point: Levinas (1985) 90 and Indaimo (2015) 209.
42. Levinas (1998/2006) 196.
43. Levinas (1998/2006) 195. In this regard, the subject is also required to advocate for the other who is victim to violent acts of their other. As an example, vegans advocating for the ethical treatment of the other's other is entirely within the spirit of this aspect of the ethics of alterity.
44. Levinas (1998/2006) 10. Levinas speaks of killing as achieving a goal, such as hunting, cutting trees or slaughtering animals. 'I can want to [kill]. Yet this power is the complete opposite of power. The triumph of this power is its defeat as power. At the very moment when my power to kill is realized, the other has escaped. In killing, I can certainly attain a goal, I can kill the way I hunt, or cut down trees, or slaughter animals—but then I have grasped the other in the opening of being in general, as an element of the world in which I stand. I have seen him on the horizon. I have not looked straight at him. I have not looked him in the face.'
45. As Douzinas argues, current human rights law is not the marker of morality because it fails to function according to the principles of alterity: Douzinas (2000) 353. Levinas' thinking on this is that violence may be necessary in justice, but it must be avoided as much as possible (1998/2006 106). Regarding state endorsement of speciesist violence towards nonhumans, a rights enterprise that utilised the principles of the ethics of alterity would require limitations on state practices. Levinas maintains that state-administered violence as justice is not always legitimate (1998/2006 105).
46. As pointed out by the NhRP, establishing rights also secures nonhuman animals as 'legal persons.' 'So far as legal theory is concerned, a person is any being whom the law regards as capable of rights or duties. . . . Any being that is so capable is a person whether a human being or not.' John Salmond, *Jurisprudence* (Glanville L Williams ed, 10th edn, Sweet and Maxwell 1947) <https://www.nonhumanrightsproject.org/media-center/04–11–17-media-release-blacks-law/> accessed 13 April 2017.
47. This is discussed in more detail below, under the 'entitlement to care and assistance.'
48. In this regard, Cochrane (2013) argues that a system of human rights that became a system of 'sentient rights' in response to the call for animal rights, would have no logical grounds on which to treat humans and nonhumans differently and that the apparatus to deal with competing claims is already in place. Cochrane makes

the point that if human beings were afforded priority, it would not be on the basis of membership 'of a particular species that must always take priority, but because it protects an interest that is stronger and more compelling' than one put forward on behalf of another species. For an interesting discussion from the capabilities approach, see Nussbaum (2007) Chapter 6.

49. The ethics of alterity do not explain the normative principles of a practical justice that follows their implementation. Other scholars have considered political measures for animals. For example, Will Kymlicka and Sue Donaldson suggest that domesticated animals could become 'citizens,' wild animals could become 'sovereigns of territories' and liminal animals could be granted basic rights. Though existing ideas would need to be assessed according to the principles of the ethics of alterity, they may have some value in establishing the principles of a remorseful system of inclusive justice for other animals. See, Donaldson and Kymlicka (2011). See also Will Kymlicka and Sue Donaldson, 'Animals and the Frontiers of Citizenship' (2014) 34(2) *Oxford Journal of Legal Studies* 201.

50. Donaldson and Kymlicka prefer to locate the emancipation of nonhumans within politics, rather than in ethics, and see ethical discourse as a limiting factor in traditional animal rights theory. Mark Rowlands has contested the need for such a move, on the basis of inaccurate perceptions. This explanation of the grounding rights for animals in ethics and its practical application in justice arguably shows the continuing relevance of both strands of discourse.

51. A discussion about an entitlement to care, support and assistance follows below.

52. In 2016 The World Health Organisation disseminated informative reports about a possible association between Zika virus infection and congenital malformations and severe neurological and autoimmune complications. The Zika virus is reported to be caused by mosquitos. World Health Organisation (WHO), 'Research: Zika: The Origin and Spread of a Mosquito-Borne Virus' (*WHO*, 2016) <www.who.int/bulletin/online_first/16–171082/en/> accessed 2 June 2016.

53. Remorse for any killing is always paramount because it is conduct that is antithetical to human nature.

54. This is something that can be discussed in relation to path dependency. Path dependency is the theory that historical factors will be significant in the possibility of securing change, despite the observation of available options. The theory is a typical approach to historical scientific discourse and was adapted in the early 1980s to explain economic inefficiencies. The theory is now applied in social and political discourse, which also explains notions of weak to super-strong path dependent modes of resistance. The idea that 'things would have been better if' is also challenged through a theory of negative path dependency. For a useful background introduction, see Richard R Nelson and Sydney G Winter, *An Evolutionary Theory of Economic Change* (Harvard University Press 1982); Mark J Roe, 'Chaos and Evolution in Law and Economics' (1996) 109 Harvard Law Review 641; Paul Pierson, 'Increasing Returns, Path Dependence, and the Study of Politics' (2000) 94(2) The American Political Science Review 251.

55. BBC News, 'NWP Officers Who Killed Dog on A55 Referred to Watchdog' (*BBC News*, 24 February 2016) <http://www.bbc.co.uk/news/uk-wales-north-west-wales-35650395> accessed 27 July 2016.

56. BBC News (24 February 2016).

57. BBC News (24 February 2016).

58. For example, Regan (1988).

59. For example, Peter Singer (1983).

60. Rowlands (2002); Rowlands (accessed 4th July 2016); Cochrane (2009).

61. Nussbaum (2007) [particularly Chapter 6], 346–347.

62. Donaldson and Kymlicka (2011); Kymlicka and Donaldson (2014). See also related ideas in Rob Garner, Dan Lyons and Angela Roberts, 'How to Protect Animal Welfare: Deliberation, Democracy and Representation. Policy Research Briefing' (*Centre for Animals and Social Justice*, Sheffield 2016) <http://www.casj.org.uk/wordpress/wp-content/uploads/2016/02/How-to-Protect-Animal-Welfare.pdf> accessed 27 July 2016. For critique, see, for example, Rowlands (accessed 4 July 2016). For a critique of specific rights in favour of responsibility, see Cupp (2016).

63. See, for example, Ani Satz, 'Animals as Vulnerable Subjects: Beyond Interest-Convergence, Hierarchy, And Property' (2009) 16 (2) Animal Law Review, 65; Maneesha Deckha, 'Vulnerability, Equality and Animals' (2015) 27(1) Canadian Journal of Women and the Law 47; Stephen Thierman, 'The Vulnerability of Other Animals' (2011) Volume IX I(2) Journal for Critical Animal Studies 182.

64. For example, in a form of justice that observes the ethical origin of the 'complaint.' See Syliviane Agacinski, 'Another Experience of the Question, or Experiencing the Question Other-Wise' in E Cadava P Connor and J-L Nancy (eds), *Who Comes After the Subject* (Routledge 1991) 14.

65. There are, of course, many ways other animals and nature are brought to bear on human rights principles and provisions, such as the right to freedom of expression and assigning a status of 'legal persons' to natural and nonhuman entities. For example, see <https://www.earthjurist.org/> or Mara Tignino and Laura E. Turley 'Granting Rivers Legal Rights: Is International Law Ready for Rights-Centered Environmental Protection?' (NewSecurityBeat 19 June 2018) <https://www.newsecuritybeat.org/2018/06/granting-rivers-legal-rights-international-law-ready-rights-centered-environmental-protection/> both accessed 15 April 2020. Also, some authors, Perpich for example, might comment that whatever valuing is brought to human rights represents ethics in the political domain of Levinas' thought.

66. As observed in *Vartic v Romania* (no 2) App no 14150/08 (ECtHR, 17 March 2014). See chapter 2.

Conclusion

The purpose of this book was to discuss whether a different ethical theory, when applied to the idea of human rights and the human right to freedom of conscience, would better accommodate the rights claims of vegans that are raised to defend the right to protect other animals. The impetus for this discussion is to contribute to the essential work already being done to help bring about a paradigm shift in the current concept of justice on account of its failure to adequately respond to nonhuman animals suffering and entrench respect for their rights.

Commenting on oppression and intersecting oppression, we saw in chapter 1 that Nibert suggests a new form of justice is necessary, one in which the 'social positions humans occupy neither compel violence, nor encourage passive complicity in oppressive practices and arrangements.' The contribution this book makes to this urgent discussion, critically assesses the exclusivity of human rights and its foundational principle of human autonomy. It questions the established orthodoxy of autonomy in human rights because, as I have explained, vegans in various parts of the world can be protected in law under the individual human right to freedom of conscience, in its various interpretations and under related equality law in the United Kingdom.

The relationship of veganism to law, the protection of vegans, or rejection of their claims for protection in law raise a number of issues to consider. The position I have taken in this book cites the rights claims of vegans, not as maters of personal and private conscience, but as claims that re-present the moral significance of other animals to a protective rights enterprise that excludes them. I have suggested that the claims of vegans are unique because although subsequent to raising a claim for unlawful interference or discrimination, a successful vegan may acquire a small tangible benefit, the claim is not primarily for the self but to protect others who are oppressed and marginalised in the current system of human rights justice.

The discussion in this book revolves around a central concern, which is; given the fact that animals suffer, and matter morally, why are the rights claims of vegans, who seek to defend their right to protect other animals, regarded to be matters concerning the right to individual, personal, and private conscience? My purpose was to explain that there is a way to think about human rights that can accommodate the rights claims of vegans as entirely logical and valuable. This way of thinking about human rights rests on the idea that the project that is human rights was advanced because witnessing and permitting the suffering of others was and is always abhorrent to the human conscience. I have developed the idea that protective rights are about dealing with the suffering of others to explain that a vegan right to freedom of conscience recognises a fundamental element of what it is to be human: to respond dutifully to vulnerable, suffering others in community, including nonhuman animals others.

By exploring the suffering narrative of human rights and its explanation that human rights were devised to ameliorate suffering, I have explained that the idea of protective rights is grounded by the ethics of otherness. This theory of ethics suggests an innate human desire for community, and a productive affectivity from witnessing the presence of precarious mortal others. It is a theory to explain what it is to be human and our innate compassion for others.

In this theory, a framework for protective rights recognises that others are vulnerable to arbitrary power and already suffer precarious mortality. In this context, a framework for rights formalises the significance of the primary duty to protect others in community. This orientation of human rights, developed by critical human rights scholars, rejects the primacy of the orthodoxy of autonomy, which, they claim, has produced unethical social relations, oppression and atomised individuals who are denied their full potential. In the current system of human rights, humanity is impoverished and denied the opportunity to flourish. What is needed, they argue, is a compassionate, dutiful justice, grounded by an ethics of alterity.

This principle idea of the ethics of alterity, as applied to the rights claims of vegans, is valuable to anti-oppressive discourse. By explaining veganism as a response to suffering and explaining the relevance of this theory of the human rights claims of vegans for the nonhuman others, the suffering narrative of human rights is relevant to an anti-oppressive discourse that seeks to deal with oppression, intersecting oppression, and support animal rights.

I have conceptualised the rights claims of vegans, through which they seek to offer protection for other animals, as originating in the original justice of the ethics of alterity. I have also suggested that veganism can be regarded as a manifestation of a much wider ethical regard for nonhuman animals: in terms of the original duty to suffering others, the rights claims of vegans to manifest duty to nonhuman animals are natural and normal demands that are made in an inclusive extended community of suffering others. I have suggested that since law has, in limited contexts, validated the claims of vegans and protected their interests, exclusive human rights are brought to a threshold where otherness and the moral standing of nonhuman animals are visible and enacted.

Using the suffering narrative of protective rights, I have suggested at least some basic rights of other animals. However, since it is unlikely that the law will permit other animals to be beneficiaries of protective rights in the short-term, I have suggested that the human right to freedom of conscience, under which claims by vegans are made, can be understood, not only as the provision under which various convictions of reason are presented to the democracy for negotiation, but also as giving expression to a 'human conscience' in which duty to others is most paramount, as evidenced by the creation of the UDHR following witnessing the atrocities of war and the suffering of others. On this view, the rights claims of vegans should not be regarded as matters of personal and private conscience to be limited by what is judicially considered to be proportional in the wider interest (built on entrenched species prejudice) but seen as re-presenting the original ethical duty that is invoked by the free conscience when in the presence of the precarious, mortal other who demands a response. As such, I argue that the suffering of other animals should necessarily feature in litigation. I also noted, however, that justice in the ethics of alterity may not always produce the outcomes desired in a vegan world, but neither would they serve oppressive anthropocentric privilege. In a protective rights enterprise built upon the ethics of alterity, a vegan value for anti-oppressive, open, honest, and transparent inclusive justice, would express remorse for all unavoidable sacrifices of some among others in community.

The discussion began, in chapter 1, by considering the essence of veganism. I explained that veganism gives expression to the moral standing of nonhuman animals and can be regarded as the lived expression of ethical responsibility to them and their suffering. I explained that veganism has significance as a culture grounded by ethics that are in opposition to those that facilitate the dominant culture of the consumption of animals. In this regard, veganism has been described by Matthew Calarco as indistinction in practice, by Bob Torres as the daily lived expression of ethical commitment and protest, and by Gary Francione as a moral imperative for a humanity that cares about other animals. Inspired by Levinas, I have argued that veganism is a matter of and for justice because it re-presents the natural moral standing of nonhuman animals and their suffering to the legal system of a society that has entrenched prejudice against them.

Following an examination of the claims of vegans, Chapter 1 went on to identify that vegans experience difficulties in various social contexts, and that some of these difficulties are categorised as claims under the human right to freedom of conscience. I explained that veganism can come within the scope of human rights, but that it was considered as an individual matter of personal and private conscience, and subject to the principles of adjudication in the orthodoxy of autonomy, in which the focus is entirely on whether the applicant suffers a disadvantage and does not include duty to suffering of other animals as an element of justice.

Chapter 2, thus, assessed the centrality of the human individual in human rights. It found that there was a complex history to the idea of human rights, that modern human rights were developed in response to immense suffering, but which orient towards individual claim rights, rather than duty in community.

Noting the centrality of the human individual in the idea of human rights, I observed that the claims of vegans for the moral standing of nonhuman animals are assessed in the context of the theory of human autonomy, known as the orthodoxy of autonomy. I suggested that claims of conscience for nonhuman others challenge this notion of entrenched human identity and the orientation of human rights. In this regard, chapter 2 went on to suggest that a system of human rights, based on Levinas's ethics of alterity, may have significant utility for the claims of vegans for suffering nonhuman others. This suggestion relies on the idea that Levinas's philosophy supports a suffering narrative of human rights, in which justice recognises that the subject is naturally and inescapably responsible to others. I explained that on this view, the claims of vegans are not about the expression of individual human autonomy but duty to a moral imperative to be concerned with suffering.

Chapter 3 explained an existing branch of critical human rights scholarship that utilises Levinas's ethics of alterity. It explained that scholars, such as Upendra Baxi and Costas Douzinas, reject the individualism of human rights. The target of human rights, they argue, is to eradicate suffering. These scholars explain how human rights could function better if the same-for-self claim rights gave way to a paramount concern for duty to and responsibility for others. They argue that the idea of human rights emerged in recognition of the ethical demands of others, and that caring and compassion are innate to human identity. They further argue that current human rights-for-the-self do not address suffering and that they restrain the ethical evolution of individuals and humanity.

Chapter 3 went on to explain that the ethics of human rights could be understood in terms of Levinas's ethics of alterity. Levinas identifies that human beings live in, and desire, community. Human beings have never known isolation and can never escape the fact that the other is always and already present. In this context of being predisposed to an awareness of others, otherness (innate concern for the other), a priori responsibility (the fact that a response to the other *cannot* be avoided), and infinite duty (the awareness that there are always and already multiple others who need to be considered) are paramount because they create ethical humanity. For Levinas, at the moment a subject encounters another, the subject is forced to respond and, thus, is made responsi-ble by the other. The subject becomes aware that they have entered the world of a precarious other and is duty-bound to consider the impact they may have on the other's vulnerability. The subject is not resistant to this universal unity. My thinking at this point is that the rights claims of vegans, to manifest ethical responsibility to other animals, or, to put it another way, the moral imperative, can be understood in terms of innate duty to others in extended community.

On this basis, I asked in chapter 4 whether the ethics of alterity concern nonhuman animals. I explained that Levinas's original, exclusive thesis was inconclusive on the matter of whether his philosophy was applicable to human and nonhuman others equally, but that it did not correspond to his later publications, in which he expressed how he was motivated to respond to a dog. I also noted that he explicitly stated that nonhuman others are owed ethical duties. Despite this, he never categorically confirmed that nonhuman animals generate ethical responsibility.

Chapter 4, therefore, examined various contributions from scholars interested in 'the question of the animal.' In these examinations, I found support for the argument that Levinas's ethics of alterity logically concern ethical responsibility to other animals. Scholars have argued that nonhuman others are not 'things'—they have expressed their authenticity as mortal beings—and that human beings have long witnessed and concerned themselves with nonhuman suffering. These scholars reasoned that if ethical responsibility is grounded by an innate desire to respond ethically to difference (alterity), then the ethics of alterity do concern other animals. I concluded this chapter by summarising that if the ethics of alterity can be grounded in suffering, have utility for the basis of rights, and concern nonhuman others, then the human ethical obligation to other animals must be understood in terms of our innate predisposition for compassion in an extended community of human and nonhuman others. I noted that such a conclusion has profound implications for human rights theory and practice, and currency in the search for a paradigm shift to ethical justice.

Chapter 5 outlined the implications for nonhuman animals and vegans of a system of human rights based on the ethics of alterity. I explained that all animals have basic entitlements, such as the right to life and liberty, and the right to exist free from being categorised in terms of oppressive themes that emerge from the totality of anthropocentric reason. I acknowledged that accommodating other animals in a rights enterprise is complex, but that it would begin from the recognition of their basic rights and a non-anthropocentric administration of legal justice that would be known as remorseful justice. This clearly requires a tremendous shift in thinking, from a prejudicial anthropocentrism to an inclusive non-anthropocentric form of reasoning that undoubtedly presents enormous theoretical and practical challenges, including a fair and honest assessment of whether the current speciesist prejudice—exemplified most predominantly in the commodification of nonhuman animals—reflects human integrity, or whether it simply serves the totality of anthropocentric reason. I conceded that a transformative paradigm shift in protective rights is unlikely to take place in the near future and the possibility of basic rights for other animals did not seem plausible.

Notwithstanding this concession, I suggested that the suffering narrative of rights and the ethics of alterity had value for the litigation of claims of conscience for nonhuman animals. Although the right to freedom of conscience is a significant value in human rights, I pointed out that it does not go far enough in facilitating evolution of the normative values that are no longer personal and private and that the claims of vegans can re-present nonhuman others, their precarious mortality, and the ethical imperative to attend to their suffering more effectively. I concluded that in cases of conscience that concern the moral standing of nonhuman animals, adjudication should reorient to recognise the collective desire for an ethical response to responsibility. In this application of the ethics of alterity to the claims of conscience for nonhuman animals, their suffering is acknowledged as a matter of ethical concern and the claims of vegans are articulated in the context of the original duty to vulnerable suffering nonhuman others as the grounding principle of natural justice.

On a practical, daily level, the argument developed requires public authorities and social institutions to regard veganism as a manifestation of a much wider ethical regard for nonhuman animals. The goal is a logical appreciation of other sentient life and the eradication of random, arbitrary and illogical prejudicial themes and categories of oppression. With regard to human rights, the argument requires a reorientation of foundational values away from the primacy of reason and towards the already acknowledged primacy of duty to others.

Chapter 5 outlined how vegans could raise the suffering narrative of human rights and bring the ethics of alterity to feature in human rights claims. It is worth explaining here, in more detail, how cases re-presenting other animals can be interpreted in the light of an ethics of alterity for human rights.

In *H v UK*,[1] the applicant was duty-bound to respond to the resource status of nonhuman animals. *H's* claim presented the commodification of a life that had been reduced to existing as a means for human ends. It was a plea for the lives of others that had been appropriated as objects of biological apparatus, on which dyes (that would eventually be made available to humans) could be tested for safety. From the perspective of the ethics of alterity, *H* presented an asymmetrical desire and the a priori duty to care. He re-presented and expressed the reduction of heterogeneous, mortal life, suffering, and death. Though we saw that his vegan convictions were held to be within the scope of the Convention, the finding was made only in relation to a system that prioritised and promoted *his* personal and private rational autonomy to believe in the seriousness of these matters, rather than on the basis that these matters of ethical responsibility, reduction, oppressive categorisation, and killing were serious, in themselves, in the free human conscience.

When discussing the merits of this case according to the ethics of alterity, the heterogeneity of life that cannot be known, and the duty to be compassionate in the face of vulnerability and suffering are paramount. Since any calculation for justice must be based on the original ethical opening—that is, the demand for responsibility as presented in an original face-to-face encounter—legal reasoning cannot rely on a principle of existing law if, in doing so, it overlooks the reduction of the legitimate other to commodity status and the dismissal of their oppression, suffering, and death.

H presented alterity to the extent that it is not limited by observable differences. In the application of the ethics of alterity, heterogeneous nonhuman animals are entitled to life and to a self-authored identity, in which their sapience is recognised. On this basis, *H* would be allowed a request to be exempt from participating in the practice of the reduction of legitimate others to a status of commodified resource, their appropriation, or their death.

Similarly, the alterity, precariousness and suffering of others were not considered in *Jakóbski* or in *Vartic*. Both cases re-presented the mortal, suffering other, and in both, personal disadvantage was paramount. In *Herrmann*,[2] Judge Pinto de Albuquerque took a novel approach in his partly dissenting judgment. In his dissent, he defended the presentation of the moral standing of nonhumans under the right to freedom of conscience. Though Pinto's views do not correlate to the argument of this book in that he promotes their protection under the Convention in other ways—such as through their property status—his views, nonetheless, give credence to the need to develop a better process of litigation for claims that represent the moral standing of nonhuman animals. Moreover, Pinto's comments recognise the scope for alterity to feature in existing human rights.

In this case, a landowner's right to object, under the human right to freedom of conscience, to an obligation to allow hunting to take place on his land was relegated by sixteen judges to one in favour of an apparently more important principle: the right to peaceful enjoyment of private property.[3] In a partly dissenting statement, Judge Pinto raised a sustained and lengthy point to support his judgment that the applicant had suffered a breach of his right to freedom of conscience. In this statement, Judge Pinto remarked on the creation of a developing interface of human and nonhuman interests at the ECtHR.

In relation to the applicant's conscientious objection to hunting, Judge Pinto commented on legal rules and on the importance of addressing higher ethical values, which he noted was '[m]ankind's true moral test.'[4] Judge Pinto remarked that this case was not only about property rights but also centred on the way in which the Convention protected animals.[5] For Pinto, the presentation of animals under the right to freedom of conscience is an important constituent part of a clear and uncontested broad trend towards the acceptance of the moral standing of nonhumans and their protection; a trend that the Convention and the ECtHR recognise.

Judge Pinto's dissenting statement was in response to the Court's prioritisation of property rights over a claim under the right to freedom of conscience. It supported the recognition of the moral standing of nonhuman animals by citing the works of philosophers who advocate positive changes in the human-animal relationship, in recognition of a 'shared nature' of human and nonhuman animals. Supporting his dissent, Pinto noted the clear and uncontested burgeoning of international and national constitutional animal protection, the developing interface of human and nonhuman interests at the ECtHR, works of compassionate philosophy in favour of the moral standing of animals, and the undisputed, widespread, compassionate, public voice (I rest my case for the need for vegan jurisprudence and a reorientation of human rights.)

From the perspective of the ethics of alterity, the claims of *H, Jakóbski, Vartic* and *Herrmann* can be reconceptualised as the recognition of ethical otherness. Each claim promoted ethical duty and responsibility to nonhuman animals. They reflected the fact of intertwined co-existence and human responsibility to precarious, mortal, nonhuman others.

What *H*, *Jakóbski*, *Vartic* and *Herrmann* communicate to law is the essence of the free human conscience in its function to respond to the ethical demand, and the pressing reality of affective ethical duty. As such, nonhuman animals have the right to be included in an extended administration of justice. This requires, in the first instance, a respectful, non-oppressive thematisation and categorisation, and a pro-active endeavour to re-present their legitimate value formally. This is unlikely to happen in the near future, but the recognition, in litigation, of affective otherness would serve to contest the principle of personal and private conscience in the human rights claims of vegans and counter the unethical totality of reason that facilitates and manifests convenient categories of oppressive anthropocentrism.

This articulation of rights, presented in the claims of vegans, forces adjudicators to face compassionate duty and ethical engagement with nonhuman others as a matter of and for human rights. The rights claims of vegans can bear witness to responsi-bility and re-present the authentic other that signifies their presence in a silent saying that precedes human reason and language in the free conscience. This silent saying can be articulated as animating ethics, or, on Perpich's view, opening valuing: the moment of intersection when the other 'speaks' to the subject: 'It is me,' 'I have a purpose,' 'I will one day die,' 'I am vulnerable and subject to mortality, how will you respond?' To ignore or reject this ethical event of absolute responsibility is to reside in the totality of reason. It stagnates human evolution, entrenches dogma, and fails to facilitate human freedom. The totality prevents the subject from enacting responsibility for others, rendering it ipso facto unethical.

Applying the principle of a priori responsibility (as invoked in the free conscience) to the cases referred to above requires the recognition of infinite responsibility to the a priori saying of the other and a commitment to responsibility as a constituent of human identity. This would then deal with the dismissal of nonhuman animals in the 'said' of the totality of reason that grounds and justifies lawful interference in the manifestation of vegan ethical responsibility. The application of a priori responsibility in adjudication works to dissolve the autonomy orthodoxy and supports animal rights infinitely.

H's claim related to the commodification of nonhumans that are designated as apparatus for chemical testing. This can also point to the infinity of the ethical demand. In two of the other cases, the plaintiffs refused to eat food derived from others they had not known or ever come into contact with. In one case, the applicant objected to the hunting of vulnerable others, who were also not observed in direct close proximity. In recognition of infinite responsibility, these subjects presented the demand of the third party under the right to free conscience. An explanation from the ethics of alterity is that the plaintiffs, in these cases, were practising infinite ethical responsibility. They were looking to defend their right to manifest the ethical obligation. They were dealt with in the context of an anthropocentric system of protective rights that is built on, but denies, ethical responsi-bility to nonhuman animal others. Though all were successful in that it was acknowledged that their beliefs could be protected under the right to freedom of conscience, all were considered in the context of individual conscience and the wider human interest which, when applying protest scholar logic, represses human flourishing.

Currently, the calculation and balancing conducted under the right to freedom of conscience are from within the totality Levinas explains. They concern only whether the individual self-of-the-ego suffers a disadvantage in circumstances of an entrenched totality of reason that has oppressed and commodified nonhuman animals. These conditions perpetuate speciesism and what Melanie Joy has called the invisible belief system of carnism that protects, perpetuates and maintains the (false) natural, normal and necessary justification for the oppressive conditions for nonhumans defined as 'food.'[6] Resistant to these systems, veganism expresses the infinity of responsibility by re-presenting the suffering nonhuman other as the relational third party who is not in direct proximity. Keeping in mind that the principle of infinity requires that the third party be owed the same ethical consideration as those in close proximity, intentional reduction, harm or killing must be prohibited.[7]

This approach to settling the human rights claims of vegans covers a range of situations that vegans currently find intolerable, such as a requirement that school pupils dissect nonhumans in class. Under the ethics of alterity, rather than primarily assessing the degree of disadvantage to the applicant, the emphasis would be on the suffering and death of the nonhuman animal in question. In these reoriented conditions, a school's attempt to limit its duty towards nonhuman others (and vegans) would be rejected on the basis that the teaching objective sought is disproportionate to the suffering of nonhuman animal others—because it requires their reduction, commodification, and death.

The same considerations apply to cases presented by public sector employees who are required to wear protective personal equipment and uniform items that are derived from the skin of nonhuman animals. In these cases, although rules and regulations exist for safety, the court would, under the ethics of alterity, have to consider the duty to nonhumans in line with the original ethical facing. Given that there are suitable alternative uniform items that meet the requirements of health and safety policies, the court would have no option but to conclude that the interference with conscience and duty to the other is disproportionate.[8]

To be clear, the application of the ethics of alterity to human rights honours the unique individuality of each and every human and nonhuman animal. It acknowledges the transcendence of the subject by the other as the process by which human beings become ethical. On this basis, it honours the moral standing of all lives as unique, ethics-inducing others, who invoke responsibility and facilitate acts of duty.

In this system, responsibility and duty are inseparable from the awareness of a universally shared characteristic of precariousness and the understanding that all life is subject to the forces of mortality. A rights enterprise protects the world of the other from the actions of the subject, regardless of actual, observed suffering. As such, all nonhuman animals have moral and legal status on the basis that they are perceived as mortal and vulnerable, and duties can be articulated as rights.

In this theory, individuals in infinity have rights, but a system of remorseful justice will, necessarily but remorsefully, limit duties owed. Though the idea of rights for singular others is complex, to accommodate uniqueness of Being, any necessary thematisation or categorisation undertaken remorsefully must not be done in order to automatically relegate, or deny the self-defined identity of, or duty owed to, the other.[9] In an inclusive application of the ethics of alterity, there is a commitment to non-oppressive categorisations and themes that demonstrate an intention to acknowledge duty and responsibility to the other.

Remorseful justice, unfortunately, requires that balance is brought to the infinite obligatory demand. The ethics of otherness offers general principles, but does not prescribe a detailed set of normative categories to suit all circumstances. It is, though, a philosophy that is sensitive to the potential for a totality of reason to subjugate in the interests of the human subject. In this regard, contemporary theory on animal rights may help to ascertain the (remorseful) principles of the way forward. In addition, an inclusive adaptation of the theory of the Saturated Marginalised Other, developed by Simmons, may also be helpful in developing principles for practice by introducing the idea of phenomenological saturation of subjugation and suffering.

Thus, the claims of vegans in a human rights built upon the ethics of alterity have strength and potential because vegan values are paramount and claims for nonhuman animals are deemed to re-present inescapable ethical facing. The idea of a universal, infinite ethical responsibility to animals to bear upon current human rights deposes the personal and private element in the claims of conscience for other animals and does not rest on personal human disadvantage. Though the right to freedom of conscience remains significant to negotiating matters of individual conscience to a democracy, when it is used by vegans to re-present the vulnerability and suffering of others to the community, it facilitates the ethics of alterity to promote the formative ethical value of duty to the other and restores the notion of duty in community.

In this system, litigation in cases, such as *H*, *Jakóbski*, *Vartic* and *Herrmann*, no longer submits to the centrality of the human individual and its associated primary concepts (such as personal disadvantage and significant disadvantage); nor does the judiciary override ethical regard for nonhuman animals in favour of a different protocol that does not 'face' animals (right to property). Instead, it acknowledges existing ethical regard for other-than-human animals and permits a natural justice based on ethical reasoning that is induced by the primacy of responsibility to the other.

I have already stated that my attention to the issues raised in this book is to contribute to the paradigm shift needed to bring about a social justice that seeks to ameliorate suffering, oppression, intersecting oppression, and the violence of injustice. I have argued that the suffering of other animals is relevant to the postmodern critique of the orthodoxy of autonomy of human rights and its grounding principle to reorient human right to the ethics of alterity. The argument developed in this book is that veganism gives expression to the moral standing of nonhuman animals that is resisted by the orthodoxy of autonomy of human rights and that there are important discussions to be held about a human rights practice that does accommodate vegans, and a human rights practice that does not. I have explained that both the accommodation of vegans and continued resistance against vegans are a matter for and of human rights, its ontology, philosophy, and practice.

The conclusion that Levinas's ethics of alterity has a place in this pressing discourse has been reached, following identifying a suffering narrative of veganism, linking this with the existing suffering narrative of human rights and reviewing the logic of Levinas's own thesis and literature, available in the domain of animal ethics. Existing scholarship on this subject identifies two positions that support the inclusion of nonhuman animals. The first is the recognition that both Levinas and social humanity in general are ethically motivated by nonhuman animals because a life force, vulnerable to the forces of mortality, is witnessed. Humans bestow care and compassion on nonhuman others, willingly, in response to the unspoken 'saying' that asks for compassion to be extended as a matter of natural social justice. In this relationship is the expression of 'face.' It is an epiphany that animates ethics. The other halts the unrestrained ego of the self, facilitating innate responsibility. This first position promotes the idea that nonhuman animals have intrinsic value to generate ethics through an encounter and, thus, are owed ethical duties.

The second position is offered by Diane Perpich. This theory holds that Levinas's priority of the human face does not exclude nonhuman others from ethical concern. Levinas's priority of the human face merely means that it is human beings who create ethics by bringing ethical openings to be negotiated within the context of a democracy. This position supports the conclusion of this book, because humans have long held nonhuman animals to be a matter of ethical justice. Evidence given for this view included both the recognition in various treaties and national constitutions of the sentient status of nonhumans and examples of case law that recognises the human concern for vulnerable nonhuman animals. That nonhuman animals matter to the human community is also recognised through the fact that veganism has been deemed to be within the scope of human rights protection.

These conclusions are important for anti-oppressive human rights discourse. Human rights, at a basic level, recognise the right of the other to live and to be free from arbitrary oppression. They aim to secure emancipation in the face of suffering and bring the suffering of the marginalised to the centre. Protest scholars explain that the idea of human rights could only ever have emerged in recognition of duty to others, but, they argue, human rights have been derailed by a focus on claim rights-for-the-self in the context of an entrenched orthodoxy of autonomy. They further maintain that the idea of a homogeneous autonomous self is a most oppressive component of a protective rights enterprise whose target is the elimination of suffering. In this historical and contemporary discourse, even that of the postmodernist, the moral standing of nonhuman others and their suffering has been largely ignored.

These observations are important because the community of living beings on planet Earth extends beyond human beings. The orthodoxy of autonomy, human exceptionalism, and human supremacy are outdated ideas that are slowly giving way to a richer understanding of interconnected life and the need for systems of justice to recognise the impact of human activities on the planet and other life. The idea of protection for life and liberty, for self-authorised identity, and for care and support no longer concerns only human beings in a society that has already recognised the sentient status of other, mortal life and acknowledged that human activities can (and do) cause further harm. In the case of nonhuman animals, the harms imposed, and the suffering endured are not just accidentally off the scale. Rather, suffering is a direct result of both an entrenched denial that nonhuman others have lives that should be lived according to their own modes of being, and of their exclusion from the moral community.

On the view I have presented, human rights are built upon a false ontology of species prejudice. In the orthodoxy of autonomy, they transmit the crime of entrenching a 'said' in denial of the clear, but silenced, metaphorical 'saying' of nonhuman others. In this context, the claims of vegans that re-present the suffering of nonhuman animals are, in many jurisdictions, disadvantaged by the established orthodoxy, while in others, the established orthodoxy covertly suppresses vegan values by negotiating the claims of conscience for nonhuman others as originating in the personal and private sphere of human reason. These manifestations of speciesist prejudice should surface to speak with and for those most marginal and most distant.

My ideas, are of course, counter to those of scholars who seek to defend the ethics of human rights on their own terms. James Griffin explains human exceptionalism to make sense of human rights and its self-perpetuating anthropocentric body of theory. In this context, advocates for nonhuman animals attempt to assign human characteristics to nonhuman others to support their cause—but in the ethics of alterity, this is merely a reduction of the other to the same: in the ethics of alterity, justice acknowledges and respects difference and suffering.

In a challenge to the autonomy orthodoxy, this book describes veganism as a response to the natural ethical demand of the suffering other. There will no doubt be objections, but in looking to the philosophy of otherness, it not only grounds the inclusion of nonhuman others within a concrete, non-abstract ethical experience of them as authentic others—it also supports the call of protest scholars for otherness to operate as the inclusive postmodern principle of justice for the idea of human rights. In this regard, the universal principle to be established in a non-anthropocentric rights enterprise is not cognitive competence, suffering, or sentience, because these are the a posteriori categories used to describe (ineffectively) the reasons for the meaning and significance of the relational encounter, intrinsic to the idea of duty and protective rights.[10] Rather, the first principle to be established is universal responsibility; but a specific kind of responsibility. It requires an acknowledgment that human beings are ethically responsive in the presence of the other, who presents their mortal existence to us. It requires an understanding that human identity is co-constructed in relational experiences with others, who are always and already present and constitutive of who we are. Reason, on the other hand, is merely subsequent, but instrumental, to an ethical humanity that is burdened with developing and implementing a system of justice that must remorsefully limit competing ethical demands.

Ultimately, the importance of this book to anti-oppressive discourse that seeks a paradigm shift to restorative justice lies in its support for the idea that ethical duties are owed to others because it is in our interest, and in our nature, to desire to live in community, without killing, oppressing, and harming vulnerable others. This is the bedrock of a protective rights enterprise that can only be conceived of from within the context of apprehending and being already concerned with, and dutiful to, others. This does not imply, of course, that applying the ethics of alterity to vegan rights to protect other animals is an easy case.

Levinas's philosophy on the ethics of alterity is complex, demanding, and so 'blisteringly obscure'[11] that interpretive accounts run the risk of representing nothing more than, as Desmond Manderson suggests, a simple understanding.[12] It is true that there is much to be explored, reflected on, and revisited in Levinas's work: for example, the command not to kill that is issued in the ethical encounter, and the idea that a remorseful justice may (remorsefully) be required to implement violence in the protection of the self and the other's other. In his development of an exceptionally dense and complex philosophy of the merits of such violence, Levinas offers a pre-social, gracious humanity no practical guidance in its quest to create and maintain a social harmony that also permits a utility of violence.

Moreover, reading and attempting to decipher Levinas's philosophy involves many optimistic highs, twists, and turns, but also intense lows that together culminate in the frustrating acknowledgment that it is a philosophy that does not easily lend itself to the formulation of exacting principles for the application of law.[13] Apart from extracting the basic ground rules on which a case for the inclusion of nonhumans can be made, Levinas's ethics of alterity and the creation of positive law are at odds: the first requires an acceptance of a priori affectivity and of notions of singularity, unique otherness, and infinity; the second provides for the reason of man and the potential need in justice for homogeneous themes and categories. What is required is a way to thematise and categorise that does not overcomplicate singularity but at the same time does not cause oppression through unjust and prejudicial themes and categories.

With the exception of the developments for practical justice put forward by Simmons, existing critical human rights scholarship does not develop a workable system of justice from Levinas's ethics of alterity. This is also characteristic of this book—save for utilising the foundational principles to argue for a reorientation in the foundations of human rights, from individualism to a non-anthropocentric inclusive otherness.

This book has explained though, an alternative model for thinking about the idea of human rights, the right to freedom of conscience, and litigating and adjudicating the human rights claims of vegans by invoking otherness, responsibility, and duty to nonhuman others. It is a starting point to consider not just the idea of the impact of exclusive human rights on nonhuman animals, but the implications of veganism in human rights in the context of manifestations of speciesist prejudice.

My discussion is necessarily rooted in the human mode of thought, in that it is concerned with the principles of Levinas's ethics of alterity that describe the normativity of the relational experience that invokes responsibility. This lack of emphasis on animal sentiency should not be regarded as lacking in the search for redirection to justice. As Jill Stauffer suggests, the ethics of alterity may present the basis for an emancipatory justice that stems from a reconceptualised understanding of human subjectivity.[14] Such a reconceptualisation of human subjectivity can accommodate an understanding of veganism being the re-presentation of the nonhuman other that has been caught up in the totality of the orthodoxy of human autonomy.

In the development of a theory of relational Becoming with other animals that can be used to underpin an extension of justice and a vegan jurisprudence of human rights, it is not only the articulation of concrete principles for everyday practice that remains a significant challenge. In an endeavour to deal with oppression, intersect oppressions, and ascribe moral and legal standing to nonhuman animals in terms of relational ethical responsibility, discourse is and will continue to be challenging.[15] It must not centre on the established orthodoxy, vegans, or nonhuman animals and their sentiency, but on human modes of thought: 'change regarding the moral standing of animals is not necessarily about animals. It is about us. Facing animals is about facing ourselves and others.'[16] In facing ourselves, our enquiries and discussions about intersubjective becoming with other animals must not only focus on becoming with other animals in close proximity but must necessarily include those most distant.

The ethics of alterity is a philosophy that is able to move forward a vegan jurisprudence of human rights on the basis that, if nothing else, Levinas's goal, as Robert Bernasconi remarks, was a 'reorientation of thinking . . . [that] impacts on our approach to concrete situations so that we come to see them as ethical.'[17] Including veganism in law as an issue for anti-oppressive discourse will help further understand what is at stake in a reorientation of thinking to ground human rights in an ethics of alterity that does not explain how to live according to what it prescribes—but certainly concerns vegans and nonhuman others. This endeavour also comes with a warning for scholars.

Baxi cautioned about the potential for 'Vulgar Levinasianism.' This was based on Alford's reference to the 'Levinas Effect,' in which scholars interpret Levinas to 'say whatever [they] wanted to say in the first place.'[18] With regard to the re-presentation of nonhuman animals and their visibility in the human rights claims of vegans, the idea of veganism as a response to a priori ethical responsibility is, admittedly, a moot point—but no more so than the traditional and historical idea of the immanence and the original violence of (exclusive) human rights.

If Levinas's philosophy on the ethics of alterity is anything at all, it is a response to and in the service of the other. As such, even a simplistic understanding and application to justice and law is better than a deep, comprehensive understanding and application of an alternative that exalts the primacy of the self and privileges some automatically, at the unexamined expense of suffering others. In this regard, discourse could do much worse than to explore further the potential of the ethics of alterity to ground a protective rights enterprise that seeks universality and aims to attend to suffering, emancipate, and liberate. This is especially so in the current era of scepticism about the institution that is human rights, the escalating urge to attend to the off-the-scale suffering of nonhuman animals, and the interface of human and nonhuman moral standing, currently observed in human rights theory and practice. Such an exploration is, after all, implicit in the existence of human rights and (as Levinas goes to great lengths to argue) is constitutive of a humanity that is always and already trying to work out how to respond to responsibility. If, even at a basic level of understanding, Levinas's ethics of alterity communicate the principles of justice that accommodate suffering others, veganism does this work at the heart of human rights and in the foundation of the right to freedom of conscience.

The argument presented in this book is not limited to a consideration of one system of human rights that seeks to comply with an interpretation of what is considered to be established, normative and universal principles. It extends to a critique of the false ontological assumptions, entrenched in the idea of human rights, that justify the exclusion of other animals. The ontologically justified exclusion of other animals does not only subjugate and deny them their basic rights, it also denies the ethical obligation innate to a compassionate humanity that, according to the critical scholars, is restrained and sucked into a paradigm of violence and prejudice, which it finds so objectionable.

In conclusion, exclusive human rights are under pressure from veganism. The human rights claims of vegans 'shake the pillars of justice' and demand human rights to account for failing to deal with the vulnerability and suffering of animals. If accommodated, the legal claims of vegans for the right to practically manifest ethical duty may be seen to be super-disruptive with huge transformative potential. Where they are denied, vegans are supressed in, what Derrida might agree, is an oppressive, established orthodoxy reminiscent of the unjust totality, in which protests and appeals for other animals are supressed and marginalised as that of an invalid minority. However, vegan voices are gaining traction and may no longer be:

> little assured of their discourse, of their right to discourse, and of the enactment of their discourse within the law, as a declaration of rights—in order to protest, in order to appeal . . . to what is still presented in such a problematic way as *animal rights, in* order to awaken us to our responsibilities and our obligations.[19]

NOTES

1. (1993) 16 EHRR.
2. *Herrmann v Germany* App No 9300/07 (ECtHR, 26th June 2012).
3. See Page 30 of the judgment: the Court 'holds by sixteen votes to one that it is not necessary to examine separately the complaint under Article 9 of the Convention.' Instead, a Protocol 1 right to peaceful enjoyment of property took precedence. Convention for the Protection of Human Rights and Fundamental Freedoms (European Convention on Human Rights, as amended) (ECHR) Protocol to the Convention for the Protection of Human Rights and Fundamental Freedoms, Article 1.
4. See Paragraph 1 of Judge Pinto's partly dissenting statement.
5. Pinto observes protection of animals in the form of the property right of humans, as beings in themselves and in the context of environmental balance.

6. Melanie Joy, *Why We Love Dogs, Eat Pigs and Wear Cows* (Conari Press 2010).

7. Subject to a notion of 'just' (but remorseful) killing.

8. This does not mean that if there were no alternatives there would be a justification for the resource status of nonhumans.

9. Derrida's thoughts on singularity (see Derrida (2008)), in which he cites the story of the cat that looks, are too complex to help develop a universal system of protective rights because of the emphasis on absolute singularity. This is a position from which it is difficult to provide any ethical categories through which universal principles would be regarded ethical.

10. These remain important concepts of reason that undoubtedly play a significant role in the remorseful balancing required in the administration of legal justice.

11. Manderson (2009) 3.

12. Manderson (2009) 4.

13. For discussions on a variety of topics on Levinas and law, see Marinos Diamantides (ed), *Levinas, Law, Politics* (Routledge-Cavendish 2007) and Manderson (2009).

14. Jill Stauffer, 'Productive Ambivalence: Levinasian Subjectivity, Justice, and the Rule of Law' in Manderson (2009).

15. For a discussion of the way philosophy currently deals with ascribing moral standing to nonhuman others, see Mark Coeckelbergh and David J Gunkel, 'Facing Animals: A Relational, Other-Oriented Approach to Moral Standing' (2014) 27(5) Journal of Agriculture and Environmental Ethics 715. doi:10.1007/s10806–013–9486–3.

16. Coeckelbergh and Gunkel (2014) 715.

17. Robert Bernasconi, 'What is the Question to Which Substitution is the Answer?' in Simon Critchley and Robert Bernasconi (eds), *The Cambridge Companion to Levinas* (Cambridge University Press 2002) 250.

18. C Fred Alford, 'Levinas and the Limits of Political Theory' in Marinos Diamantides (ed), *Levinas, Law, Politics* (Routledge-Cavendish 2007) 107.

19. Derrida (2008) 26.

Bibliography

Acampora R R, *Corporal Compassion: Animal Ethics and Philosophy of Body* (University of Pittsburgh Press 2006)

Adams C J, *The Sexual Politics of Meat* (Polity Press 1990)

——— *Neither Man nor Beast: Feminism and the Defence of Animals* (The Continuum Publishing Company 1995)

Adams C J and Gruen L, 'Introduction' in Adams C J and Gruen L (eds), *Ecofeminism: Feminist Interactions with Other Animals and the Earth* (Bloomsbury 2014)

Adorno R, 'Human Dignity and Human Rights as a Common Ground for a Global Bioethics' (2009) 34(3) *Journal of Medicine and Philosophy* 223

Agacinski S, 'Another Experience of the Question Other-Wise' in Cadava E, Connor P and Nancy J-L (eds), *Who Comes After the Subject* (Routledge 1991)

Agamben G, *The Open Man and Animal* (Attell K tr, Stanford University Press 2004)

American Vegan Society, 'History' <www.americanvegan.org/history.htm>

Animals Australia, 'The Voice for Animals' (*Animals Australia*, nd) <http://www.animalsaustralia.org/media/videos.php?vid=factoryfarming>

ALFSG, 'Animal Liberation Front Supporters Group' December 2011 <http://www.alfsg.org.uk/mags/SG_Dec_2011.pdf>

Andersen S S, 'Proximity: A Levinasian Approach to Justice for Animals' (2015) 1 Global Journal of Animal Law (GJAL) <https://ojs.abo.fi/index.php/gjal/article/view/1381/1686>

Animal Aid, 'You can help stop this suffering' (2011) 165 Outrage supplement Winter 2011

Atterton P, 'The Talking Cure: The Ethics of Psychoanalysis' in Atterton P and Calarco M (eds), *Radicalizing Levinas* (State University of New York Press 2010)

———, 'Levinas and our Moral Responsibility to Other Animals' (2011) 54(6) Inquiry 633

——— 'The Emanuel Levinas Web Page' <www.levinas.sdsu.edu/>

—— and Calarco M, 'Editors Introduction: The Third Wave of Levinas Scholarship' in Atterton P and Calarco M (eds), *Radicalizing Levinas* (State University of New York Press 2010)

Baxi U, 'Concepts of Human Rights' in Baxi U and Mann K (eds), *Human Rights Learning. A People's Report* (*PDHRE*, 2006) <www.pdhre.org/pdhre-report-2006.pdf>

—— *Human Rights in a Posthuman World* (Oxford University Press 2007)

—— 'Judging Emmanuel Levinas? Some reflections on reading *Levinas, Law, Politics'* (Book review of Diamantides M (ed), *Levinas, Law, Politics* (Routledge-Cavendish 2007)) (2009a) 72 (1) *The Modern Law Review* 116

—— *The Future of Human Rights* (3rd ed, 2nd impression, Oxford University Press 2009b)

—— 'Random Reflections on the [Im]possibility of Human Rights Education' (*PDHRE*, no date) <www.pdhre.org/dialogue/reflections.html>

BBC News, 'Animal Activist Dies on Hunger Strike' (*BBC News*, 5 November 2001) <http://news.bbc.co.uk/1/hi/england/1639225.stm>

—— 'Austrian driver allowed 'pastafarian' headgear photo' (*BBC News*, 14 July 2011) <http://www.bbc.co.uk/news/world-europe-14135523>

—— 'NWP Officers Who Killed Dog on A55 Referred to Watchdog' (*BBC News*, 24 February 2016)

Becker S, 'Patricia MacCormack Talks About Ahuman Theory, Importance of Non-Speciecist Ways' (*Daily Nexus*, 6 November 2013) <http://dailynexus.com/2013–11–06/patricia-maccormack-talks-about-ahuman-theory-importance-of-non-speciecist-ways/>

Bell R H, *Simone Weil: The Way of Justice as Compassion* (Rowman & Littlefield Publishers 1998)

Berger J, *About Looking* (Pantheon Books 1980)

Bernasconi R, 'What is the Question to Which Substitution is the Answer?' in Critchley S and Bernasconi R (eds), *The Cambridge Companion to Levinas* (Cambridge University Press 2002)

—— and Critchley S, *Re-Reading Levinas* (The Athlone Press 1991)

—— and Wood D, *The Provocation of Levinas: Rethinking the Other* (1st paperback edn 2014, Routledge 1988)

Bhasin K and de la Cruz N, 'Here's What You Need To Know About The Ground Up Insects Starbucks Puts in Your Frappuccino' (*Business Insider*, 29 March 2012) <www.businessinsider.com/how-cochineal-insects-color-your-food-and-drinks-2012–3?IR=T>

Bielefeldt H, 'Freedom of Religion or Belief: A Human Right Under Pressure' (2012) Oxford Journal of Law and Religion 1(1), 24 doi 10.1093/ojlr/rwr018

Bird Rose D, *Wild Dog Dreaming: Love and Extinction* (University of Virginia Press 2011)

Bobbio N, *The Age of Rights* (Allan Cameron tr, Polity Press 1996)

Bourke J, *What it Means to be Human: Reflections From 1791 to the Present* (Virago Press 2011)

Brambell F W R; Technical Committee to Enquire into the Welfare of Animals kept under Intensive Livestock Husbandry Systems, 'Report of the Technical Committee to Enquire into the Welfare of Animals kept under Intensive Livestock Husbandry Systems' (Ministry of Agriculture Fisheries and Food, Cmnd 2836. Her Majesty's Stationery Office [ca. 1965])

British Dietetic Association, 'Complimentary Feeding (weaning)' <https://www.bda.uk.com/foodfacts/WeaningYourChild.pdf>

British Dietetic Association, 'Food Facts Sheet: Vegetarian Diets' <https://www.bda.uk.com/foodfacts/vegetarianfoodfacts.pdf>

Brown A, *Who Cares for Animals? 150 Years of the RSPCA* (Heinemann Ltd 1974)

Bunch M, 'Posthuman Ethics and the Becoming Animal of Emmanuel Levinas' (2014) 55(1) Culture, Theory and Critique 34

Burggraeve R, *The Wisdom of Love in the Service of Love: Emmanuel Levinas on Justice, Peace, and Human Rights* (Marquette University Press 2002)

Butler J, *Precarious Life* (Verso 2004a)

—— *Undoing Gender* (Routledge 2004b)

Calarco M, 'Deconstruction is Not Vegetarianism: Humanism, Subjectivity, and Animal Ethics' (2004) 37 Continental Philosophy Review 175

—— *Zoographies: The Question Of the Animal from Heidegger to Derrida* (Columbia University Press 2008)

—— 'We Are Made Of Meat: Interview With Matthew Calarco' (Interviewer Caffo L 2013) 1 (2) Relations: Beyond Anthropocentrism <www.ledonline.it/index.php/Relations/issue/view/3>

Cambridge Declaration on consciousness <http://fcmconference.org/img/CambridgeDeclarationOnConsciousness.pdf>

Casey E, 'Taking a Glance at the Environing World' in Martino D J (ed), *Confluences: Phenomenology and Postmodernity, Environment, Race, Gender* (Duquesne University Silverman Phenomenology Centre 2000)

Castricano J and Simonsen R R (eds), *Critical Perspectives on Veganism* (Palgrave Macmillan 2016)

Caspero A, 'Building a Healthy Vegetarian Meal: Myths and Facts' (*Eat Right: Academy of Nutrition and Dietetics*, 28 January 2014) <www.eatright.org/resource/food/nutrition/vegetarian-and-special-diets/building-a-healthy-vegetarian-meal-myths-and-facts>

Cavalieri P, *The Animal Question, Why Non-Human Animals Deserve Rights* (Oxford University Press 2005

Clark D, 'On Being the Last Kantian in Nazi Germany: Dwelling with Animals After Levinas' (1999) in Ham J and Senior M (eds), *Animal Acts: Configuring the Human in Western History* (Routledge 1997)

Clement G, *Care Autonomy and Justice: Feminism and the Ethic of Care* (Westview Press 1996)

Cochrane A, 'Do Animals Have an Interest in Liberty?' (2009) 57(3) Political Studies 660

—— *Animal Rights Without Liberation: Applied Ethics and Human Obligations* (Columbia University Press 2012)

—— 'From Human Rights to Sentient Rights' (2013) 16(5) Critical Review of International Social and Political Philosophy 655 doi:10.1080/13698230.2012.691235

Coeckelbergh M and Gunkel D J, 'Facing Animals: A Relational, Other-Oriented Approach to Moral Standing' (2014) 27(5) Journal of Agriculture and Environmental Ethics 715. doi:10.1007/s10806–013–9486–3

Cohen R A, 'Foreword' in Levinas E, *Otherwise Than Being or Beyond Essence* (Alphonso Lingis tr, Duquesne University Press 1998/2011)

——— 'Introduction' in Levinas E, *Humanism of the Other* (Poller N tr, University of Illinois Press 2006)

Cole M and Morgan K, 'Vegaphobia: Derogatory Discourse of Veganism and the Reproduction of Speciesism in UK National Newspapers' (2011) 62 1, 134 The British Journal of Sociology

Collard A and Contrucci J, *Rape of the Wild: Man's Violence against Animals and the Earth.* (The Women's Press Ltd 1988)

Compassionate Action for Animals, 'Embrace Your Empathy' <www.exploreveg.org/stories/>

Compassion in World Farming, 'The life of: dairy cows' <www.ciwf.org.uk/media/5235185/the-life-of-dairy-cows.pdf>

Council of Europe, Collected Edition of the 'Travaux Préparatoires' Volume 1: Preparatory Commission of the Council of Europe, Committee of Ministers, Consultative Assembly 11 May-8 September 1949 (Martinus Nijhoff-The Hague 1975)

Council of Europe, 'Compass: Manual for Human Rights Education with Young People: Makah Whaling' <http://www.coe.int/en/web/compass/makah-whaling>

Council of Europe/European Court of Human Rights, 'Practical Guide on Admissibility Criteria' (2011) <http://www.justitsministeriet.dk/sites/default/files/media/Arbejdsomraader/International/Guide_pratique_ENG.pdf>

Cranston M, *What Are Human Rights?* (Bodley Head 1973)

Critchley S, 'Introduction' in Critchley S and Bernasconi R (eds), *The Cambridge Companion to Levinas* (5th printing, Cambridge University Press 2002/2008)

——— *Infinitely Demanding: Ethics of Commitment, Politics of Resistance* (Verso 2012)

——— and Bernasconi R (eds), *The Cambridge Companion to Levinas* (Cambridge University Press 2002)

Cruft R, Liao S M and Renzo M (eds), *Philosophical Foundations of Human Rights* (Oxford University Press 2015)

Cupp R L Jr, 'Focusing on Human Responsibility Rather than Legal Personhood for Nonhuman Animals' (2016) Paper Number 2016/17 Legal Studies Research Paper Series (Pepperdine University School of Law) <http://papers.ssrn.com/sol3/papers.cfm?abstract_id=2784890>

Curtin D, 'Compassion and Being Human' in Adams C J and Gruen L (eds), *Ecofeminism: Feminist Interactions with Other Animals and the Earth* (Bloomsbury 2014)

Damian C, 'Avoiding meat and dairy is 'single biggest way' to reduce your impact on Earth' (The Guardian, 31 May 2018) <https://www.theguardian.com/environment/2018/may/31/avoiding-meat-and-dairy-is-single-biggest-way-to-reduce-your-impact-on-earth>

Davis C, *Levinas: An Introduction* (University of Notre Dame Press 1997)

Davis J, 'Veganism from 1806' (*Vegsource*, 2011) <www.vegsource.com/john-davis/veganism-from-1806.html>

Deckha M, 'Vulnerability, Equality and Animals' (2015) 27(1) Canadian Journal of Women and the Law 47

Dembour M-B, *Who Believes in Human Rights*? (Cambridge University Press 2006)

Derrida J, ''Eating well,' or the calculation of the subject: An interview with Jacques Derrida' in Cadava E, Connor P, Nancy J-L (eds), *Who Comes After the Subject* (Routledge 1991)

——— *The Animal That Therefore I Am* (Wills D tr, Mallet M L ed, Fordham University Press 2008)

Diamantides M (ed), *Levinas, Law, Politics* (Routledge-Cavendish 2007)

Donaldson S and Kymlicka W, *Zoopolis: A Political Theory of Animal Rights* (Oxford University Press 2011)

Douzinas C, *The End of Human Rights: Critical Legal Thought at the Turn of the Century* (Hart Publishing 2000)

——— 'The End(s) of Human Rights' (2002) 26 (2) 445 Melbourne University Law Review <www5.austlii.edu.au/au/journals/MelbULawRw/2002/23.html>

——— 'The Many Faces of Humanitarianism' (2007) 2, 1 Parrheisa <parrhesiajournal.org/parrhesia02/parrhesia02_douzinas.pdf>

——— 'The Poverty of Rights Jurisprudence' in Gearty C and Douzinas C (eds), *The Cambridge Companion to Human Rights Law* (Cambridge University Press 2012)

——— 'Seven Theses on Human Rights: (6) Desire' (*Critical Legal Thinking: Law and the Political*, 2013) <criticallegalthinking.com/2013/06/03/seven-theses-on-human-rights-6-desire/>

——— and Warrington R, 'Antigone's Law: A Genealogy of Jurisprudence' in Douzinas C, Goodrich P and Hachamovitch Y (eds), *Politics, Postmodernity and Critical Legal Studies: The Legality of the Contingent* (Routledge 1994)

Edelglass W, 'Levinas on Suffering and Compassion' (2006) 45(2) Sophia 43

———, Hatley J and Diehm C (eds), *Facing Nature: Levinas and Environmental Thought* (Duquesne University Press 2012)

Eisnitz G, *Slaughterhouse: The Shocking Story of Greed, Neglect, And Inhumane Treatment Inside the U.S. Meat Industry* (Prometheus Books 1997/2007)

——— 'From Farm to Fork Presentation by Gail Eisnitz' (*Animal Liberation Front*, 1999) <www.animalliberationfront.com/Practical/FactoryFarm/From%20Farm%20to%20Fork.ht>

——— 'From Farm to Fork Presentation by Gail Eisnitz' (*Compassion Action for Animals*, 1999) <www.exploreveg.org/issues/farmtofork.html>

Elliot R (ed), *Environmental Ethics* (Oxford University Press 1995)

Ellis F R and Sanders T A B, 'Angina and Vegan Diet' (June 1977) 93 (6), American Heart Journal

Equality and Human Rights Commission, 'Employment Statutory Code of Practice (Draft for Consultation)' (Equality and Human Rights Commission 2009) 32, 252. The website of the Equality and Human Rights Commission (https://www.equalityhumanrights.com/en) no longer carries a copy of this document. An online copy can be viewed at <https://www.elaweb.org.uk/sites/default/files/docs/Draft%20 Employment%20Code%20of%20Practice%201109798532.pdf>

—— 'Employment: Statutory Code of Practice' <https://www.equalityhumanrights.com/en/publication-download/employment-statutory-code-practice>

Evans C, *Freedom of Religion under the European Convention of Human Rights* (Oxford University Press 2001)

Fassin D, *Humanitarian Reason: A Moral History of the Present* (Gomme R tr, University of California Press 2012)

Fineman M A, Emory University, 'Vulnerability and the Human Condition' <http://web.gs.emory.edu/vulnerability/>

Fitzgerald A J, Kalof L and Dietz T, 'Slaughterhouses and Increased Crime Rates: An Empirical Analysis of Spillover from 'The Jungle' into the Surrounding Community' (2009) 22 Organization and Environment

Food and Drug Administration, HHS, 'Listing of Color Additives Exempt From Certification; Food, Drug, and Cosmetic Labelling: Cochineal Extract and Carmine Declaration' (1 May 2009) <www.fda.gov/OHRMS/DOCKETS/98fr/FDA-1998-D-0032-nfr.pdf>

Francione G, *Animals, Property and the Law* (Temple University Press 1995)

—— *Animals as Persons: Essays on the Abolition of Animal Exploitation* (Columbia University Press 2008)

—— 'Animal Welfare and the Moral Value of Nonhuman Animals' (2014) in Anderson E, Bjork A, Jennbert K and Lonngren A-S (eds), *Exploring the Animal Turn: Human-Animal Relations in Science, Society and Culture* (Pufendorf Institute: Lund 2014)

—— 'Animal Rights: The Abolitionist Approach' <www.abolitionistapproach.com/abolitionist-intersectionality/#.VzXjJMr2YuQ>

—— and Garner R, *The Animal Rights Debate* (Columbia University Press 2010)

Fur Free Alliance, 'City of Berkeley Bans the Sale of Fur' (*Fur Free Alliance*, 10 April 2017) <http://www.furfreealliance.com/city-berkeley-bans-sales-fur/>

Garner R, Lyons D and Roberts A, 'How to Protect Animal Welfare: Deliberation, Democracy and Representation. Policy Research Briefing' (Centre for Animals and Social Justice Sheffield 2016)

Gearty C, *The Hamlyn Lectures: Can Human Rights Survive?* (Cambridge University Press 2006)

—— 'Can Animals Have 'Human Rights' Too?' (2007) 9 <https://adam1cor.files.wordpress.com/2013/12/animals.pdf>

Griffin J, *On Human Rights* (Oxford University Press 2008/2013)

Grimshaw J, *Feminist Philosophers: Women's Perspectives on Philosophical Traditions* (Harvester Wheatsheaf 1986)

Hall A, 'European Court Agrees to Hear Chimp's Plea for Human Rights' (*Mailonline*, 2008) <http://www.dailymail.co.uk/news/article-1020986/European-Court-agrees-hear-chimps-plea-human-rights.html#ixzz4FbLnblNK>

Hand S (ed), *The Levinas Reader: Emmanuel Levinas* (Blackwell 1989/1996)

Haraway D, *When Species Meet* (University of Minnesota Press 2008)

Harres C, 'Vegan Soldier Rejected by Swiss Army for Failing to Wear Leather Boots' (*International Business Times*, 26 January 2016) <http://www.ibtimes.com/vegan-soldier-rejected-swiss-army-refusing-wear-leather-boots-2280206>

Harper A B, 'Race as a 'Feeble Matter' in Veganism: Interrogating Whiteness, Geopolitical Privilege, and Consumption Philosophy of 'Cruelty-Free' Products' (2010) 8(3) Journal for Critical Animal Studies 5

Hass M, *International Human Rights: A Comprehensive Introduction* (2nd edn, Routledge 2014)

Hayden P, *The Philosophy of Human Rights* (Paragon House 2001)

Henderson F K, 'Vegan Values' (International Vegetarian Union [IVU]. The Vegetarian, winter 1947 No 4, 29–30) <www.ivu.org/history/world-forum/1947vegan.html>

Henley J, 'Documentary follows Pastafarians as they strain for recognition' (The Guardian, 18 September 2019) <https://www.theguardian.com/world/2019/sep/18/documentary-follows-pastafarians-strain-for-recognition>

Hooley D and Nobis N, 'A Moral Argument for Veganism' in Andrew Chignell, Terence Cunio and Matthew C Halteman (eds), *Philosophy Comes to Dinner: Arguments about the Ethics of Eating* (Routledge 2016).

Human Rights Watch, 'Blood, Sweat, and Fear: Workers' Rights in U.S. Meat and Poultry Plants' (*Human Rights Watch*, January 2005) <www.hrw.org/node/11869/section/2 Blood Sweat and Fear>

Hunt C, 'Vegan Values, Religious Rights: a Cultural Critique of Entrenched Ethics' Presentation for Lewis & Clark Animal Law Conference—October 2010. Available online at <http://www.lclark.edu/live/files/6665-vegan-values-religious-rights>

Hunt L, *Inventing Human Rights: A History* (W.W. Norton and Company Ltd. 2007)

Iacobbo K and Iacobbo M, *Vegetarians and Vegans in America Today* (Praeger Publishers 2006)

Ignatieff M, 'II Human Rights As Idolatry: The Tanner Lectures' (PDF Delivered at Princeton University April 4–7, 2000) <http://tannerlectures.utah.edu/_documents/a-to-z/i/Ignatieff_01.pdf>

Imaner Consultants (a), 'Vegan Profile' <www.imaner.net/panel/profile.htm>

——— (b), 'Vegan Statistics' <www.imaner.net/panel/statistics.htm#reveal>

Indaimo J A, *The Self, Ethics and Human Rights: Lacan, Levinas & Alterity* (Routledge 2015)

Jahangir A, *Elimination of all Forms of Religious Intolerance* (2005) UN Doc A/60/399

Jamieson A, 'Vegans should be protected from discrimination, says equality watchdog: Vegans and atheists should have the same protection against discrimination as religious groups according to guidance on new equality laws proposed by Harriet Harman' *The Telegraph* (2010) <http://www.telegraph.co.uk/news/religion/7392222/Vegans-should-be-protected-from-discrimination-says-equality-watchdog.html>

Jannaway K, 'Abundant Living in the Coming Age of the Tree' (*Movement for Compassionate Living*, 1991) <www.mclveganway.org.uk/Publications/Abundant_Living.pdf>

Joy M, *Why We Love Dogs, Eat Pigs and Wear Cows* (Conari Press 2010)
Kant I, *The Metaphysic of Ethics* (Semple J W tr, Thomas Clarke M.DCCC.XXXVI) available at <http://philosophyfaculty.ucsd.edu/faculty/ctolley/texts/kant.html>
Karp A P, *Understanding Animal Law* (Carolina Academic Press 2016)
Kass L R, 'Defending Human Dignity' (*Human Dignity and Bioethics: Essays Commissioned by the President's Council on Bioethics*, 2008) <https://bioethicsarchive.georgetown.edu/pcbe/reports/human_dignity/chapter12.html>
Kearney R, *Dialogues with Contemporary Continental Thinkers: The Phenomenological Heritage* (Manchester University Press 1984)
Kellert S, 'Attitudes Towards Animals' (*Vegetarian Times*, Sept-Oct 1978)
Kheel M, 'From Heroic to Holistic Ethics: The Ecofeminist Challenge' in Gaard G (ed), *Ecofeminism: Women, Animals, Nature* (Temple University Press 1993)
——— 'Toppling Patriarchy With a Fork—The Radical Potential of Veganism, Lecture by Marti Kheel; Part 2—Why Aren't More People Vegan?' ([video clip] Internet Archive Community Video website 2008b) <www.archive.org/details/toppling_patriarchy_part_2_of_8>
Klaper M, 'Plant-only medicine man' (video clip 2010) <www.vegsource.com/news/2011/09/dr-klaper----plant-only-medicine-man-video.html >
Kymlicka W and Donaldson S, 'Animals and the Frontiers of Citizenship' (2014) 34(2) Oxford Journal of Legal Studies 201
Lacey R, *Unfit for Human Consumption: Food in Crisis: The Consequences of Putting Profit Before Safety* (Souvenir Press 1991)
Larkin L, 'Turning face-to-face with Limobius Mixtus' (2002) 7(1) Journal for the Study of Religion Nature and Culture, Ecotheology 30
Larsson C L, Ronnlund U, Johansson G and Dahlgren L, 'Veganism as a Status Passage: the Process of Becoming a Vegan Among Youths in Sweden' (2003) 41 Appetite 61
Lechte J, 'Emmanuel Levinas' In *Fifty Contemporary Thinkers: from Structuralism to Post Modernity* (Routledge 1994)
Levinas E, 'Is ontology fundamental?' in Peperzak A T, Critchley S and Bernasconi R (eds), *Emmanuel Levinas: Basic Philosophical Writings* (Atterton P tr, Indiana University Press 1951/1996)
——— 'Substitution' in Peperzak A T, Critchley S and Bernasconi R (eds), *Emmanuel Levinas: Basic Philosophical Writings* (Atterton P tr, Indiana University Press 1968/1996)
——— *Totality and Infinity: An Essay on Exteriority* (Lingis A tr, The Hague 1969/2000)
——— *Ethics and Infinity: Conversations with Philippe Nemo* (Cohen R A tr, Duquesne University Press 1985)
——— *Of God Who Comes to Mind* (Bergo B tr, Stanford University Press 1986/1998)
——— *Outside the subject* (Smith M B tr, Continuum International Publishing Group 1987/2008)
——— 'Ideology and Idealism' in Hand S (ed), *The Levinas Reader* (Blackwell 1989a)

—— 'Ethics as first philosophy' in Hand S (ed), *The Levinas Reader* (Blackwell 1989b)
—— *Difficult Freedom: Essays on Judaism* (The John Hopkins University Press 1990)
—— *Entre Nous: Thinking of the Other* (Smith M B and Harshav B trs, Continuum Publishing Group 1998/2006)
—— *Otherwise Than Being or Beyond Essence* (Lingis A tr, Duquesne University Press 1998)
—— *Alterity and Transcendence* (Smith M B tr, Columbia University Press 1999)
—— *Humanism of the Other* (Poller N tr, University of Illinois Press 2006)
Lifskofsky S, 'The UN Declaration on the Elimination of Religious Intolerance and Discrimination: Historical Perspectives' in Wood J E (ed), *Religion and the State: Essays in Honour of Leo Pieffer* (Baylor University Press 1985)
Lingis A, 'Practical necessity' (1998) 20/21(2/1) Graduate Faculty Philosophy Journal 3
Linzey A, 'Does Animal Abuse Really Benefit Us?' (2009) in Linzey A (ed), *The Link Between Animal Abuse and Human Violence* (Sussex Academic Press 2009)
Llewelyn J, 'Am I Obsessed By Bobby? (Humanism of the Other Animal)' in Bernasconi R and Critchley S (eds), *Re-reading Levinas* (Indiana University Press 1991)
Luke B, 'Justice, Caring, and Animal Liberation' in Donovan J and Adams C (eds), *The Feminist Care Tradition in Animal Ethics* (Continuum Press 1996)
MacNair R, 'McDonalds 'Empirical Look At Becoming Vegan'' (2001) 9 1, 63 Society & Animals
Mahoney Rev J, 'The Challenge of Human Rights' (*Gresham College*, 17 May 2007) <http://www.gresham.ac.uk/lectures-and-events/the-challenge-of-human-rights>
Manderson D (ed), *Essays on Levinas and Law* (Palgrave Macmillan 2009a)
—— 'Introduction' (2009b) in Manderson D (ed), *Essays on Levinas and Law* (Palgrave Macmillan 2009)
Marcus E, *Meat Market* (Brio Press 2005)
Marino L and Colvin C M, 'Thinking Pigs: A Comparative Review of Cognition, Emotion, and Personality in Sus Domesticus' (2015) International Journal of Comparative Psychology 28 available at <animalstudiesrepository.org/cgi/viewcontent.cgi?article=1042&context=acwp_asie>
Martin R M, *The Philosophers Dictionary* (2nd ed, Broadview Press 1994)
McDonald B, 'Once You Know Something, You Can't Not Know It: An Empirical Look At Becoming Vegan' (2000) 8 (1), 1 Society & Animals
Monaghan K, *Equality Law* (Oxford University Press, 2007)
Moran V, *Compassion The Ultimate Ethic: An Exploration of Veganism* (3rd edn, The American Vegan Society 1991)
Morsink J, *The Universal Declaration of Human Rights: Origins, Drafting and Intent* (University of Pennsylvania Press 1999)
—— *Inherent Human Rights: Philosophical Roots of the Universal Declaration* (University of Pennsylvania Press 2009)

Morss J, 'Saving Human Rights from Its Friends: A Critique of the Imaginary Justice of Costas Douzinas' (2003) 27 (3) Melbourne University Law Review 889 <http://www.law.unimelb.edu.au/mulr/issues/previous-issues/2003-volume-27/2003-volume-27–3>

Mountain M, 'Lawsuit Filed Today on Behalf of Chimpanzees Seeking Legal Personhood' (*Nonhuman Rights Project*, 2 December 2013) <http://www.nonhumanrightsproject.org/2013/12/02/lawsuitfiled-today-on-behalf-of-chimpanzee-seeking-legal-personhood/ [https://perma.cc/6BDE-85B8]>

Müller-Amenitsch R, *Vegan im Recht* (Ventil 2016)

Nelson R R and Winter S G, *An Evolutionary Theory of Economic Change* (Harvard University Press 1982)

Nibert D, *Animal Rights Human Rights: Entanglements of Oppression and Liberation* (Rowman & Littlefield Publishers Inc 2002)

Nonhuman Rights Project <https://www.nonhumanrightsproject.org/litigation/>

Nussbaum M, *Frontiers of Justice: Disability, Nationality, Species Membership* (Harvard University Press 2007)

Oliver K, 'What Is Wrong with (Animal) Rights?' (2008) 22(3) Journal of Speculative Philosophy 214

—— 'Animal Ethics: Toward an Ethics of Responsiveness' (2010) 40 Research in Phenomenology 267

Peperzak A, *To The Other: An Introduction to the Philosophy of Emmanuel Levinas* (*Purdue University Press Books*, Book 20 1993) <http://docs.lib.purdue.edu/purduepress_ebooks/20>

Perpich D, *The Ethics of Emmanuel Levinas* (Stanford University Press 2008)

Perry M J, *Toward a Theory of Human Rights: Religion, Law, Courts* (Cambridge University Press 2007)

Personick M E and Taylor-Shirley K, 'Profiles in Safety And Health: Occupational Hazards of Meat Packing' Monthly Labor Review (United States Department of Labor, Bureau of Labor Statistics, 1989) <www.bls.gov/mlr/1989/01/art1full.pdf>

Peters A, 'Global Animal Law: What It Is and Why We Need It' (2016) 5(1) Transnational Environmental Law 9.

Pierson P, 'Increasing Returns, Path Dependence, and the Study of Politics' (2000) 94(2) The American Political Science Review 251

Plant B, 'Welcoming Dogs: Levinas and the Animal Question' (2011) 27(1) Philosophy and Social Criticism 49

Plato, *The Republic* (380BC Lee D tr, 2nd edn, Penguin 1987)

Plumwood V, 'Nature, Self, and Gender: Feminism, Environmental Philosophy, and the Critique of Rationalism' in Elliot R (ed), *Environmental Ethics* (Oxford University Press 1995)

Porter E, 'Can Politics Practice Compassion' (2006) 21 (4) Hypatia

—— *Peacebuilding: Women in International Perspective* (Oxon 2007

Prisco C, *The Right to Vegetarianism* (Hamilton Books 2017)

Regan T, *The Case For Animal Rights* (2nd edn, Routledge 1988)

—— and Singer P, *Animal Rights and Human Obligations* (2nd edn, Prentice Hall 1989)

Robbins J (ed), *Is it Righteous to Be?: Interviews with Emmanuel Levinas* (Stanford University Press 2001)

Rodger G D, 'Interview With Donald Watson On Sunday 15 December 2002' <www.vegansociety.com/sites/default/files/DW_Interview_2002_Unabridged_Transcript.pdf>

Roe M J, 'Chaos and Evolution in Law and Economics' (1996) 109 Harvard Law Review 641

Rousseau J-J, *Discourse on Inequality* (1754) (Cole G D H tr) <https://www.aub.edu.lb/fas/cvsp/Documents/DiscourseonInequality.pdf879500092.pdf>

—— *The Social Contract or Principles of Political Right* (Cole G D H tr, public domain, Foederis æquas Dicamus leges 1762) <https://www.ucc.ie/archive/hdsp/Rousseau_contrat-social.pdf>

Rowlands M, *Animal Like Us* (Verso 2002)

—— 'Making Light of the Ethical? The Ethics and Politics of Animal Rights' (nd) (Penultimate Version. To appear in Woodhall A and Garmendia da Trindade G (eds), *Ethical and Political Approaches to Nonhuman Animal Issues: Towards an Undivided Future* (Palgrave Macmillan)). This version available at <https://www.academia.edu/24880242/Making_Light_of_the_Ethical_The_Ethics_and_Politics_of_Animal_Rights>

Royal Society for the Prevention of Cruelty to Animals 'Trustees Report and Accounts 2018' <https://www.rspca.org.uk/documents/1494939/0/TrusteesReportsAndAccounts+%281%29.pdf/d9beb013–28e1-c7e2–1948-f34bbe484fe3?t=1557490023015 >

Rushprnews, 'Statistics: 55% of Population on Mainly Vegan Diet by 2020 Predict Vegfest UK' (*rushprnews*, 25 April 2013) <rushprnews.com/2013/04/25/statistics-55-of-population-on-mainly-vegan-diet-by-2020-predict-vegfest-uk>

Russell B, *History of Western Philosophy* (Routledge 1994)

Ryder R D, *Victims of Science: The Use of Animals in Research* (Davis-Poynter 1975)

—— *The Political Animal: The Conquest of Speciesism* (McFarland Jefferson 1998)

—— 'Speciesism Revisited' (*Think*, 2nd June 2004) 83–92, DOI: 10.1017/S1477175600002840

Salmond J, *Jurisprudence* (Williams G L ed, 10th edn, Sweet and Maxwell 1947) <https://www.nonhumanrightsproject.org/media-center/04–11–17-media-release-blacks-law/>

Sapon S M, 'Vegan Values: A Philosophy of Vegan Values' (2007–2009) <www.veganvalues.org/>

Satz A, 'Animals as Vulnerable Subjects: Beyond Interest-Convergence, Hierarchy, And Property' (2009) 16 (2) Animal Law Review, 65

Sawyer P, 'Owner 'flabbergasted' as hundreds join Walnut the whippet on his final walk after Facebook invitation' (*The Telegraph*, 12 November 2016) <http://www.telegraph.co.uk/news/2016/11/12/hundreds-join-walnut-the-whippet-on-his-final-walk/>

Scheinin M, 'Article 18' in Eide A and others (eds), *The Universal Declaration of Human Rights: A Commentary* (Scandinavian University Press 1992) 263–264

—— 'Freedom of Thought, Conscience and Religion' (2000) (Studia Theologica 54) 5

Schlosser E, 'The Chain Never Stops' Mother Jones (July/August 2001) para 12 <motherjones.com/politics/2001/07/chain-never-stops>

Seeker, 'Zoo Chimp Has Legal Rights, says Judge in Argentina' (*Seeker*, 7 November 2016) <https://www.seeker.com/zoo-chimp-has-legal-rights-says-judge-in-argentina-2083850453.html>

Sen A, 'Elements of a Theory of Human Rights' (2004) 32(4) Philosophy & Public Affairs <http://www.jstor.org/stable/pdf/3557992.pdf>

Simmons W P, *Human Rights Law and the Marginalised Other* (Cambridge University Press 2014)

Simonsen R R, 'A queer vegan manifesto' (2012) 10(3) Journal for Critical Animal Studies 51

Singer P, *Animal Liberation* (1st paperback edn, Thorsons Publishers Limited 1983)

—— and Mason J, *The Ethics of What We Eat: Why Our Food Choices Matter* (Rodale Inc 2006)

Sobbrio P, 'The Relationship Between Humans and Other Animals in European Animal Welfare Legislation' (2013) 1 (1) Relations: Beyond Anthropocentrism doi: 10.7358/rela-2013–001-sobb

Soifer S, 'Vegan Discrimination: An Emerging and Difficult Dilemma' (2003) Loyola of Los Angeles Law Review 1709

Stauffer J, 'Productive Ambivalence: Levinasian Subjectivity, Justice, and the Rule of Law' in Manderson D (ed), Essays on Levinas and Law: A Mosaic (Palgrave Macmillan 2009)

Stepaniak J, *The Vegan Sourcebook* (Lowell House 1998)

—— *Being Vegan: Living with Conscience, Conviction and Compassion* (Lowell House, a division of NTC Contemporary Publishing Group Inc. 2000)

Sylvester C, *Feminist International Relations: An Unfinished Journey* (Cambridge University Press 2002)

Tahzib B G, *Freedom of Religion or Belief: Ensuring Effective International Protection* (The Hague, Kluwer Law International 1996)

Taylor N and Twine R, 'Introduction: Locating the 'Critical' in Critical Animal Studies' in Taylor N and Twine R (eds), *The Rise of Critical Animal Studies: From the Margins to the Centre* (Routledge 2014)

—— and Twine R (eds), *The Rise of Critical Animal Studies: From the Margins to the Centre* (Routledge 2014)

Taylor P M, *Freedom of Religion: UN and European Human Rights Law and Practice* (Cambridge University Press 2005)

The Connexion, 'Vegan mother has baby taken away' (*The Connexion*, 8 Jan 2014) <https://www.connexionfrance.com/Archive/Vegan-mother-has-baby-taken-away>

The European Pet Food Industry Federation (FEDIAF), 'Facts and Figures 2014' [PDF] <http://www.fediaf.org/facts-figures/>

The International Vegan Rights Alliance, '1st International Symposium on the Right to a Plant Based Diet' <www.theivra.com/symposium.html>

The Vegan Society, *Animal Free Shopper* (8th edn, The Vegan Society 2008)
—— 'Ripened by Human Determination' (70 Anniversary) (The Vegan Society 2014) <http://www.vegansociety.com/sites/default/files/uploads/Ripened%20by%20human%20determination.pdf>
—— 'Definition of veganism' <www.vegansociety.com/go-vegan/definition-veganism>
—— 'History' <https://www.vegansociety.com/go-vegan/definition-veganism>
—— 'There Are Three And Half Times as Many Vegans as There Were in 2006, Making it the Fastest Growing Lifestyle Movement' (*The Vegan Society*, 17 May 2016) <https://www.vegansociety.com/whats-new/news/find-out-how-many-vegans-are-great-britain>
—— 'Why Go Vegan' <https://www.vegansociety.com/go-vegan/why-go-vegan>
Thierman S, 'The Vulnerability of Other Animals' (2011) Volume IX I(2) Journal for Critical Animal Studies 182
Thomas D, The Law And Animals (2005) 149 (7) Solicitors Journal <www.alaw.org.uk/articles/thelawandanimals.pdf>
Tolstoy L, 'Introduction—The First Step' in Williams H, *The Ethics of Diet: An Anthology of Vegetarian Thought* (White Crow Books 2009)
Torch: The Oxford Research Centre in the Humanities <http://torch.ox.ac.uk/towards-vegan-theory>
Torres B, *Making A Killing: The Political Economy of Animal Rights* (AK Press 2007)
—— and Torres J, *Vegan Freak: Being Vegan in a Non-Vegan World* (Tofu Hound Press 2005)
Turner B S, *Vulnerability and Human Rights* (The Pennsylvania University Press 2006)
Twine R, 'The Industrialisation of Animals: What Happened to Ethics?' (*The Scavenger*, 12 December 2010) <www.thescavenger.net/social-justice-sp-24912/animals/538-the-iindustrialisation-of-animals-where-are-the-ethics-89912.html>
—— 'Ecofeminism and Veganism: Revisiting the Question of Universalism' in Adams C J and Gruen L (eds), *Ecofeminism: Feminist Interactions with Other Animals & the Earth* (Bloomsbury 2014)
United Nations A/PV.183, 'One Hundred and Eighty Third Plenary Meeting. Continuation of the Discussion on the Draft Universal Declaration of Human Rights: Report of the Third Committee (A/777)' A/PV.183, <https://documents-dds-ny.un.org/doc/UNDOC/GEN/NL4/812/23/PDF/NL481223.pdf?OpenElement>
United Nations Commission on Human Rights (UNCHR) (Krishnaswami A, Special Rapporteur of the Sub-Commission on Prevention of Discrimination and Protection of Minorities), 'Study Of Discrimination In The Matter Of Religious Rights And Practices' (1960) UN Doc E/CN.4/Sub.2/200/Rev.1
United Nations Food and Agriculture Organisation, 'Livestock's Long Shadow—Environmental Issues and Options' (United Nations FAO Corporate Document Repository 2006) <ftp://ftp.fao.org/docrep/fao/010/a0701e/a0701e00.pdf>

United Nations Human Rights Committee (HRC), 'CCPR General Comment No 22: Article 18 (Freedom of Thought, Conscience and Religion)' (30 July 1993) UN Doc CCPR/C/21/Rev.1/Add.4

United Nations Human Rights Committee (HRC), 'CCPR General Comment No 23: Article 27 (Rights of Minorities)' (8 April 1994) UN Doc CCPR/C/21/Rev.1/Add.5

United Nations Human Rights Committee (HRC), 'CCPR General Comment No 31 [80]: The Nature of the General Legal Obligation Imposed on States Parties to the Covenant' (26 May 2004) UN Doc CCPR/C/21/Rev.1/Add. 13

United Poultry Concerns <http://www.upc-online.org/>

United States Department of Labor, 'Injuries, Illnesses and Fatalities' <www.bls.gov/iif/oshsum.htm#13Summary_News_Release>

—— 'Meat Packing Industry' <https://www.osha.gov/SLTC/meatpacking/index.html>

—— 'Occupational Safety and Health Administration: Accident Search Results' <https://www.osha.gov/pls/imis/AccidentSearch.search?acc_keyword=%22Meat%20Slicing%20Machine%22&keyword_list=on>

University of Oxford, Oxford Martin School, 'Plant-based diets could save millions of lives and dramatically cut greenhouse gas emissions' (21 March 2016)< https://www.oxfordmartin.ox.ac.uk/news/201603-plant-based-diets/>

Vegan World Network <www.vegansworldnetwork.org/world_vegan_directory_vcountries.php>

Vialles N, *Animal to Edible* (Cambridge University Press 1994)

Watson D, 'The Vegan News' (*The Vegan Society*, November 1944 No 1) > https://issuu.com/vegan_society/docs/the_vegan_news_1944>

Watson L, 'Yorkshire's Vegan Cricket Coach Stumps Sponsors after Questioning Use of Leather Balls and Calling for Entire Dairy Industry To Be Shut Down' (*The Telegraph*, 7 June 2016) <http://www.telegraph.co.uk/news/2016/06/07/yorkshires-vegan-cricket-coach-angers-sponsors-after-calling-for/>

Wild J, 'Introduction' in Levinas E, *Totality and Infinity: An Essay on Exteriority.* (Lingis A tr, The Hague 1969/2000)

Williams H, *The Ethics of Diet: A Catena of Authorities Deprecatory of the Practice of Flesh Eating* (University of Illinois Press 1883/2003)

—— *The Ethics of Diet: An Anthology of Vegetarian Thought* (White Crow Books 2009)

Winders B and Nibert D, 'Consuming the Surplus: Expanding 'Meat' Consumption and Animal Oppression' (2004) 24 (9) International Journal of Sociology and Social Policy 76

Wood D, 'Introduction' in Bernasconi R and Wood D (eds), *The Provocation of Levinas: Rethinking the Other* (1st paperback edn 2014, Routledge 1988)

—— 'Comment ne pas Manger—Deconstruction and Humanism' in Steeves H P (ed), *Animal Others: On Ethics, Ontology and Animal Life* (State University of New York Press 1999)

World Health Organisation (WHO), 'Research: Zika: The Origin and Spread of a Mosquito-Borne Virus' (*WHO*, 2016) <www.who.int/bulletin/online_first/16–171082/en/>

Wren C L, 'Human Supremacy, Post-Speciesist Ideology, and the Case for Anti-Colonialist Veganism' in Moorehead D (ed), *Animals in Human Society: Amazing Creatures Who Share Our Planet* (University Press of America 2016).

Wright T, Hughes P and Ainley A, 'The Paradox of Morality: An Interview with Emmanuel Levinas' (Benjamin A and Wright T trs) in Bernasconi R and Wood D (eds), *The Provocation of Levinas: Rethinking the Other* (1st paperback edn 2014, Routledge 1988)

Wynne-Tyson J, *Food for a Future* (Davis-Poynter Ltd 1975)

—— *The Extended Circle: An Anthology of Humane Thought* (3rd edn, Sphere Books Ltd 1990)

LIST OF CASES

European Court of Human Rights Cases

Bladet Tromsø And Stensaas v Norway App no 21980/93 (ECtHR, 20 May 1999)

C v UK (1983) DR 142

Campbell and Cossans v UK (1982) Series A no 48

Friend, The Countryside Alliance And Others v UK App no 16072/06 and 27809/08 (ECtHR, 4 November 2009)

Golder v UK (1975) Series A no 18

H v UK (1993) 16 EHRR (Commission Decision)

Handyside v UK (1976) Series A no 24

Hashman and Harrup v UK App no 25594/94 (ECtHR, 25 November 1999)

Herrmann v Germany App no 9300/07 (ECtHR, 26 June 2012)

Jakóbski v Poland App no 18429/06 (ECtHR, 7 December 2010)

National Union of Belgium Police v Belgium App no 4464/70 (ECtHR, 27 October 1975)

Rukavina v Croatia App no 770/12 (ECtHR, 6 January 2015)

Soering v UK (1989) 11 EHRR 439

Stibbe v Austria App no 26188/08 (ECtHR, 4 May 2008)

Vartic v Romania (no 2) App no 14150/08 (ECtHR, 17 March 2014)

Verein Gegen Tierfabriken Schweiz (Vgt) v Switzerland App no 32772/02 (ECtHR, 30 June 2009)

United Nations Cases

Angela Poma Poma v Peru Comm no 1457/2006 UN Doc CCPR/C/95/D/1457/2006, 27 March 2009

Chief Bernard Ominayak and the Lubicon Lake Band v Canada Comm no 167/1984 UN Doc CCPR/C/38/D/167/1984, 10 May 1990

Kitok v Sweden Comm no 197/1985 UN Doc CCPR/C/33/D/197/1985, 10 August 1988
Länsman et al v Finland (no 1) Comm no 511/1992 UN Doc CCPR/C/52/D/511/1992, 8 November 1994
Länsman et al v Finland (no 2) Comm no 671/1995 UN Doc CCPR/C/58/D/671/1995, 22 November 1996
Länsman et al v Finland (no 3) Comm no 1023/2001 UN Doc CCPR/C/83/D/1023/2001, 15 April 2005

British Cases

BC v EF (Parental Responsibility: Immunisation) [2016] EWFC 69 (05 December 2016)
F v F (Welfare of Children: Immunisation) [2013] EWHC 2683 (Fam)
S (CHILDREN) [2012] EWCA Civ 210
R (Williamson) v Secretary of State for Education and Employment [2005] 2 AC 246.

United States Cases

Friedman v Southern California Permanente Medical Group 102 Cal, App 4th 39, 125 Cal Rptr 2d 663 (2002)

Canadian Cases

H (Re) 2011 CanLII 63119 (ON CCB)
Melville v Muller 2006 BCSC 895 (CanLII)
WCAT-2012–02217 (Re) 2012 CanLII 54414 (BC WCAT)

Israeli Cases

Academic Center of Law and Business v Minister of Finance HCJ 2605/05
Let the Animals Live v Hamat Gader LCA 1684/96

German Cases

Life Imprisonment Case (1977) 45BVerfGE 187 Ger, fed, Const. Ct.

South African Cases

Smit NO and Others v King Goodwill Zwelithini Kabhekuzulu and Others (10237/2009) [2009] ZAKZPHC 75 (4 December 2009)

Australian Cases

Genna & Dennis [2010] Fam CA 1161 (30 November 2010)

Employment Tribunal Cases

Alexander v Farmtastic Valley Ltd and Others [2011] 2513832/10 (ET)
Hashman v Milton Park Dorset Limited [2011] EqLR 426 (ET)
Conisbee v Crossley Farms Limited [2019] 3335357/2018 (ET)
Mr J Casamitjana Costa v The League Against Cruel Sports: [2020] 3331129/2018 (ET)

TREATIES AND DECLARATIONS

Convention for the Protection of Human Rights and Fundamental Freedoms (European Convention on Human Rights, as amended) (ECHR) Article 9
Convention for the Protection of Human Rights and Fundamental Freedoms (European Convention on Human Rights, as amended) (ECHR) Article 10
Convention for the Protection of Human Rights and Fundamental Freedoms (European Convention on Human Rights, as amended) (ECHR) Protocol 1
Convention for the Protection of Human Rights and Fundamental Freedoms (European Convention on Human Rights, as amended) (ECHR) Protocol 14
Declaration on the Elimination of all Forms of Intolerance and Discrimination Based on Religion or Belief, UNGA Res 36/55 (25 November 1981)
International Covenant on Economic, Social and Cultural Rights (adopted on 16 December 1966, entered into force on 3 January 1976) 993 UNTS 3 (CESCR)
International Covenant on Civil and Political Rights (adopted 16 December 1966, entered into force 23 March 1976) 999 UNTS 171 (ICCPR)
Treaty of Amsterdam Amending the Treaty on European Union (Amsterdam Treaty)
Universal Declaration of Human Rights (adopted 10 December 1948 UNGA Res 217 A) (III) (UDHR)
Vienna Convention on the Law of Treaties (adopted 23 May 1969) 1155 UNTS 331
Other legal instruments
Animal Welfare Amendment Act (No 2) 2015 (NZ)
Cruelty to Animals Bill to Parliament: HL Deb 15 May 1809 vol 14 cc553–71

Index

About the Author

Dr Jeanette Rowley is a British animal rights and vegan advocate. She founded the International Vegan Rights Alliance in 2012, to bring together a global community of legal professionals committed to defending those who seek the right to live with respect for nonhuman animals. She conducted a ground-breaking 'vegan equality' survey in 2013, produced the UK's first short guide on vegan rights in 2014, and has brought about changes that advance veganism in education, consumer, and workplace policies. She has secured out of court settlements for vegans in a variety of unlawful discrimination cases, given evidence in court, and on vegan rights to the All-Party Parliamentary Group on Veganism. She currently works at The Vegan Society as advisor and chair of the International Rights Network. She also manages the Society's vegan rights department as a non-practicing personal advocate.

www.ingramcontent.com/pod-product-compliance
Ingram Content Group UK Ltd.
Pitfield, Milton Keynes, MK11 3LW, UK
UKHW041842031026
15587UKWH00002B/954

9 781793 623669